Toward an Urban Ecology

Toward an Urban Ecology

Kate Orff
SCAPE

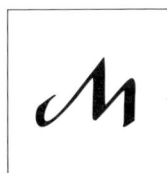

Library of Congress
Cataloging-in-Publication Data

Names: Orff, Kate, 1971–
Title: Toward an urban ecology / Kate Orff.
Description: First American edition. |
New York, NY : Monacelli Press, [2016]
Identifiers: LCCN 2015043350
Subjects: LCSH: Urban landscape
architecture—United States. |
Urban landscape architecture—
Environmental aspects. | City planning—
Environmental aspects—United States.
| Urban ecology (Sociology)—United
States. | Urbanization—Environmental
aspects—United States. | Urbanization—
Environmental aspects—United States. |
Sustainable development—United
States. | Human ecology. | Nature—Effect
of human beings on.
Classification: LCC SB472.7 .O74 2016 |
DDC 712/.5—dc23
LC record available at
http://lccn.loc.gov/2015043350

ISBN 978-1-58093-436-7

Printed in China

Design by MTWTF, New York
Michela Povoleri, Sarah Dunham,
Aliza Dzik, and Glen Cummings,
with Benoit Lemoine, Pedro Gonçalves,
Camille Gervais, and Hanna Rullmann

Production by Michael Vagnetti

Monacelli
A Phaidon Company
111 Broadway
New York, NY 10006

Phaidon SARL
55, rue Traversière
75012 Paris

phaidon.com/monacelli

—

INTRODUCTION
Kate Orff

"Change has become the essential element of our time."[1]
—Lawrence Halprin

Human activity has become such a dominant, disruptive source of change on a planetary scale that the biologist Eugene Stoermer coined the term *Anthropocene* to describe our current planetary epoch. Trends in climate change, a loss of biodiversity, and dissolution of social fabrics can seem already beyond our control or influence. We are at a critical juncture. What does it mean to practice design in the Anthropocene Age? How should we modify our methods, techniques, and strategies when every process and cycle is accelerating along an unknowable trajectory? What is the agency of the urban designer? How do we not just make landscapes, buildings, and public spaces, but make *change*? These questions are central to our work at SCAPE—and this book maps the philosophy, methodology, and potential of our practice.

Toward an Urban Ecology is part monograph, part manual, part manifesto.[2] Its objective is to reconceive urban landscape design as a form of activism, within which landscape itself is both a *frame* and a *solution*. Our intention is that the spatial and physical tools explored here will help designers and citizen activists to conceptualize their local environment in new ways and inspire them to sustainably remake the built-natural world.

SCAPE was founded in 2005 with a mission to bring a holistic, activist approach to questions of urban nature. Our work aspires to capture the epochal shift away from a top-down, monocultural program for infrastructure and the environment and toward a collaborative, community-stewardship-driven methodology that acknowledges change and uncertainty.

Rather than creating a chronological or typological survey of SCAPE projects, we designed this book to be widely understood, easily referenced, and put to work. It advances a new framework for conceiving landscape: design-driven, participatory, and science-based. It offers a set of strategies for motivating, informing, and changing existing patterns of occupying, making, and being in urban landscapes. To reveal our thought lines and research threads—in the context of a creative network of like-minded collaborators—it highlights what happens "behind the scenes," the messy process of synergistic design, including the kinds of questions we ask, how we construct narratives of projects, and how we've engaged in a constellation of sites, issues, and communities in a way that we hope will be useful for the next generation of urban designers and activists.

Issues as massive as global climate change can feel well beyond our capacity to effect positive outcomes. By bringing together large-scale strategic planning practices and community-based participatory initiatives that expand environmental awareness in ways that enable change, however, we believe that we can spur a larger public debate about achievable solutions and the collective responsibilities necessary for their implementation. The concept of a designed neighborhood landscape is a manageable scale for thought and action, for example, from which we can productively scale down to the unit of individual behavior and up to the frame of regional politics. SCAPE aims to overlay the regenerative capacity of living infrastructure with the methods of community organizing.

NATURE AND THE CITY

This approach to landscape architecture builds on insights gained from my interdisciplinary undergraduate thesis titled *Ecofeminism*, which explored why women were leading environmental and humanitarian movements; not because of innate gender difference but due to how "women's work"—gathering firewood, drawing well water, gathering food and caring for children—engendered a perception of the interconnected nature of economy and environment.[3] Due to their concrete, lived experiences, the women profiled in the thesis, like Wangari Maathai, founder of the Green Belt Movement in Kenya, were drawing connective lines between extractive landscapes, waste, and environmental degradation; they didn't see health and well-being as an externality of industrial processes.

It also builds upon working methods explored in my graduate thesis that looked closely at the reality of what was happening relative to global urbanization processes in the world at large—in zones that, at the time, were not in architecture's purview. The 1997 Pearl River Delta project, completed by a small team of six architecture students, including myself, positioned global urbanization front and center as the primary challenge of, and to, design.[4] This approach, which relies on travel, investigation, interview, photography, and writing, has informed SCAPE's working method, as well as subsequent book projects, including *Gateway: Visions for An Urban National Park* (2011) and *Petrochemical America* (2012).[5]

Since the 1990s, the landscape field has reinvented itself in different guises including, but not limited to: landscape-as-art, landscape urbanism, and landscape infrastructure. Each of these frameworks combines new ways of thinking about the city as an environmental system with varying emphases on form, performance, and program. Further, technological advances in digital terrain modeling, Google Earth, diagramming, and the use of computer programs to generate photorealistic perspectives have all changed the content of landscape architectural design processes and content.

Beyond technology, the field has been expanded and enriched by an expanded understanding of process derived from evolving ecological theory, including the systems-based emphasis of landscape ecologists such as

Eugene Odum, who developed the modern notion of ecology as an integrated discipline. Odum's work has provided a ground for further evolution in the topic by Richard T.T. Forman, Steward Pickett, Steven Handel, and Nina-Marie Lister, among many others. This emphasis provides a crucial corrective to the traditional, interventionist mode of landscape architecture, and the emphasis on ecological systems in this vein can to be further enriched with an equal attention to sociology and political science. Moving forward, we need to think analytically about the interconnectedness of social and physical systems, knit these strands together, and derive new territories for action.

FRAMING URBAN ECOLOGY

This book aims to define this territory for action and posits a new definition of urban ecology as a mode of transformation where an infrastructural system is overlaid on and connected with a unit of engaged citizenry. In order to effect positive change in a world in constant flux, landscape architects and urban designers have to synthesize other disciplines—from science to storytelling to community organizing—and must be able to foster connections between communities and their environments in support of more informed, just, and sustainable spatial practices. Moving forward, landscape architects and urban designers should contribute their skills to shared, positive, purposeful civic-scale interventions that interweave science, policy, and art. Even design ideas as massive as Living Breakwaters (see pp. 237–59), have emerged from this impulse to engage the world in its current state by using contextual, holistic, and collaborative work processes.

Landscape architecture is a combination of two terms: architecture as an applied art, and the site-driven prerogatives of living landscape systems. The strategy of combining disciplines is therefore, in a way, embedded in the profession. Frederick Law Olmsted, often called the father of modern landscape architecture, coalesced art and agricultural techniques to create lasting and significant public parks. He shaped parks to anticipate city growth 150 years ago, when settlements along the eastern seaboard were growing increasingly dense amid a public health crisis and rapid modernization. As sewers and water mains were placed underground and roads and canals cut through the countryside, Olmsted seamlessly hid infrastructural features like reservoirs and drainage ways within the English pastoral form of his iconic landscapes. His aim was to provide a visual and natural "counterpoint" to the unsanitary and generally squalid urban conditions of the city. Not only did public parks such as Central Park serve as a forum for discussion about the nature of what was "public" in the aggressively capitalist and socially divided city of early New York, but the very presence of the countryside in the city, or *rus in urbe*, sharpened the idea of city by contrast.[6] At the time, Central Park's sinuous and stylized version of an artfully arranged "natural landscape" designed to provide a respite for city dwellers, in its contrast to the gridiron of Manhattan, cemented a visual dichotomy between nature and urban culture.

Anne Whiston Spirn began to write about the city as a garden in her book *The Granite Garden* (1965):

> [Nature in the city] is the consequence of a complex interaction between the multiple purposes and activities of human beings and other living creatures and of the natural processes that govern the transfer of energy, the movement of air, the erosion of the earth, and the hydrologic cycle. The city is part of nature.[7]

Working in the 1980s, at another moment of urban upheaval, Spirn remains a groundbreaking figure who helped shape what a generation of landscape architects and planners studied, but we can take her notions further yet—beyond the idea that the city alters but is also complement to nature, and befitting of what we know is possible in our own era. SCAPE is building a practice that combines urbanism and ecology as mutually engendering and interdependent systems. This shift in landscape architecture is a response to the ethical imperatives of climate change, uncertainty, and the need to act now.[8]

As a frame, "urban ecology" has been the most useful term to describe the joint social and natural, systems-based interdependency that SCAPE seeks to define and regenerate in every project we take on. Since the 1970s, when urban ecology became a subset of field biology and ecology, significant reevaluation of each term has provided more context. "Urban" as a term has moved beyond the confines of the traditional city border to describe global urban fabrics and networks of energy, food, infrastructure, and living systems that support human settlement. "Ecology" has exceeded the purview of the nonhuman to describe relationships and interactions between organisms and their constructed environment—to include people, institutions, and even governance. Together, unbound, the terms *urban* and *ecology* describe a permanent relationship of designed life support on the engineered globe.[9]

SHIFTING BASELINES

Ian McHarg introduced the concept of shifting baselines, or the notion that there is a continual degradation of our own standards and knowledge of pre-industrial ecosystems over generations, in *Design With Nature* (1969). To counter this perception gap, a primary task of the designer is to visualize landscape history and interconnectedness. This extends from the invisible causal relationships at the root of socio-environmental changes—such as the impacts of resource extraction and pollution on health—to water-quality systems and biodiversity loss, requiring new forms of drawing as a starting point for design.[10] As opposed to a flattened plan, power relationships and orders of cause-and-effect can be comprehended more effectively in section or in animation through time. SCAPE's work has been promulgating a reading of the city that "acknowledges the complex ecological and biogeochemical processes taking place above, below, and within the urban ground" through the use of the thick, rendered, and heavily notated section.[11] Illustrative cases about how effective these can be in engaging the public include the subsurface pollution of the Gowanus Canal in Brooklyn, New York, or the almost imperceptible creep of sea level rise in New York's Outer Harbor. Catastrophic events like historic typhoons, floods, and droughts—and the human suffering and mass migration that result from these events— abruptly bring climate change issues to the forefront of public discussion. However, on a day-to-day basis, it's difficult to perceive the global crisis on a personal level and to imagine its long-term effects. So, the first point of order is to find new ways of seeing and sharing information that can communicate and shape a common purpose, that can bear witness to shifting baseline conditions.

An early investigation of Jamaica Bay, the massive salt marsh estuary near New York's JFK Airport, served as a launchpad for multiple threads of research for our office in this regard. Jamaica Bay, on the city's periphery, was at one point in its history radically, visibly altered by a profusion of garbage dumps, sewage pools, and steaming horse-rendering factories.[12] More recently, however, Jamaica Bay has been altered in less obvious ways. The conditions of disappearing salt marshes, declining migratory bird populations, and increasingly fishless bays developed slowly over time, and are therefore difficult to register. The horseshoe crabs that once swarmed the gradually sloped beaches of the New York region, and which lived through mass extinctions eons ago, are now in dramatic decline; they are succumbing to the combined effects of water pollution, habitat loss, and overfishing. The same hardening of shorelines that reduces habitat for crabs also makes surrounding communities increasingly vulnerable to hurricane events and flooding. But aside from midnight beach excursions to observe mating horseshoe crabs or a once-in-a-generation storm that reveals infrastructural vulnerabilities and inequities, we have few occasions to perceive these complex and interrelated landscape phenomena.

Designers therefore face a compound challenge. We first have to make visible the new systemic challenges of the petrochemical era—which are ubiquitous yet nearly invisible: nitrogen pollution, hypoxia, estrogenic compounds in our water system, carbon dioxide atmospheric pollution, and gradual sea level rise. The stakes are high: failing to perceive what is happening to our landscapes is obviously devastating environmentally, but also architecturally and politically. It is hard to rally efforts or resources around invisible damages, and it is impossible to imagine better practices without first unearthing the flaws in the infrastructural systems we already have. The challenges we face today are different from those of the past.

Confronting threats to terrestrial and marine ecosystem function—from deforestation or ocean acidification to the obliteration of biodiversity—requires new forms of visualization and spatial solutions that go beyond piecemeal architectural addition or accumulation. Scales of ecosystem function do not mesh with scales of policy or decision making. Landscape can help pair ecology with scales of governance and policy.

ACTIVISM

Climate change requires us to imagine this different scale of action, to generate a magnified understanding of the interconnectedness of systems and processes, to be science based, and to scale up our work to effect larger behavioral modifications. And we need to do it now. But this type of action is not usually commissioned by a specific client or municipality in a typical Request for Qualifications. Rather, a pervasive, activist stance needs to be consciously brought to bear on all our endeavors to effect change. The point of research is not only to generate white papers, but tangible, accessible, and replicable experiments. We need to convene conversations about social justice and sustainable development models, certainly, but also to move the conversation forward into action. Landscape architects and, more broadly, all design professions, can become activist leaders and meld research agendas with achievable spatial goals.

Environmental and political advocates of the last few decades prefigure this stance on urban ecology. Rachel Carson, author of the classic environmentalist texts *Under the Sea-Wind* (1941) and *Silent Spring* (1962); Wilma Subra and Marylee Orr of the Louisiana Environmental Action Network; and, more recently, colleagues at Columbia University, including economist Jeffrey Sachs and climatologist James Hansen, all broke out of purely observational economics and sciences to call for policy reform. These individuals embody the conviction to do more about the conditions around them. Landscape architecture offers us the same potential—we can expand a traditionally service-based discipline by bridging the physical and the social.

How do we start to make change? First, we recognize that landscape design in particular holds a useful potential for forming coalitions. We reimagine the design process from this new starting point. When we look at a site, we see ways to redefine it and acknowledge its underlying physical, political, and social foundations. We ask questions about who is stewarding the landscape and develop time-based approaches to solutions. We educate ourselves to evaluate all the complexity at work in landscapes—a necessary precursor to any kind of design intervention and to generating productive dialogue that is public and shared, thus the argument for new kinds of visualization as a key tool for the twenty-first-century landscape architect.

Second, further to the effort of making latent forces visible, we draw visually intuitive, deeply explanatory maps and integrate previously separated silos of information—both qualitative and quantitative. We combine narrative and intuitive insights with the best available data to advance perception and create a context for informed decision making.[13] In The Shallows (see pp. 220–3), we overlaid existing land-use maps with the floodplains demarcated by the Federal Emergency Management Agency, records of Superstorm Sandy's impacts, and the National Oceanic and Atmospheric Administration's bathymetric data to define not only who and what is most immediately at risk, but also to demarcate a proposed zone of operation. The Shallows map served as both a template and catalyst: with it as a base, we were able to ask new kinds of questions and bring together fishermen, teachers, public officials, the US Army Corps of Engineers, and community advisory committees around a shared set of observations and values.

Third, we define a new platform of multiparty engagement scaled according to the needs of diverse coalitions of partners. The landscape of Jamaica Bay represents all the complexity of confronting systemic change at a global scale. Restoration of the Jamaica Bay Marsh Islands is an inspiring case study in successful collaboration between community groups and city, state, and federal entities. Implementation of the restoration effort combines dredged material from the Army Corps channel-deepening projects to rebuild the base structure of the marshes, with the hand-harvesting, seeding, and planting of the islands done by hundreds of volunteers through the efforts of the American Littoral Society and the Jamaica Bay Ecowatchers.[14]

Jamaica Bay participatory restoration

The story of how restoration was initiated and how it has been implemented highlights the importance of local citizens as stewards of their environments. It also argues for design interventions and infrastructural solutions that connect waterfront communities to their shorelines, rather than divide them. Had it not been for Jamaica Bay's fisherman, kayakers, windsurfers, bird-watchers, and scuba divers—members of the community already on the ground and intimately engaged with the recreational use of the bay—the Jamaica Bay Marsh Islands might have already disappeared. And were it not for the continued advocacy and action of local citizenry, there might never have been sufficient motivation and volunteer power to restore or maintain the marshes.

Engaging with an example such as Jamaica Bay forces the landscape architect to grapple with the knowledge that there is no single problem and thus no single solution that could make a sufficient difference. We need to widen our scope and activate new models of collaboration; a final design must do more than result in a beautifully photographed "completed project"—it must provide a framework for behavioral change. We know that one of the most effective ways of engaging the waters of the bay itself, for example, would be to work in the watershed and sewershed on land to capture and slow rainwater and prevent combined sewage overflow. Accomplishing this would require a range of actions at various levels: creating policy-level bans on phosphates and detergents to reduce nutrient loads; spraying sand marsh-lands with reclaimed dredge; planting thousands of street-side, pollution-filtering bioswales within the urban street grid on land; and changing personal behavior habits away from petrochemical-based personal care products. As we learned from Jamaica Bay, one way to scale up is to foster education and stewardship and to promulgate a methodology of intervention that ties together big infrastructural interventions with many small actions by community members. We should start conceiving of landscape as a visible and manageable record of actions from which we can both scale up to the level of city and regional policy, or down to the level of the organism—be it spartina plug, oyster spat, horseshoe crab, local volunteer, or science student.

This convergence of coordinated visioning and ground-up action can create a template for change. Designers, politicians, and individuals share a growing recognition that dispersed but coordinated, localized actions mark a way forward, toward lasting positive effects at the scale of the bioregion. Against the grim backdrop of conflicts over dwindling resources, war, famine, and disease, there is one thing that's proven to work: people coming together to be creative and to imagine solutions. By understand-ing the contexts we work in and fostering new connections between social and environmental systems, we can reverse what is too often a downward spiral of degradation and community alienation. We can create a positive, holistic cycle, and this cycle can be regenerative. It can also bind commu-nities more strongly to landscapes. Mirroring the shift toward thinking of urban ecology as an emerging hybrid category, so too can we envision and start to build new practices around community landscape. Through immersive and participatory landscapes and experiences, we can create new urban ecosystems that transcend the inherited tropes of "healing" industrial lands or "bringing nature into the city," which are too simplistic to apply to our globalized reality. This is the work of the twenty-first century. We hope you agree.

HOW TO USE THIS BOOK

The title of this book references critic and historian Kenneth Frampton's essay "Toward an Urban Landscape," published in Columbia University *Documents* in 1994. In the essay, Frampton discreetly calls on designers to rally behind an "ecological stance in the broadest possible sense."[15] This volume aims to describe exactly this stance in SCAPE's practice, which builds on a set of ideas and advances and expands them in multiple forms, from essays and pilot projects to built works and installations. More important, it aims to show that a practice is a stance, an attitude, a way of thinking and operating in the world. Its roots may be in the discipline of landscape, but its outcomes branch out into the political, scientific, and social realms. Four key principles serve as the framework for this book: *Revive*, *Cohabit*, *Engage*, and *Scale*.

Revive explores a design ethic that overlays natural and cultural systems toward the common purpose of generating eco-awareness. It features projects that rethink how public space can hold water and how cities and downtowns can redefine and reveal their relationships with natural systems. The chapter clusters projects inspired by the logic of regional water and geology systems and their place-making potential.

Cohabit features projects that extend design thinking beyond our own species and that enliven the public realm in a way that expands social justice and ecological connections.

Engage illustrates designs that are inspired and informed by ground-up community programs and processes. Rather than the one-way expositions with "stakeholders" that are typical of planning processes, we advance a philosophy and technique for engagement that generates new community formats around a shared purpose and that is education-driven and downright fun.

Scale demonstrates the integration and scalability of the ideals and methodologies espoused in the previous three chapters. It shows the potential for landscape to radically cross what seem to be competing interests and to integrate multidisciplinary expertise—from micro-installations and ecological experiments to the macro scales of planning and analysis. It suggests a trajectory for moving forward that brings together social systems and education with environmental stewardship models in a way that builds landscape-based culture over time.

Together, these four chapters chronicle the forward-thinking and celebratory design provocations of our office and arm the reader with a way of thinking and acting ecologically across systems. The chapters are interspersed with essays by several esteemed contributors: Jane Hutton focuses on materiality and the fundamentals of geology and hydrology as a means of revealing time and change in the landscape; Thaïsa Way explores historic and contemporary urban ecological design as a feminist practice; Emily Eliza Scott's essay inverts the normative assumptions of infrastructure as huge and monofunctional and describes how infrastructure might instead be based in art and social practice; and finally, Brian Davis asks us to rethink the concept of "the public" as something that is not only passively "responded to," but that can also be actively generated by design.

In our first ten years of practice, SCAPE has worked hard to chart a path for design in the age of the climate crisis. We have combined design, research, art, and environmental knowledge in order to advance landscape architecture as a form of activism. We have imagined landscape as a zone of collective engagement—of direct, lived connection, of hands building together, and of people working toward a common purpose. We have been inspired by landscape-change processes, connected them to granular scales of community stewardship, and defined their joint regenerative potential in a way that is fundamentally optimistic and transformative. Our first decade has yielded a synthetic vision of landscape, infrastructure, and community. We hope that it will inspire you to synthesize everything that you know, to marshal your own personal talents, and to work toward an urban ecology.

1. Lawrence Halprin, *Cities* (New York: Reinhold Publishing Corp., 1963). Halprin played a significant role in developing the concept of urban landscape design. Beyond his well-known built works in urban spaces, such as Lovejoy Plaza, he pioneered along with Anna Halprin the "RSVP Cycle" (1969) as a collaborative, intuitive, and consensus-based design process.
2. Or as our office has coined in the process of developing the book, a *manufestograph*.
3. Thesis by Kate Orff for the Political and Social Thought Degree Program, University of Virginia.
4. The author worked with a small group of students on a research thesis with the Dutch architect Rem Koolhaas on the urbanization of the Pearl River Delta at Harvard's Graduate School of Design. The group studied how the highrise city of Shenzhen, China, along with many hectares of golf courses and vast undeveloped areas reclaimed as fill from the estuary, had been built within a matter of years in a paroxysm of construction. The group's work was later published as Chihua Judy Chung, Jeffrey Inaba, Rem Koolhaas, and Sze Tsung Leong, eds., *The Great Leap Forward* (Cambridge, Mass.: Harvard Design School; Cologne: Taschen, 2002). Our office moniker, SCAPE, came from the title of the first essay in the 2002 publication.
5. *Petrochemical America* (New York: Aperture, 2012) was a close collaboration with the photographer Richard Misrach. Through photography, mapping, and storytelling, it brings into focus the industrialized landscape of the Mississippi River Corridor that stretches from Baton Rouge to New Orleans—a place that first garnered attention as "Cancer Alley" because of unusually high reports of cancer and other diseases in the area.
6. As documented in Roy Rosenzweig and Elizabeth Blackmar's excellent book *The Park and the People: A History of Central Park* (Ithaca: Cornell University Press, 1992), 4.
7. Anne Whiston Spirn, *The Granite Garden: Urban Nature and Human Design* (New York: Basic Books, 1984), 4.
8. The greater profession of architecture is confronting a similar shift, with the need for buildings to perform environmentally, consume less energy, and enable flexible uses. Design professionals are more aware than ever that most of the world is constructed in ways—quickly and at a large scale—that largely don't involve architects. The proliferation of self-built slums, or favela settlements, in the Global South has provoked a shift in the role of the architect toward one that enables others to build. Overlaying trends of global climate change and decarbonized economies onto these scenarios challenges us to redefine what architecture is now and how to engage with a world that has been made and not found, a world where biodiversity is being erased, and where the urbanization of poverty and climate-driven conflict is on the rise.
9. See Andrew C. Revkin's important article in the *New York Times*, "Forget Nature. Even Eden is Engineered" (August 20, 2002).
10. See the Infrastructure and Displacement chapters in *Petrochemical America*.
11. Stephanie Carlisle and Nicholas Pevzner, "The Performative Ground: Rediscovering the Deep Section," *Scenario 02: Performance* (Spring 2012).
12. See *Envisioning Gateway, an Atlas of the Gateway National Recreation Area* (2007). This comprehensive report, produced by the Urban Landscape Lab at Columbia University and SIDL, visualized the landscape of New York's forgotten outer harbor, and put forth a new framework for thinking about Jamaica Bay. My essay, "Cosmopolitan Ecologies: Jamaica Bay as Pilot Project" is published in Alexander Brash, Jamie Hand, and Kate Orff, eds., *Gateway: Visions for an Urban National Park*, (New York: Princeton Architectural Press, 2010), 50–73.
13. For example, the book *Petrochemical America* overlaid sites of chemical manufacture, toxic release inventory data, and neighborhood health metrics with stories and anecdotes from people living in Louisiana's "Cancer Alley."
14. The American Littoral Society, NYS DEC, NYC DEP, NFWF Foundation, US Army Corps of Engineers, Jamaica Bay Ecowatchers, Gateway National Recreation Area, and NYC DPR were the core project team here.
15. This essay was influential and led me (eventually) to seek out and teach alongside Professor Frampton at Columbia University.

Revive

"Water is life. It's the briny broth of our origins, the pounding circulatory system of the world . . ."[1]
—Barbara Kingsolver

To *revive* is to restore to life, to bring back from disuse. It also means to renew in the mind or memory. At SCAPE, our ambition is to achieve a hybrid design goal that builds on both of these meanings: to create places that magnify the immediate experience and perception of regional landscape identity, and to link systems at multiple scales to regenerate ecosystem structure and function. These revived landscapes can inspire community identity and literally reconnect severed neighborhoods and habitats. Observing the way water moves through a landscape can reveal hidden potential—geological, industrial, agricultural, cultural—in the urban landscape. For us, water un-locks the design process.

In contrast to "restoration," revival is a creative, forward-looking act not driven by nostalgia for the past. An anthropogenic ecology with completely unique soil chemistry and structure has transformed our urban landscapes well beyond a point of realistic or practical restoration. Urban dwellers have removed and replaced the soils and biota from territories as we've built cities. We have buried streams, filled in estuaries, dammed rivers, merged watersheds with sanitary sewersheds, and replaced rainwater cycles with timed irrigation. Exposing the physical parameters of water in the urban landscape—Where does it go? How is it absorbed? Where is it piped? Who is drinking it? Where is it being "disposed" as a waste product?—is revelatory, and leads to potential new and positive spatial relationships that can link urban form with water programs.

Water is also a primary place-making and identity driver. It takes the form of what it touches, roiling sediment and nutrients on continental scales, splashing over obstructions, and dispersing pollutants. It transports flora, fauna, and deathly viruses. As glaciers in motion, water has carved canyons, transported boulders, and shaped the earth's surface to give our landscapes their regional character, from Boston's drumlins to New York State's Finger Lakes. Throughout most of history, human settlement occurred where water took an advantageous form—a floodplain reliable for agriculture, a river confluence for expanding trade, a protected harbor safe for anchoring ships, estuaries with nutritious shellfish, or falls powerful enough to turn the wheels of industry. This economic and ecological context forms a distinct regional urban terroir.

Water can also help us rediscover unique and camouflaged regional elements missing in the homogenized urban landscape. With few exceptions, urban development patterns typical of the last century have been characterized by flattened contours—hills cut, valleys filled, and surfaces neutered into impermeable concrete, asphalt, or turf grass. Water flow that once nourished a range of plant and animal species has been recast as "drainage," and is engineered to be piped away as expeditiously as possible. In this scenario, urban vegetation takes the limited form of an approved list of street trees that can tolerate massive quantities of road salt and pollution. Uncovering and rebuilding—or in many cases reimagining altogether—the geologic, vegetal, and hydraulic properties of the region can improve ecological performance and renew wonder and curiosity in residents about how these systems work. The two are critical in moving us toward healthier lives and in generating an adaptive stance toward the future.

In the modern era, our power to manipulate the landscape and the flow of water has grown manifold. We've diverted monumental volumes of water from their natural courses, dredged their paths, and extracted prehistoric water from deep reservoirs. Globally, water—too much or too little—reveals climate change dynamics in our overbuilt and overheated world. It is visibly vanishing from lakes, rising incrementally and then surging over our shores, and falling unpredictably in preposterous quantities. At this writing, the state of California "is now pumping water that fell some 15,000–20,000 years ago."[2] In Central Asia, the freshwater Aral Sea, once a thriving home for civilization, is transforming into a desiccated wasteland due to upland irrigation projects. Its Eastern Basin has become completely dry for the first time in six hundred years. In contrast, with almost every rain event in New York City, hot, contaminated rainwater is flushed together with raw sewage into overflows that suffocate basic aquatic life, and rising tides threaten to submerge the feet of the Statue of Liberty.

Water's unique properties and characteristics make it a compelling starting point for design. It can engage our senses as ice, steam, or spray, and cycles from bedrock to sky. Through inundation or scarcity, it is the most probable vehicle of our destruction. As Barbara Kingsolver writes, Mother Water is "the gold standard of biological currency."[3] While carbon dioxide invisibly pollutes the atmosphere, water is our most tangible, physical link to the effects of climate change and direct life support. By valuing water as an environmental and civic common asset, it can be designed back into the city fabric to regenerate biological and social life.

The physical properties of water in a sense defy scale—it cycles from raindrop to ocean and back again. But we must define scales of action, whether governmental, community-based, or personal, in order to revive our water bodies. For example, at a national scale, policy regarding pesticide, nitrogen, and phosphate fertilizer can combine with seemingly the most trivial acts of personal behavior (don't flush in a rainstorm) to rebuild the water commons. At a site scale, significant landscape deconstruction and reconstruction projects like demolishing pavement, daylighting culverts, and replacing bulkheads with stepped, absorptive edges are required.

Designers can integrate water in design to help shape, give form to, and lend identity to the public realm. Human civilization will always depend on access to waterways, but we can no longer afford to build antagonistically against water or despite water, as we have done. Rather we must live and build with water, understanding it as a source of inspiration and as a tool for creating robust systems within the fabric of our cities.

Water has been key in shaping some of the world's most memorable spaces, from Islamic Spain's Court of the Lions at the Alhambra to Rome's Trevi Fountain to the solemn reflecting pool at the Lincoln Memorial in Washington, D.C. But water is typically expressed in the urban environment as an idealized abstraction of the water found in nature, which only exacerbates its plight. Designers need to develop more nuanced and flexible solutions for experimenting with water design in the public realm. Due to the demands of irrigation, freshwater rivers are reduced to trickles before they empty into the sea, lakes are clogged with algae, and streams are scoured. In the coastal context, too much water leads to repeat flooding at high tide, whereas inland too little water has given rise to the term "mega-drought." Moreover, the gritty realities of water design—broken fountains, frozen pipes, disease and contamination issues, Board of Health regulations, litigation, access, and safety—largely determine how we experience water in the city.

We also need to understand and correct the pollution and contamination of water systems, damage that has been wrought by rapid urbanization. A case in point is Seoul, South Korea's Cheonggyecheon "River"—a long, linear fountain in the city center, comprising water piped for seven miles from the Han River, then filtered through a decorative streambed lined with plantings. While admirable in its aspiration to reclaim "nature in the city" and to create beloved cool, tranquil social spaces, it represents a fantasy world—the pristine surface of clean, sparkling water conceals polluted stormwater and the original creek culverted beneath the surface.

Moving forward, a key challenge for landscape architects will be to at least dip their toes into the realities of regional water systems and take on their hypoxic, fecal coliform-choked, and generally polluted physical condition. It's time to start valuing water as a shaping, connective force and designing space for regionally connected, robust water systems within our urban fabric. There is still plenty of room for ornamental fountains and pleasurable water play—but let's not settle for only piped fountains.

CASE STUDY: TOWN BRANCH COMMONS
SCAPE's project for Town Branch tests this concept of a water commons in downtown Lexington, Kentucky (see pp. 26–45). The strategy is to actively and intentionally not create an image of a river, or a continuous blue shiny fountain, but to understand how water actually moves through the landscape, deal with the reality of its degraded status, and reintegrate it into city streets and civic perception.

Lexington was founded on the banks of Town Branch, described as "a magnificent spring . . . whose green banks were gemmed with the brightest flowers."[4] Later, its waters were walled into a trough called the "public spring" which eventually the defined the center of Lexington and become known as the "Commons."[5] However, as in so many other cities, the font that was the birthplace and birth-reason of Lexington was celebrated, then impinged upon, then soured by industry and eventually channeled and completely hidden beneath a state roadway that severs neighborhoods. The differential impact of land and water management practices and policies on the local environment is startlingly clear at the border of Lexington's urban growth boundary, where the Town Branch is more clearly understood as a stream system. Our design proposal for Town Branch Commons is driven by complex forces at play: rates of urban development, economic shifts, ecological flows of plants and animals, hydrological systems, and circulation systems, to name just a few. So here we design not only as a means to reveal these regional systems—to make their traces legible—but also as an opportunity to combine, act within, and act upon them.

Town Branch in rural Bluegrass Country

What makes Kentucky's regional landscape unique is its karst topography. Ancient seabeds rose and eroded into a picturesque topography of rolling hills, with Lexington at its center. Rainfall absorbs atmospheric carbon dioxide, and the resulting weakly acidic groundwater dissolves the calcite bedrock into almost fantastical, thick three-dimensional sculpted ground of pockets, caves, and sinkholes.

Karst topography forms unique subterranean drainage patterns and is the real secret of Lexington. Rainfall penetrates quickly through the limestone bedrock and over time expands along natural cleavages to reveal a wonderland of typological features. Its riverine form is almost the opposite of a sinuous, blue, idealized river. Water flows in surprising combination with this eroding rock, emerging in pools, disappearing into caves, dramatically resurfacing as boils and springs when least expected. SCAPE designed an array of new public spaces that interpret these features along the Town Branch. The waterway is strategically daylit to create a series of spaces that thread through downtown, making safe pockets for pedestrians and filtering rainwater before it gets into the network.

Lexington urban growth boundary

The geology of the karst landscape and the patterns of use downtown provide a joint urban-ecology framework for design that is adaptable to a diversity of urban conditions along the length of Town Branch. Retaining, capturing, slowing, or even quickening water for dramatic effect and aligning it strategically with urban space typologies—such as water absorbing sidewalks and water-filled plazas—set the latent ecological and public-realm potential of Lexington into motion. Understory shrubs and streamside rushes can establish when cleaner streams flow more slowly. Water can pool and puddle, making intuitive resting points and gathering spaces.

You can't love what you can't see. Concurrent with the design of the physical spaces, SCAPE advanced a community engagement strategy with University of Kentucky students and local civic leaders and volunteers, through developing a "Water Walk" tour that traces the path of Town Branch as it moves through and under the city in parallel culverts or erupts into "urban boils" of sewage on the streets of local neighborhoods (see pp. 180–1).

The fact that the Branch can surface and disappear again within the city fabric not only makes for a more feasible design, but it generates its own topography of difference and sparks new opportunities for making places along its length. These public spaces are deeply site-specific and magnify the existing urban districts that have emerged organically. Town Branch

Commons revives by revealing. It improves hydrologic health of the creek and the historical relationship between Lexington's urban space and its now-hidden waterway. This hybridized infrastructure makes the public realm a critical element within the city's traffic and water distribution networks. By renewing the creek's centrality in the city's identity and in the public life of its residents, downtown Lexington becomes a place of gathering and meaning. Rather than recreating a singular precolonial ecology, the project revives Town Branch as a series of diverse and resilient ecosystems, local in character yet responsive to the needs of a twenty-first century city.

Simon Schama structured his book *Landscape and Memory* (1995) as an exploration of the "veins of myth and memory" embedded in the elements of wood, rock, and water. He distilled these elements as the "carrier of memory."[6] *Revive* aims to take advantage of this condition to project new identities and construct future memories out of the concrete and asphalt surfaces of the contemporary city. It is undeniable that urban spaces are largely defined by introduced anthropogenic systems: parks and medians are matted with crabgrass, phragmites, or kudzu; waterbodies choked with excess nitrogen, and streets populated with pigeons and rats. But we can advance aesthetic values of textured landscapes and that favor diversity and interaction over pastoral, neutered, and debilitating forms of urbanism. Soon the monocultural grassy backdrop of the American lawn and the impermeable vertical bulkhead walls along our waterfronts will be perceived as eyesores and wasted opportunities. Grassy parks only designated for "passive or active" use will be boring to communities exposed to productive forms of working and participating in shaping their environs, as in the case of Be'er Sheva Quarry Park (see pp. 62–63). A new aesthetic is emerging from the desire to revive: one grounded in heightened eco-awareness, and the idea of landscape as a material practice rooted in the geological, hydrological, and social systems that sparked their formation.

1. Barbara Kingsolver, "Fresh Water," *National Geographic* (April 2010): 38.
2. Tom Knudson, "California Is Drilling for Water That Fell to Earth 20,000 Years Ago," *Mother Jones* (March 13, 2015): http://www.motherjones.com/environment/2015/03/california-pumping-water-fell-earth-20000-years-ago.
3. Kingsolver, "Fresh Water": 38.
4. George Washington Ranch, *The History of Lexington, Kentucky* (Cincinnati: Robert Clarke & Co, 1872), 23.
5. For more information, see Matthew Clarke's excellent Princeton School of Architecture research paper, "The Town Branch Project: A Vision for Lexington, KY" (2013).
6. Simon Schama, *Landscape and Memory* (New York: Vintage, 1995), 14.

Town Branch Commons

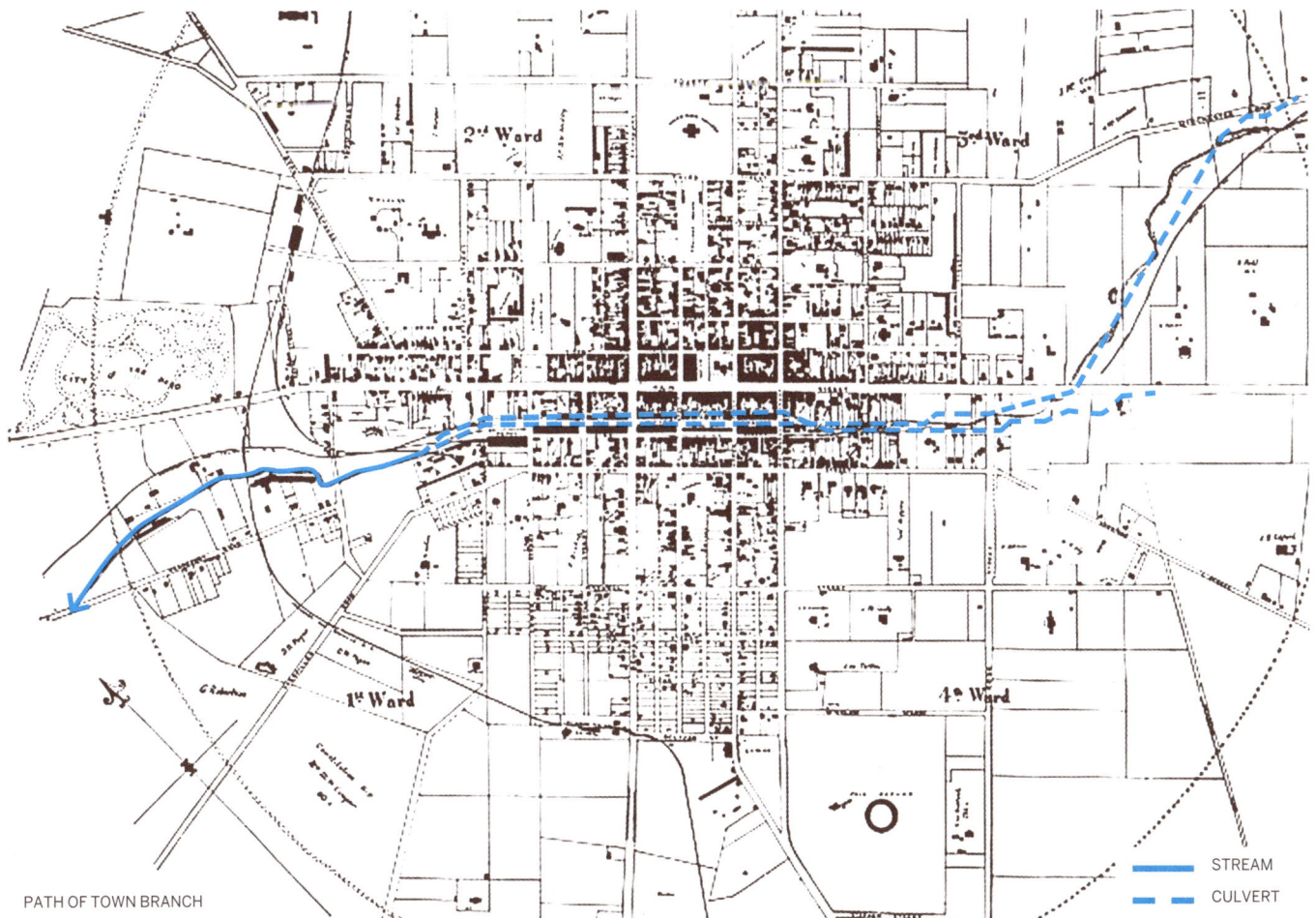

PATH OF TOWN BRANCH

STREAM

- - - CULVERT

Lexington's urban area forms the headwaters of Town Branch. Historically a waste canal, sewer, and water conduit for the city, the buried stream channel of Town Branch is a hidden remnant of public infrastructure buried beneath the city of Lexington, Kentucky. While the identity of this region is rooted in the blue-grass landscape, the downtown core of Lexington contains a series of fragmented public spaces with little connection to their landscape origins. Town Branch Commons introduces a new, water-based public realm with deep ties to the city's regional karst geology as a method for rethinking the public realm of downtown Lexington.

The Town Branch Commons proposal shown here was created for the Lexington Downtown Development Authority Town Branch Commons competition in 2013. This winning proposal has evolved as a strategic planning effort and hydrologic feasibility study, with phased construction funded through city, federal, and private dollars.

Facing page: Path of Town Branch under Vine Street

Design with Karst

Karst geology has shaped downtown Lexington—visibly and invisibly—since the city was founded. This limestone layer under the city is rumored to nourish the growth of Kentucky bluegrass (and subsequently the bones of its racehorses!) and improve the taste of Lexington's locally distilled bourbon. Unlike most stone, karst is highly porous, and creates unexpected water flow patterns, where underground waterways travel through permeable limestone layers and surface into pools, disappear into sinks, and dramatically resurface where least expected.

Rather than express Town Branch as a linear channel, the project aims to reveal a karst identity through a network of water windows, pools, pockets, fountains, and filter gardens that evoke and expose the underground stream. The public space is continuous, surface water is not; embracing this diversity allows the stream to be woven into the existing urban fabric while reconnecting Lexingtonians to their cultural landscape.

Swallet

KARST HYDROLOGY

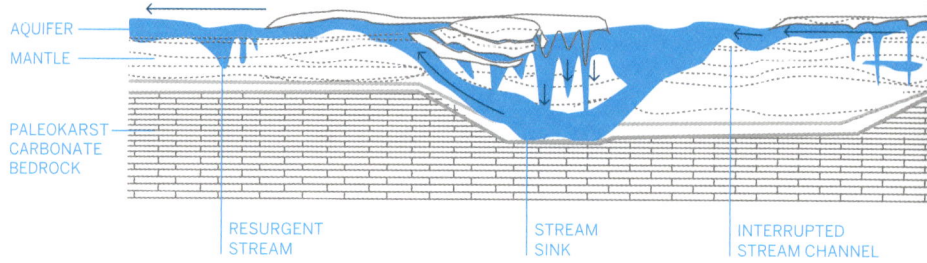

AQUIFER
MANTLE

PALEOKARST CARBONATE BEDROCK

RESURGENT STREAM

STREAM SINK

INTERRUPTED STREAM CHANNEL

URBAN INTERPRETATION AT TOWN BRANCH COMMONS

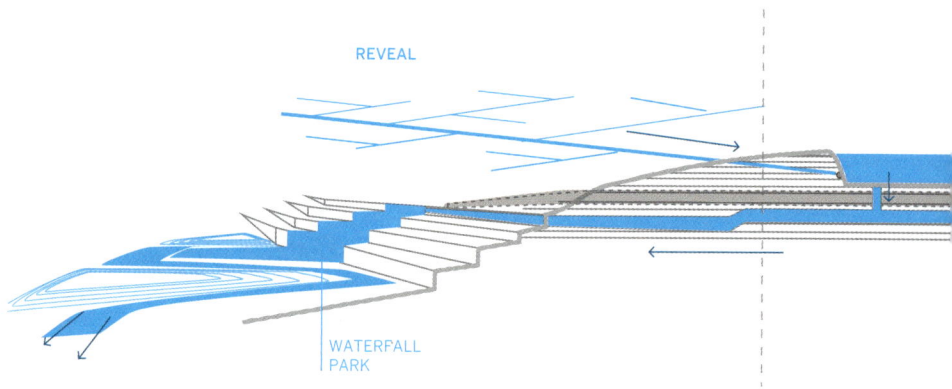

REVEAL

WATERFALL PARK

KARST OCCURENCE IN KENTUCKY

HIGH POTENTIAL
MODERATE POTENTIAL
LOW POTENTIAL

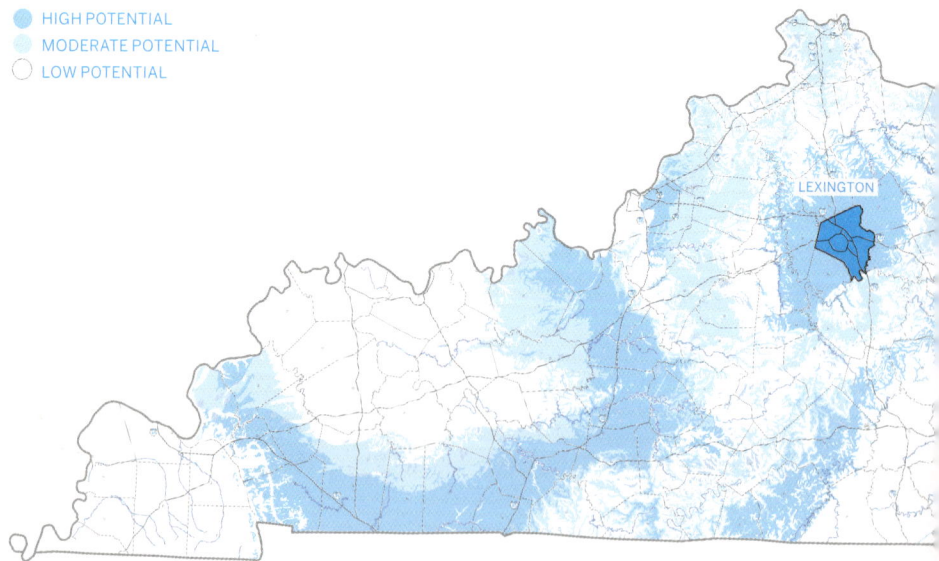

LEXINGTON

SWALLET   BOILS   SINK HOLE

CLEAN   CARVE   CONNECT

FILTRATION
GARDEN

URBAN
BOILS

KARST
CUTS

DAYLIT DIVERSION
CHANNEL

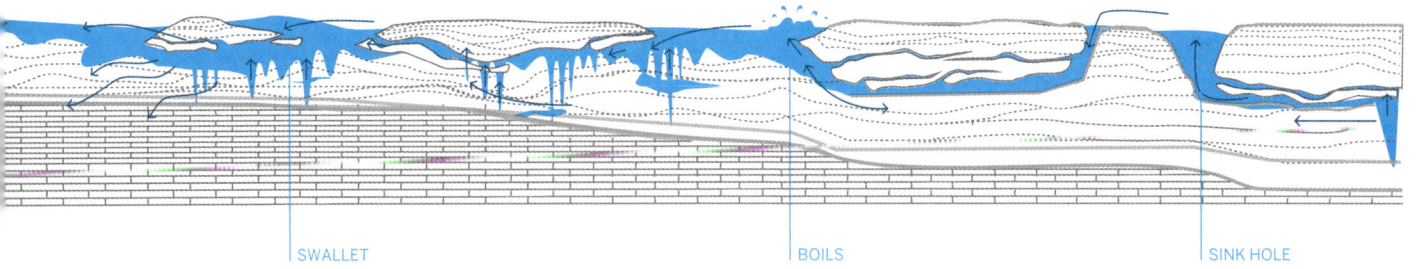

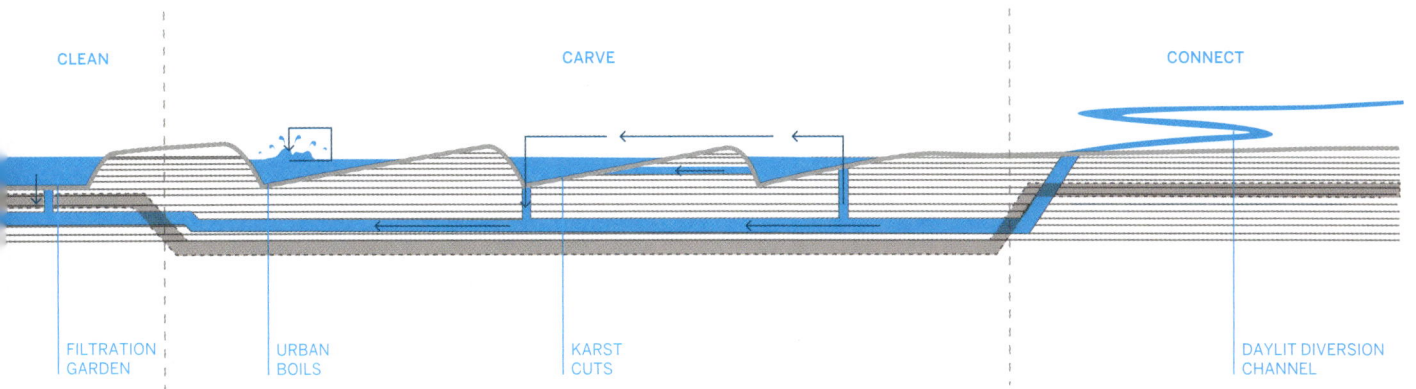

URBAN WATERSHED

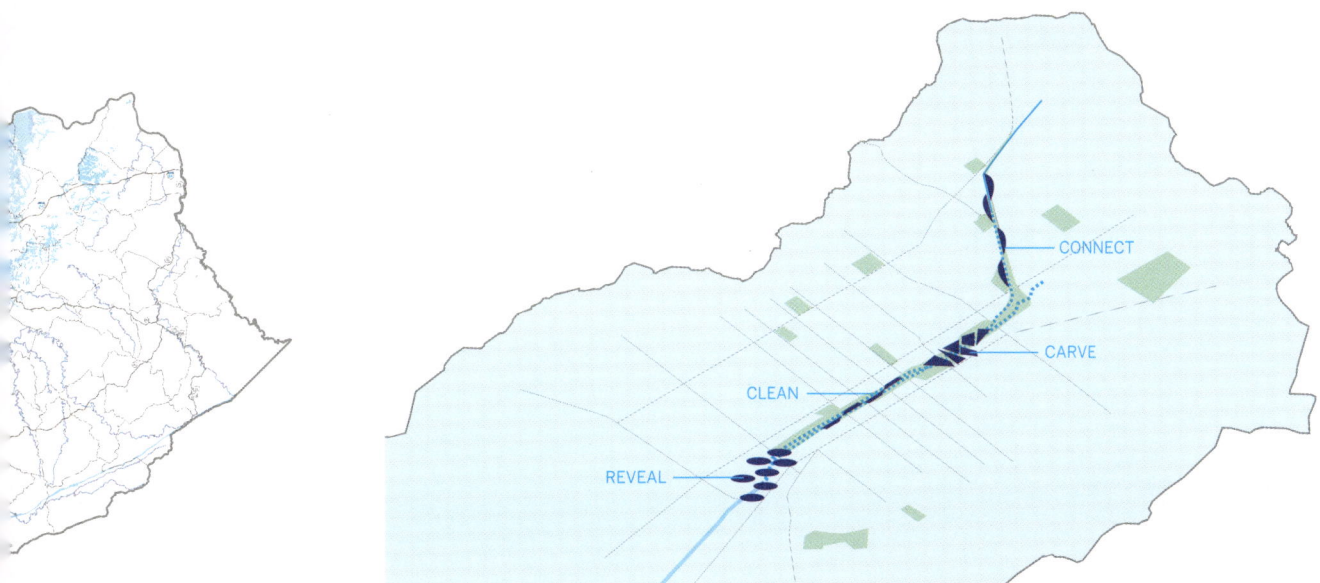

CONNECT

CARVE

CLEAN

REVEAL

Reveal, Clean, Carve, Connect

Four actions structure the approach to water: reveal, clean, carve, and connect. Each suggests a new relationship to water within the urban realm and a new typology of public space for Lexington.

REVEAL: At the Hollows, Town Branch is a fully revealed and daylit stream that connects to the Bluegrass Region and structures a new recreational park, a much needed downtown amenity.

CLEAN: In the core of downtown, Town Branch is expressed as a series of water filtration gardens that shape an ex-panded pedestrian streetscape and bicycle trail.

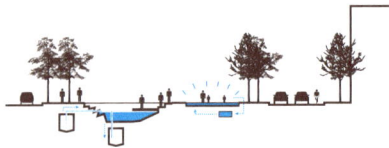

CARVE: A surface parking lot is transformed into a public event plaza, scattered with cuts and karst windows into the culverted waterbody below. Pools and other elements organize this flexible open space.

CONNECT: A small headwaters stream links two historically divided neighborhoods and provides a direct connection between the downtown and the Legacy Trail, a regional bike and pedestrian pathway.

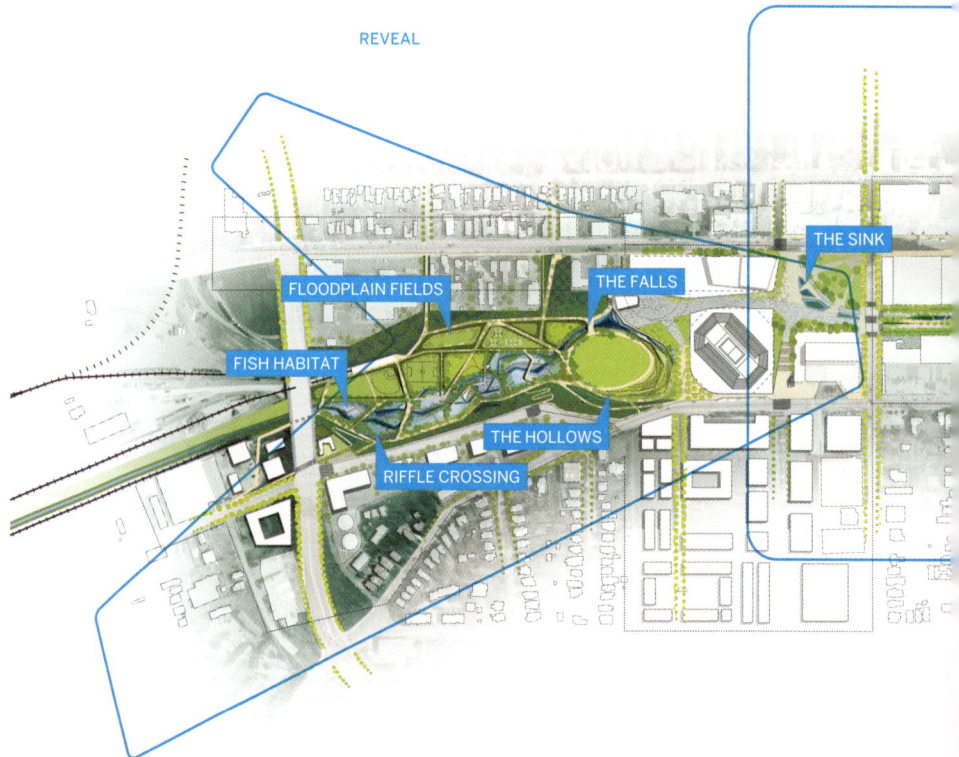

REVEAL

FLOODPLAIN FIELDS

THE SINK

THE FALLS

FISH HABITAT

THE HOLLOWS

RIFFLE CROSSING

CONNECT

CLEAN

CARVE

MIDLAND RUN

THE BIKEWAY

KARST WINDOW

THE GATEWAY MARSH

FILTER GARDEN

THE BOILS

TRIBUTARY STREET

Reveal: The Hollows

Placed at the nexus of three emerging development zones—the Arena District, West Main, and the Distillery District—The Hollows is a central park for the city that weaves civic gathering space, athletic fields, and playgrounds into an ecologically rich riparian corridor. The Hollows offers space to reestablish and fully expose the buried stream system of Town Branch, creating a series of flood-adapted recreational and ecological rooms that transform this marginalized floodplain into a new water-based entry to the city.

THE COX STREET LOT
WHAT COULD HAPPEN HERE?

Design outreach

Riparian Public Space

The daylit waterbody meets the edge of the
city as a waterfall, cascading from the layered
urban infrastructure of Rupp Arena and the
Lexington convention center into a restored
series of riparian stream channels below. As
Town Branch moves through the space, it
carves out new programmatic rooms of ball
fields, playgrounds, riffles, and wet meadows
before connecting to the Town Branch Trail
and Bluegrass Region beyond.

Town Branch waterfall at Rupp Arena

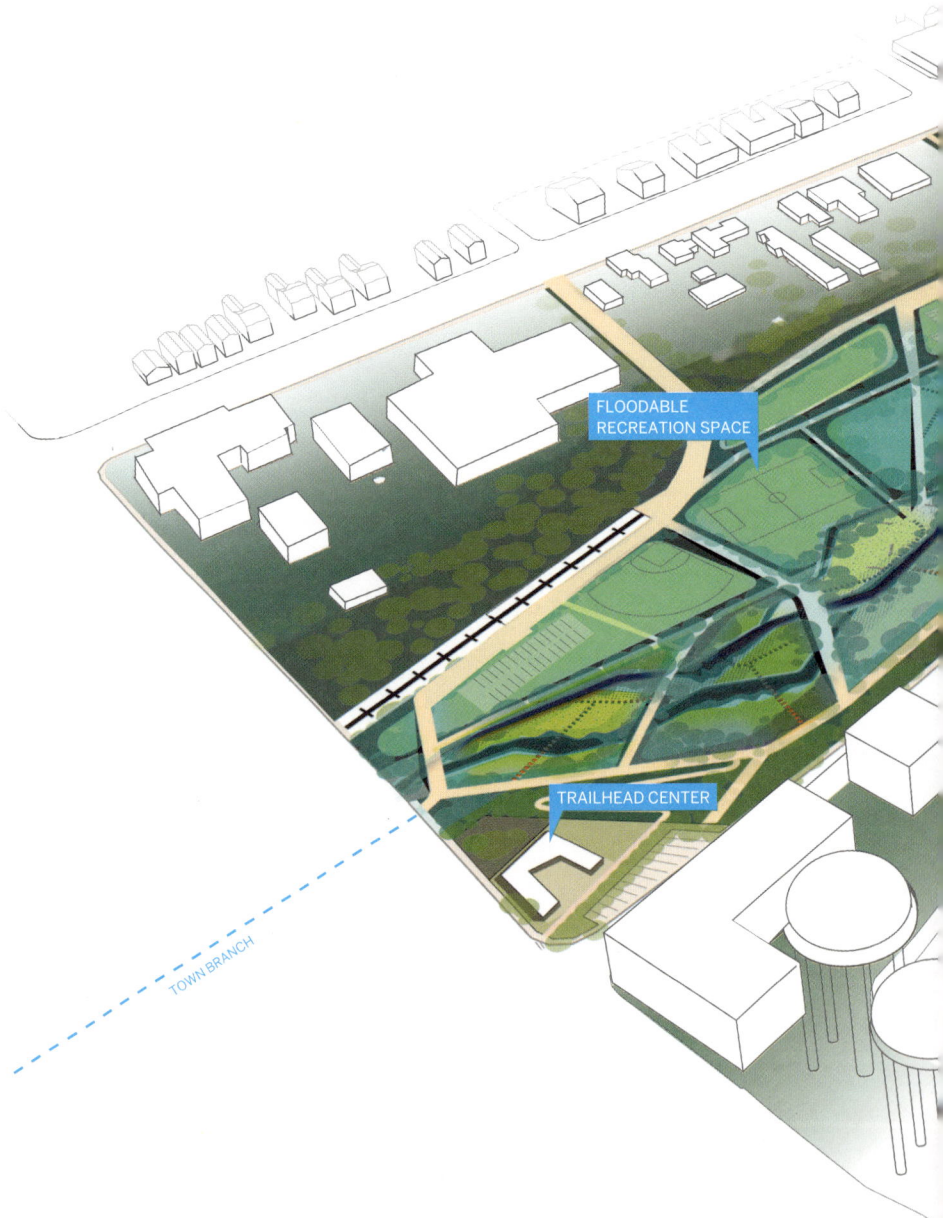

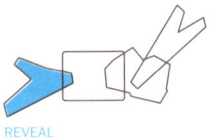

FLOODABLE
RECREATION SPACE

TRAILHEAD CENTER

TOWN BRANCH

REVEAL

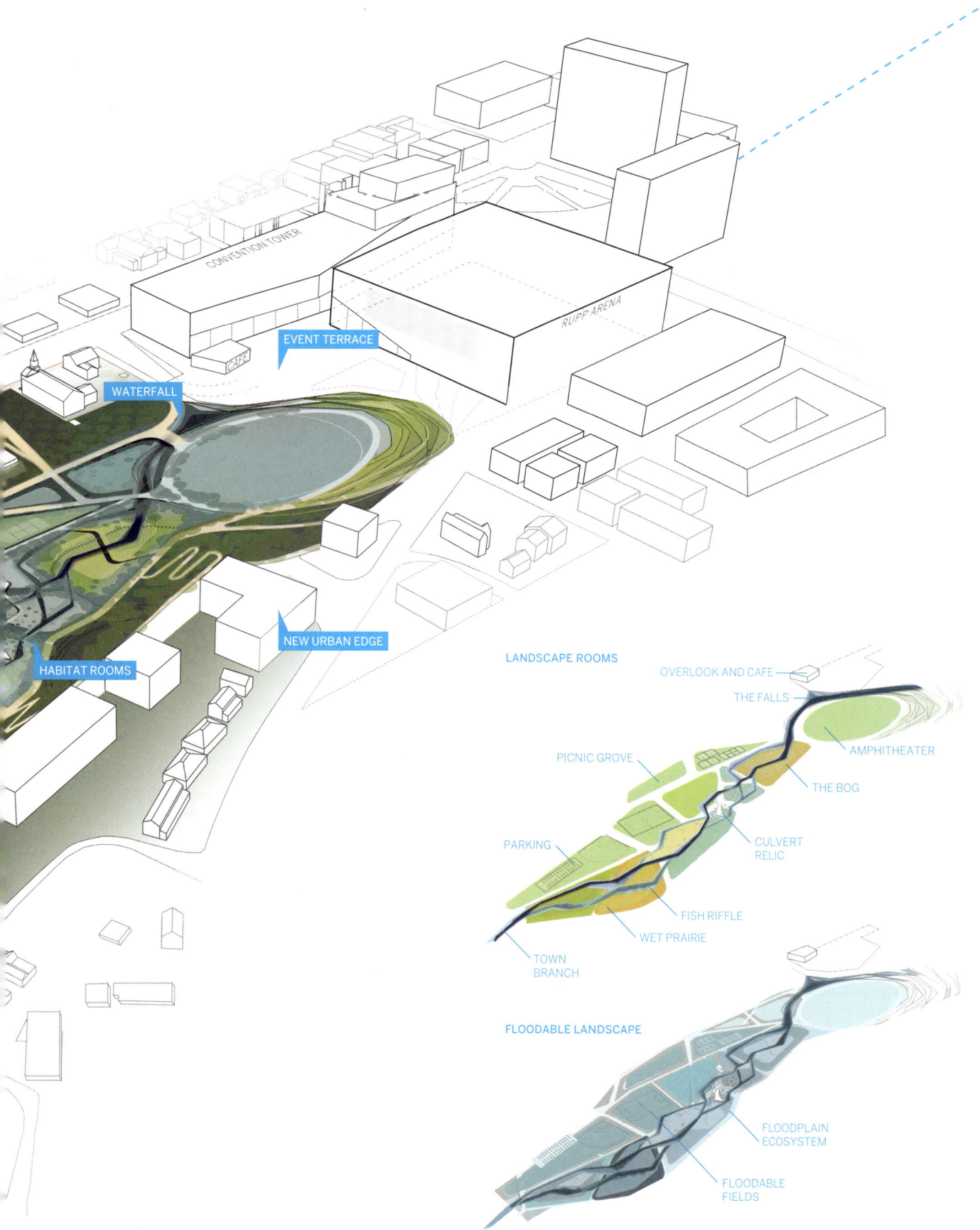

CONVENTION TOWER

CAFE

EVENT TERRACE

WATERFALL

HABITAT ROOMS

NEW URBAN EDGE

RUPP ARENA

LANDSCAPE ROOMS

OVERLOOK AND CAFE

THE FALLS

PICNIC GROVE

AMPHITHEATER

THE BOG

PARKING

CULVERT RELIC

FISH RIFFLE

WET PRAIRIE

TOWN BRANCH

FLOODABLE LANDSCAPE

FLOODPLAIN ECOSYSTEM

FLOODABLE FIELDS

Clean: Downtown Greenway

Town Branch is recast as hybrid hydrological and urban infrastructure, creating defined and safe spaces for water, pedestrians, bicyclists, and vehicles along its path. In the downtown core, streets are realigned to make way for an expanded public realm, where water is expressed not at the surface, but underground, as rainwater-fed filtration gardens clean the waters of Town Branch before entering the culvert below.

Filtration gardens

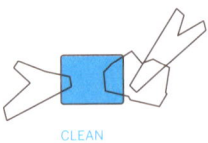

TO TRANSYLVANIA UNIVERSITY →

POP UP VENDORS

STONE FENCE

TO SOUTH HILL

CLEAN

TO CHEAPSIDE PLAZA
AND MARKET

CHEAPSIDE LINK

SEATING LAWN

FILTRATION GARDEN

PERMEABLE PAVEMENT

TO GRATZ PARK

SUPPER STREET

Geology as Materiality

The urban stream path is marked by a palette of materials adapted from karst geology and hydrology. Lexington's Bluegrass Country is marked by karst outcroppings and limestone walls. Downtown, this geologic language is repurposed to separate traffic, retain water, and provide seating. Paving, walls, and planted forms interact with water and express its flow.

Karst outcropping

SCAPE at stone fence workshop

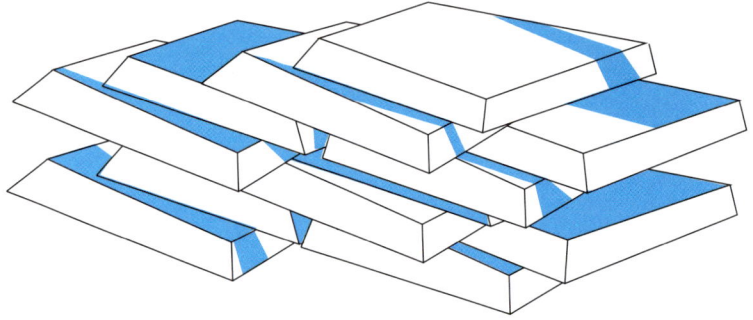

WHERE IS TOWN BRANCH?
The urban stream path is marked by a material palette adapted from karst geology and hydrology.

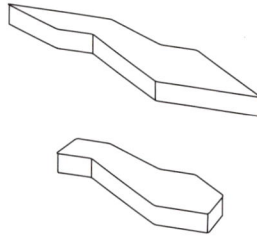

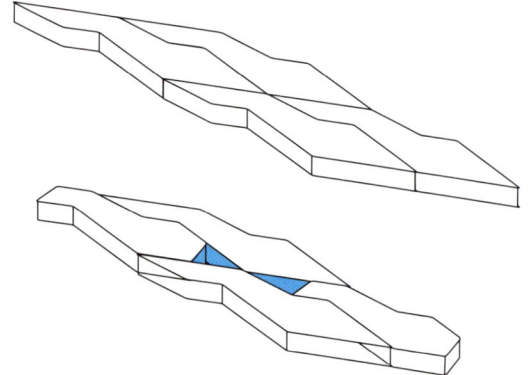

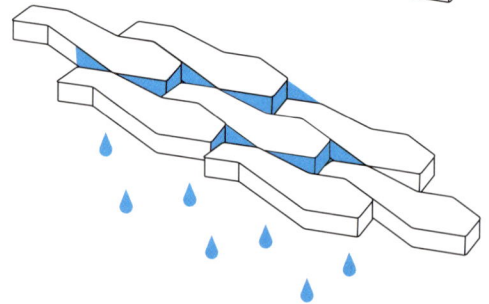

CLEAN

PAVING
Permeable paving units are designed to reflect the striated form and porous qualities of karst limestone. Surface runoff filters through and recharges Town Branch at strategic zones.

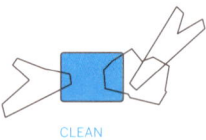

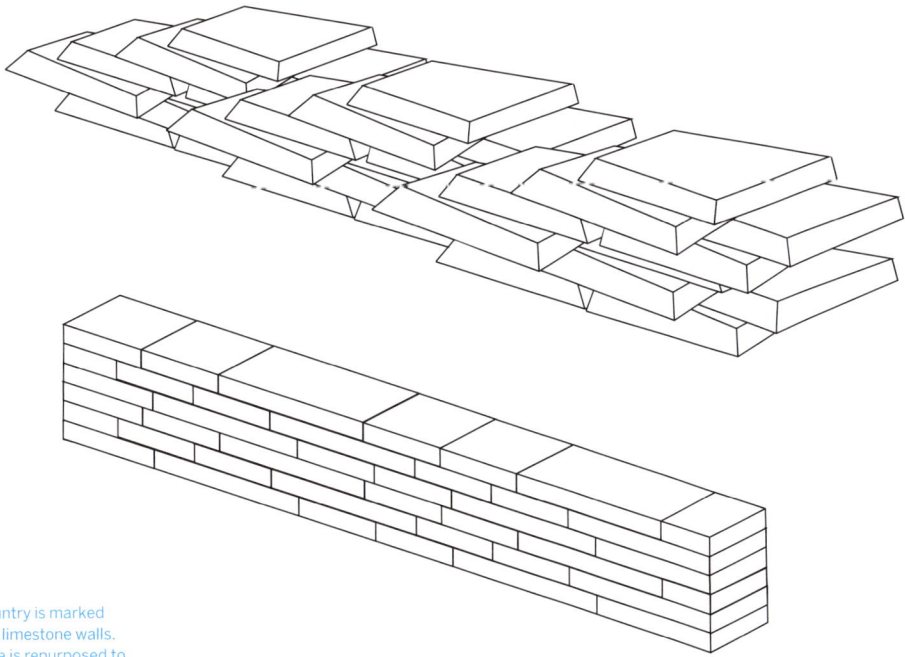

STONE FENCE
Lexington's Bluegrass Country is marked by karst outcroppings and limestone walls. Downtown, the stone fence is repurposed to serve a multitude of functions—as a median divider, as seating, and as a water retention device.

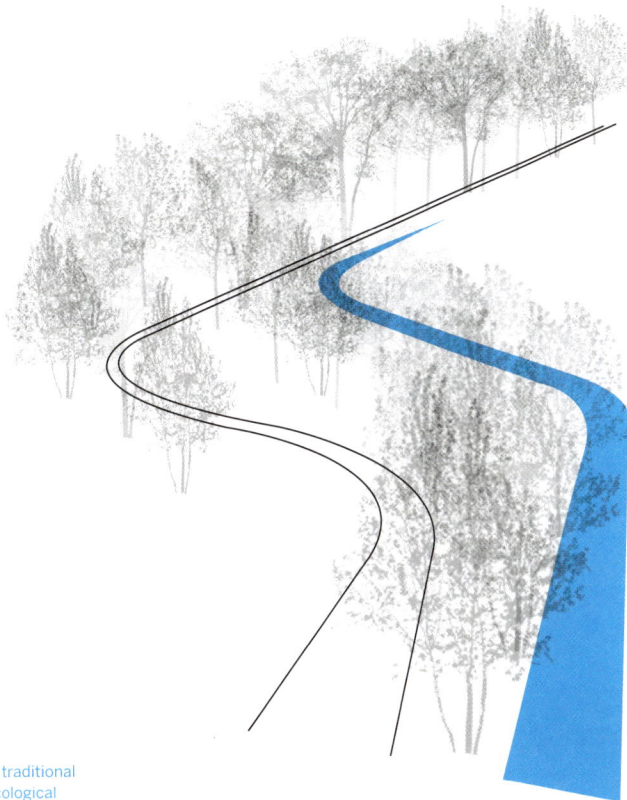

RIPARIAN FOREST
Stream bank vegetation replaces traditional street tree planting, enhancing ecological diversity and evoking the path of Town Branch.

Carve: Karst Commons

New water-based public spaces are carved into Lexington's emerging arts and entertainment district, catalyzing development of vacant sites and expanding amenities for urban living. A highly programmed public plaza accommodates multiple activities and is shaped by a series of constructed karst windows filled with diverted water from the Town Branch culvert below. Spaces for young adults, children, and grandparents are shaped by water—uniting at the central "urban boils," reminiscent of the geologic condition where upstream water pressure creates a downstream karst boil, a naturally occurring water feature.

Boils at McConnell Springs

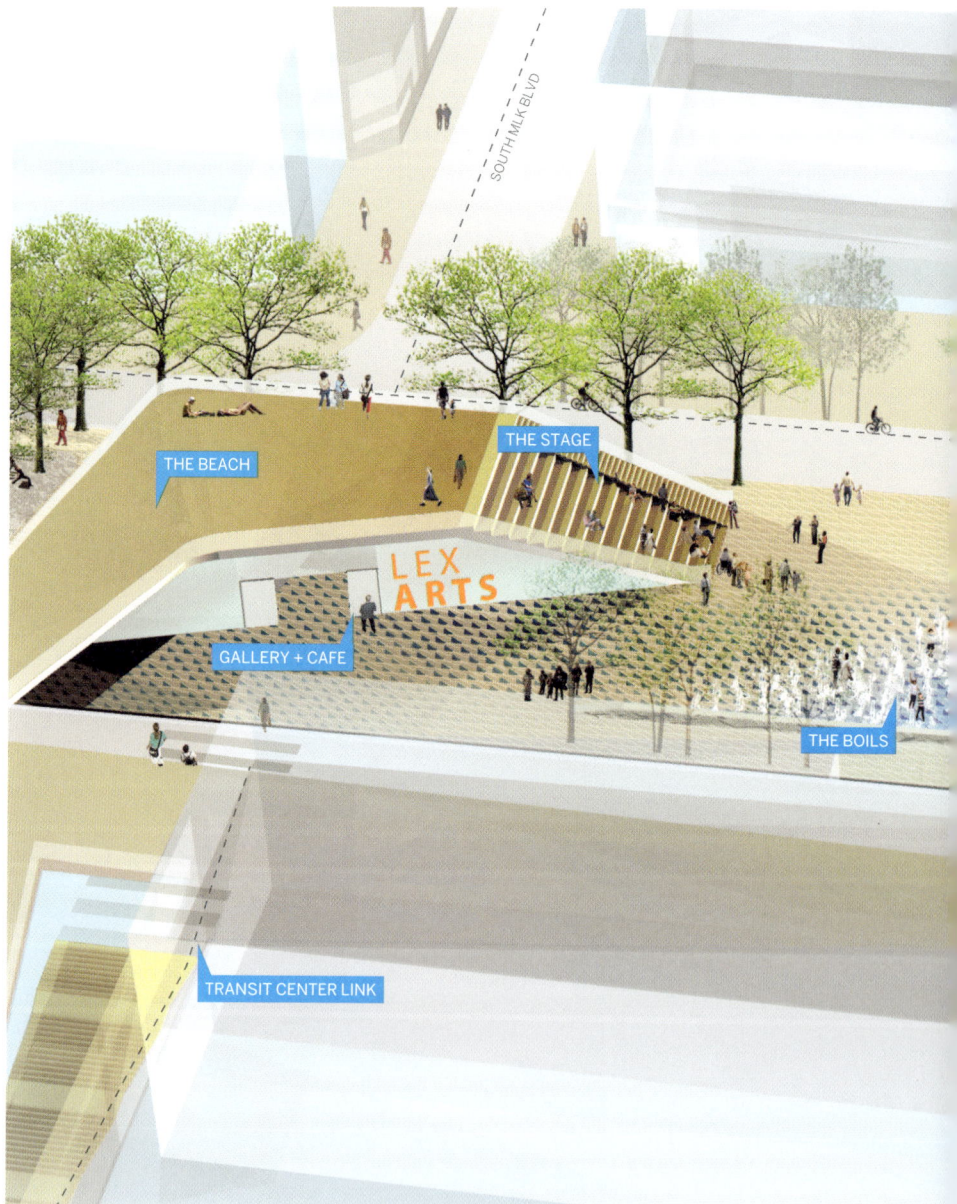

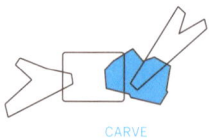

SOUTH MLK BLVD

THE BEACH

THE STAGE

LEX ARTS

GALLERY + CAFE

THE BOILS

TRANSIT CENTER LINK

CARVE

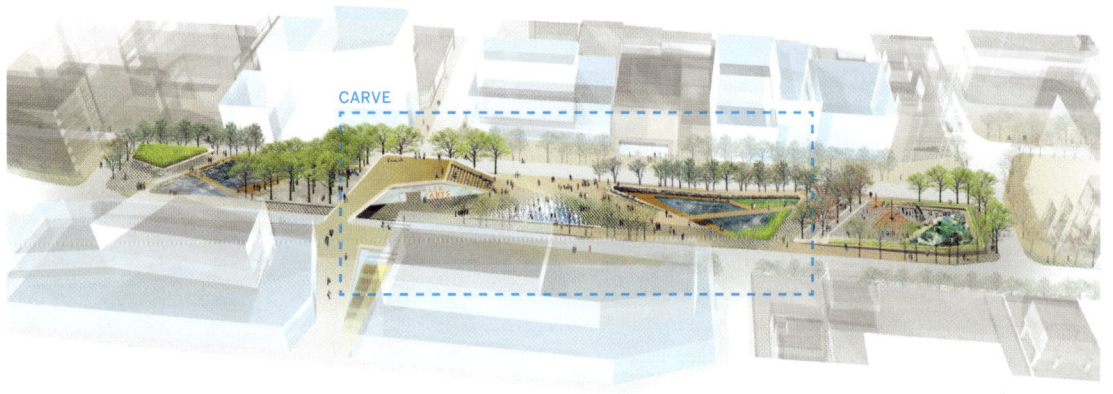

CARVE

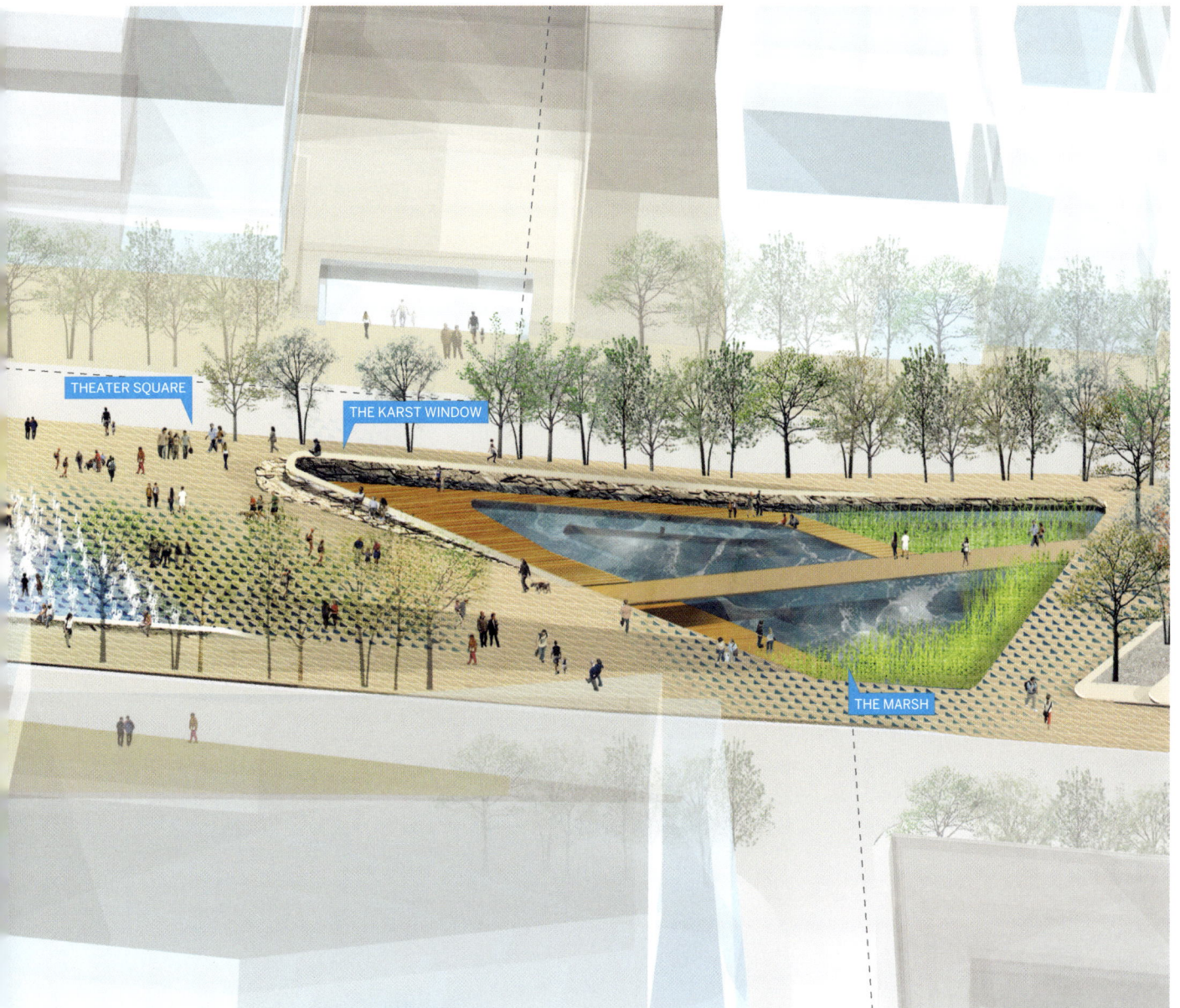

THEATER SQUARE

THE KARST WINDOW

THE MARSH

Karst Windows

In Karst Commons, Town Branch emerges, disappears, and reemerges as karst cuts and designed rock formations, creating larger windows for dynamic play, performance, and entertainment while orienting pedestrians to the underground stream below.

Karst window

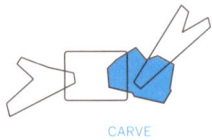

CARVE

LEX ARTS

Connect: Eastern Headwaters

Town Branch is fed by a broad field of neighborhoods in the northeast areas of Lexington. Divided by railroads and highway infrastructure, the Eastern Headwaters is designed to collect people and water along a common path, through the reduction of vehicular roadways, the introduction of water, and the addition of pedestrian crossings and connections. This "blue street" strategy accommodates new low-rise, mixed-use development while linking downtown with the Legacy Trail, a twelve-mile recreational path to the Bluegrass Region. Fully assembled, Town Branch Commons provides a critical link between almost twenty miles of continuous regional trail, connecting country and city.

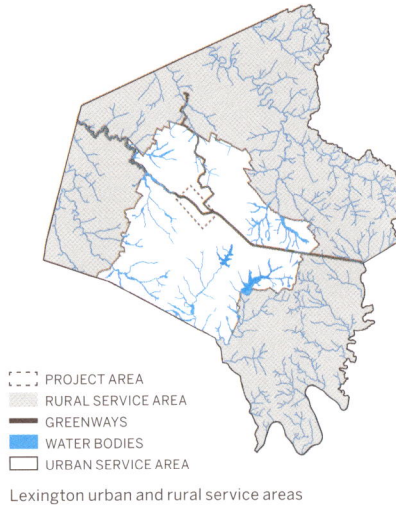

PROJECT AREA
RURAL SERVICE AREA
GREENWAYS
WATER BODIES
URBAN SERVICE AREA

Lexington urban and rural service areas

CONNECT

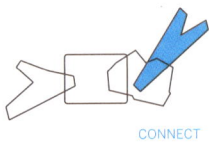

LEGACY TRAIL TRAILHEAD

LEWIS STREET

GOODLOE STREET

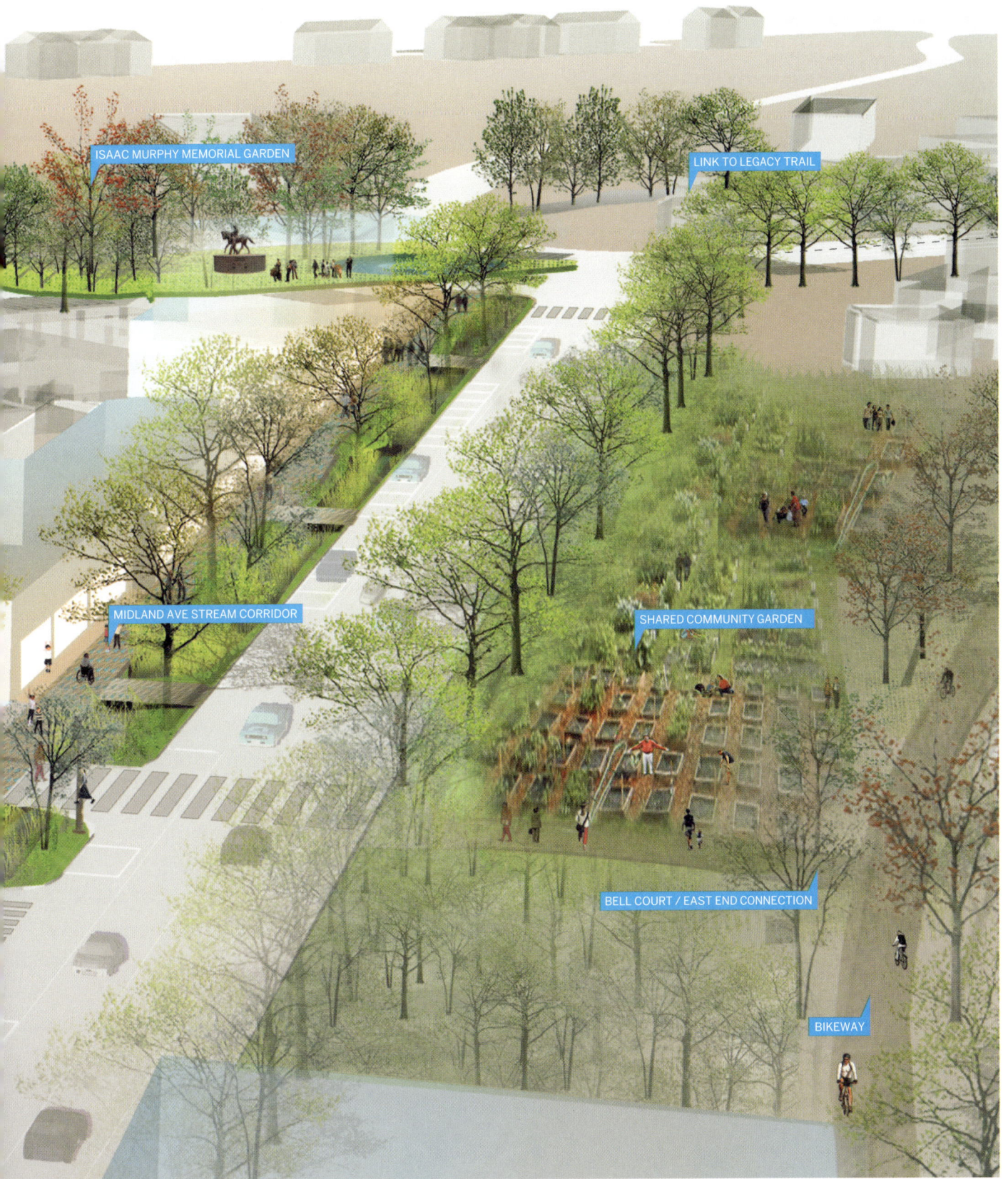

ISAAC MURPHY MEMORIAL GARDEN

LINK TO LEGACY TRAIL

MIDLAND AVE STREAM CORRIDOR

SHARED COMMUNITY GARDEN

BELL COURT / EAST END CONNECTION

BIKEWAY

WHAT
COULD
HAPPEN
HERE?
Tell us your ideas!
Leave a note.
Draw a picture.

Water Harvesting Sidewalk
Green Roof
Absorptive Street
Water Plaza
Working Landscape
Connective Ground
Urban Manager
Watershed Steward

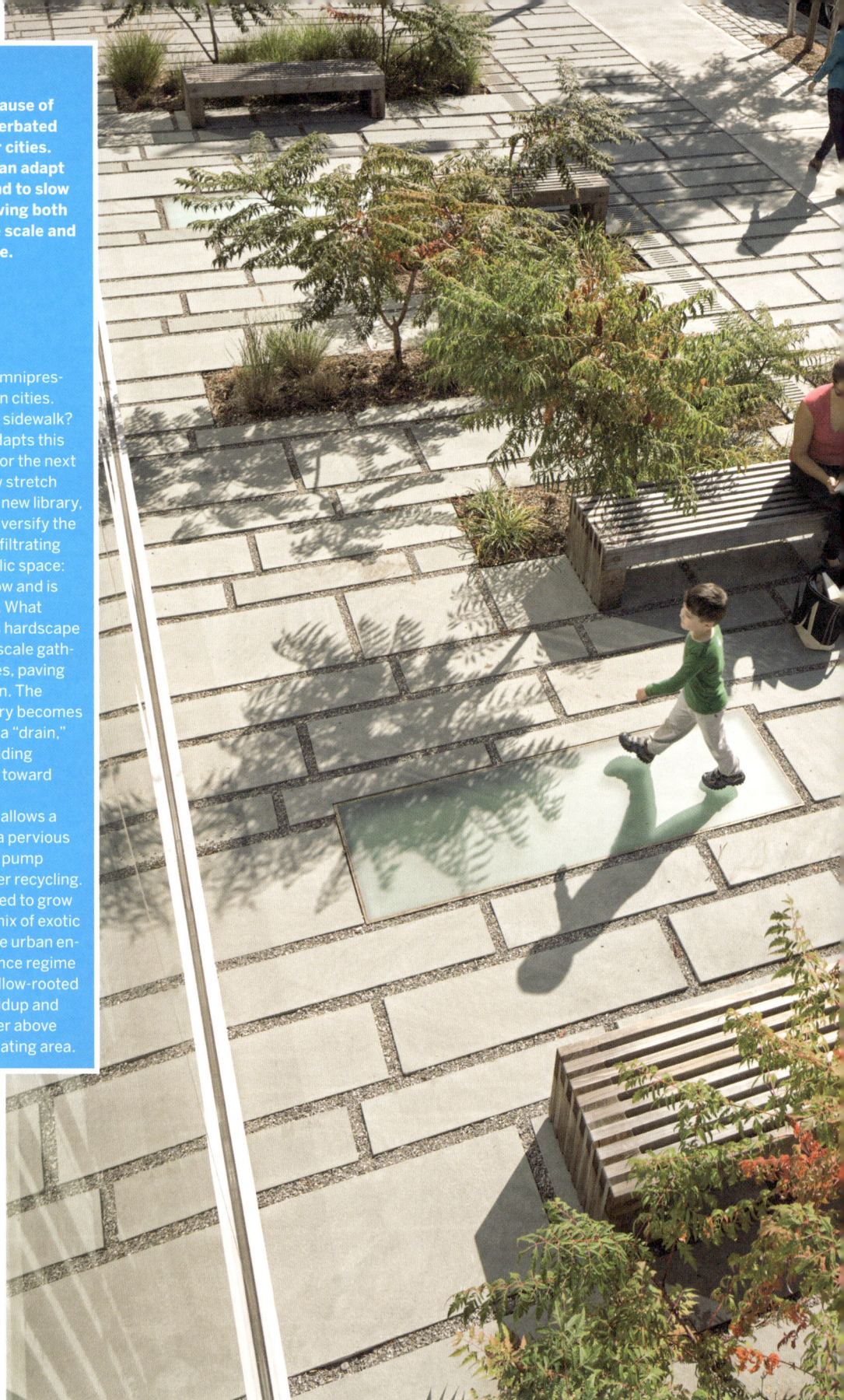

Water Harvesting Sidewalk

Stormwater runoff is a major cause of water pollution. Runoff is exacerbated by ubiquitous hardscape in our cities. The typical plaza or sidewalk can adapt to become more permeable, and to slow and clean urban waters, improving both pedestrian experience at a site scale and water quality at a regional scale.

—

Glen Oaks Branch Library
Queens, New York

Sidewalks are among the most omnipresent and typical of public spaces in cities. But what else can be done with a sidewalk? The Glen Oaks Branch Library adapts this most common of public spaces for the next century. Working within a narrow stretch of circulation space adjacent to a new library, the design aims to expand and diversify the public realm while allowing for infiltrating water. The result is a porous public space: rainwater filters into the soil below and is recycled for landscape irrigation. What would typically be an impervious hardscape is rethought as a neighborhood-scale gathering space, spotted with benches, paving texture, and emergent vegetation. The outdoor space of the public library becomes not only a reading room but also a "drain," a paradigm shift away from shedding water into the sewer system and toward on-site reuse.

Loose jointing at street level allows a field of bluestone to function as a pervious layer, feeding a large cistern and pump house within the building for water recycling. The planting, designed and pruned to grow into thick groves over time, is a mix of exotic and native species adapted to the urban environment and limited maintenance regime of public infrastructure. The shallow-rooted sumac thrives in the thin soil buildup and provides a mid-story canopy layer above passersby looking for a shady seating area.

WATER INFILTRATION

STORMWATER COLLECTION SYSTEM

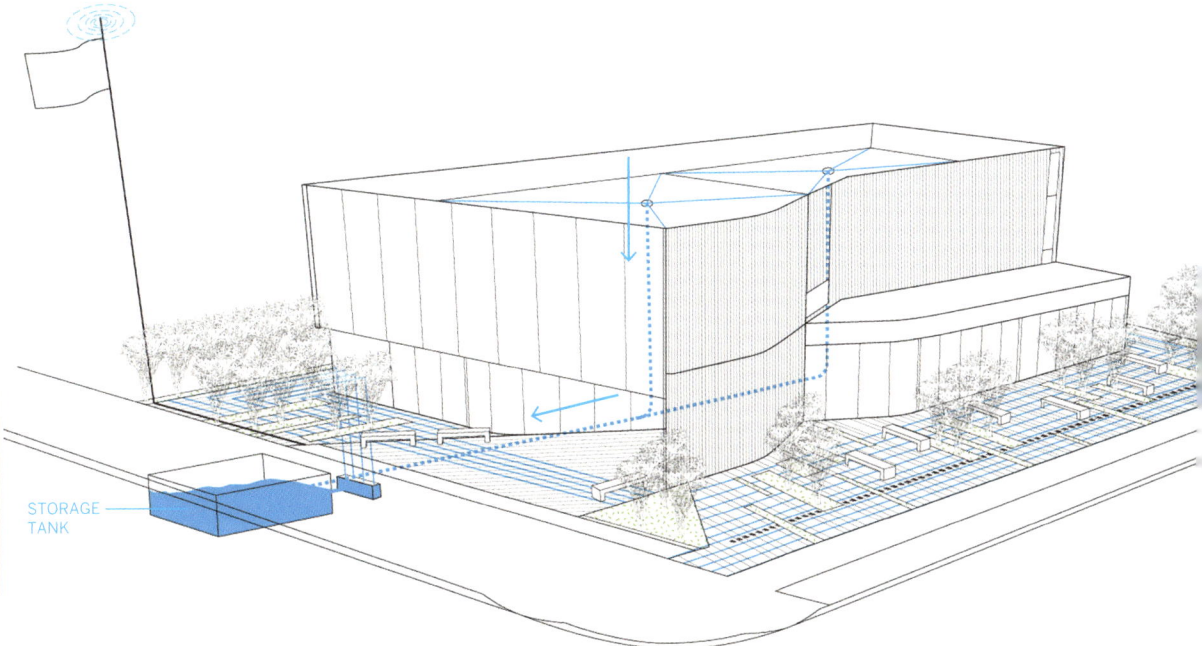

STORAGE TANK

Green Roof

A green roof serves to absorb water, provide insulation, create a home for wildlife, and help lower urban air temperatures—which are on average three to eight degrees Fahrenheit cooler than the surrounding area.

—

Milstein Hall
Ithaca, New York

The university campus is typically associated with verdant quadrangles, stately trees, and ivy-covered halls. Despite this "green" appearance, university campuses often require the environmental resources of a small city. SCAPE's work for Milstein Hall at Cornell University introduces a new campus: a landscape-on-structure that functions as both infrastructure, art, and environmental mitigation. The 26,000-square-foot green roof of the new College of Architecture, Art, and Planning building reduces the structure's environmental impact by collecting rainwater and improving insulation and cooling. Planted in a dynamic pattern of red and green sedums and designed to change over time as a successional experiment, this massive landscape insertion visually integrates the building with the spectacular colors of the surrounding forest canopy. Beneath this green roof layer, water is collected, stored, and eventually channeled into existing stormwater systems. In a 1" rain event, almost 11,000 gallons can be absorbed.

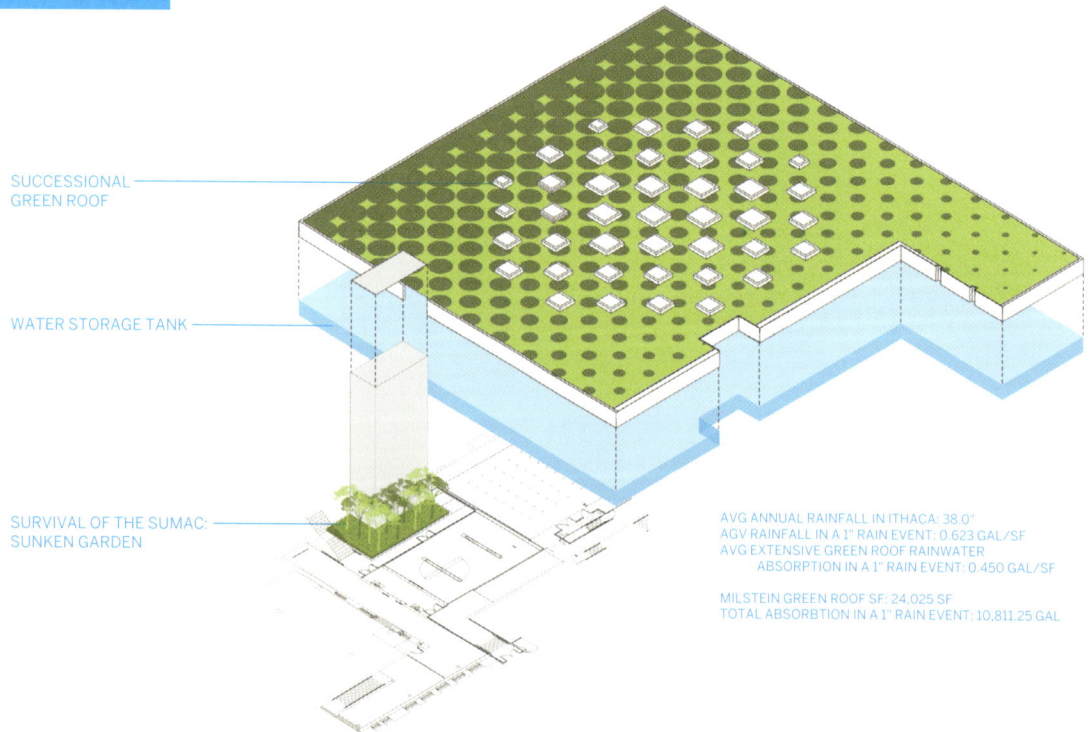

SUCCESSIONAL
GREEN ROOF

WATER STORAGE TANK

SURVIVAL OF THE SUMAC:
SUNKEN GARDEN

AVG ANNUAL RAINFALL IN ITHACA: 38.0"
AGV RAINFALL IN A 1" RAIN EVENT: 0.623 GAL/SF
AVG EXTENSIVE GREEN ROOF RAINWATER
    ABSORPTION IN A 1" RAIN EVENT: 0.450 GAL/SF

MILSTEIN GREEN ROOF SF: 24,025 SF
TOTAL ABSORBTION IN A 1" RAIN EVENT: 10,811.25 GAL

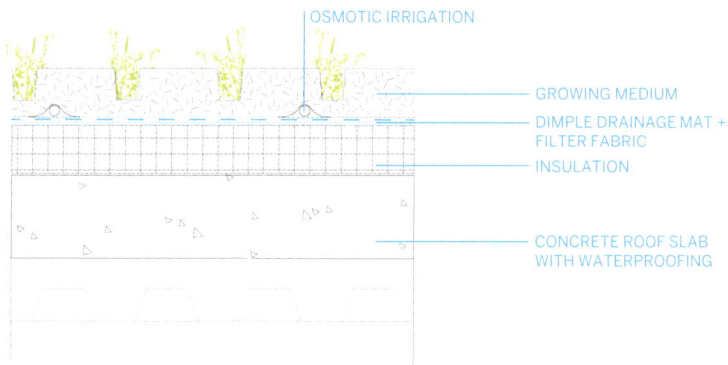

OSMOTIC IRRIGATION

GROWING MEDIUM

DIMPLE DRAINAGE MAT +
FILTER FABRIC

INSULATION

CONCRETE ROOF SLAB
WITH WATERPROOFING

Absorptive Street

Finding novel ways of increasing water infiltration in the urban environment requires redefining hard infrastructure itself. Vegetated areas help to ameliorate some of the harmful effects of this hardscape—in essence, they delete the street.

—

Buffalo Niagara Medical Campus Streetscape
Buffalo, New York

How can urban streetscapes adapt to the ecological challenges of the twenty-first century? At Buffalo Niagara Medical Center, a monotonous urban environment was ecologically barren and lacking identity. SCAPE worked as part of a larger team to reestablish a strong vegetated footprint for the site. Long angled planting beds maximize the tree-planting area while respecting the root zones of existing large street trees. A tiered system of vegetation increases permeability while cooling the space. The shrub layer, understory tree planting, and canopy tree planting are composed of a mix of native and urban-adapted species with a high tolerance to Buffalo's harsh winters and salting regime. A new experience emerges within the campus—a once homogenous edge transforms into a dynamic and ever-changing forested walkway, offering new experiences for the students, patients, and visitors who walk the path every day.

GOODRICH STREET

ELLICOTT STREET

 VIRGINIA STREET

ELLICOTT STREET

Water Plaza

Public spaces can not only carry programming and recreation, they can literally hold water. Designing for heavy rain events and occasional inundation allows public spaces to be flexible and productive within the urban fabric.

—

First Avenue Plaza
New York, New York

SCAPE's First Avenue Plaza activates the urban realm through topography, makes space for people and water, and celebrates Manhattan as a marshland-turned-megalopolis. Steps from the East River, the plaza serves as both urban civic space and a gateway to the East River Greenway. The plaza, located over a parking structure, is activated by a layered water collection system that responds to multiple types of inundation. A piped wading fountain centers the design, creating a bubbling plane of water that mitigates the noise of the FDR Drive and cools the space. Around the perimeter, a series of rock-lined swales collect stormwater runoff from the plaza while creating a sense of vegetated enclosure. In a heavy rain event, the swales are coupled with an underground retention system located below the fountain that captures and holds water before gradually diverting it to the East River. In the event of a flood, the water-plaza landscape combines with a deployable floodwall to protect the new building structure from inundation. The site responds directly to both stormwater and coastal flooding threats while creating spaces for relaxation, performance, and play.

FOUNTAIN

BIOSWALE

BALD CYPRESS GROVE

METASEQUOIA GROVE

WATER PLAZA SYSTEM

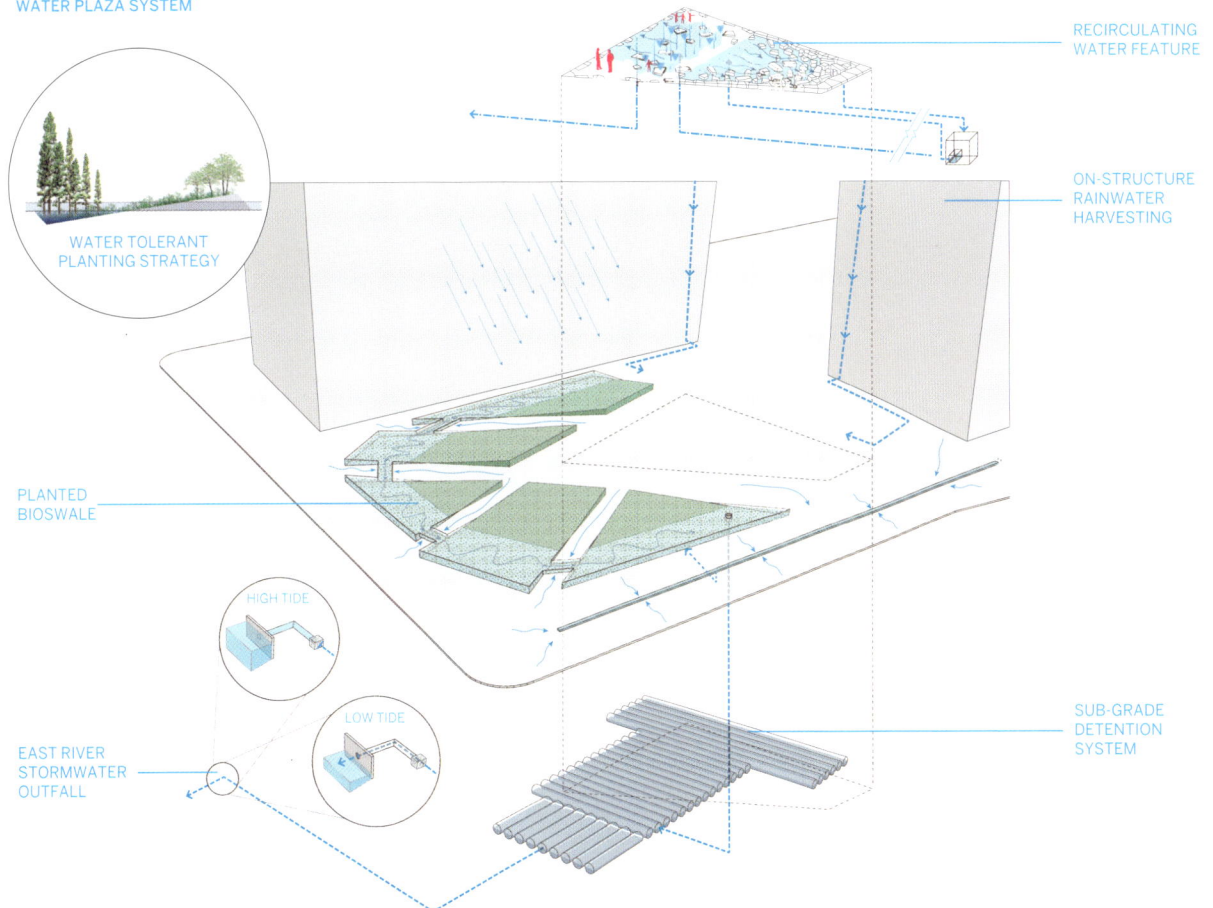

RECIRCULATING
WATER FEATURE

ON-STRUCTURE
RAINWATER
HARVESTING

WATER TOLERANT
PLANTING STRATEGY

PLANTED
BIOSWALE

HIGH TIDE

LOW TIDE

EAST RIVER
STORMWATER
OUTFALL

SUB-GRADE
DETENTION
SYSTEM

Working Landscape

Urban landscapes can produce valuable goods and services—minerals, food products, clean water—while creating new forms of public space. Essential to the creation of productive and working landscapes is an active and engaged citizenry, committed to managing and stewarding resources over the long term.

—

Be'er Sheva Quarry
Negev Region, Israel

What is the future of postindustrial infrastructure? This proposal for Be'er Sheva Quarry Park activates a retired quarry site, currently a void in the urban fabric of Be'er Sheva, and the source of forgotten origins of the base buildings materials of the old city. Rather than proposing to fill and "green" the site, SCAPE worked with LOLA Landscape Architects and TOPOTEK1 to reactivate it as a working quarry. Unique public spaces are carved through the re-initiation of quarrying operations, revealing inhabitable zones framed by the indigenous red hammer stone. Cultural education, stonework apprenticeships, and quarrying observation become part of an expanded park program that builds upon the history of the site and the city, built from the stone historically quarried here.

The design proposes constant transformation. Phasing is structured through the incremental creation of public, or park space—deep oasis cuts to cast shade and collect valuable water, carefully molded outdoor rooms for evening, early morning, and religious activities. Excess material is shaped into street furniture and paving stones for use around the city by the site's stonework apprentices, who play the dual role of craftspeople and geologic interpreters. As time advances, discreet spaces and moments are incrementally revealed and opened to the public, producing an experience that grows out of itself: through the relationship of found and constructed, residual and new, Be'er Sheva Quarry provides a new park experience that is constantly evolving.

CULTURAL CENTER

EDUCATIONAL WORKSHOP

URBAN PROMENADE

BLACK BOX THEATER

CASCADE STAIR

LUSH OASIS

FLEXIBLE PLAZA

SHADED CAVE

POOLS

PROTECTIVE DUST FENCE

1. ACTIVATE AND EDUCATE

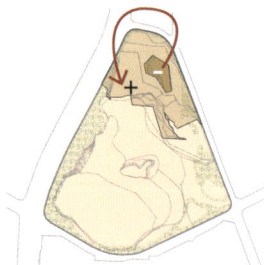

2. CARVE AND CREATE

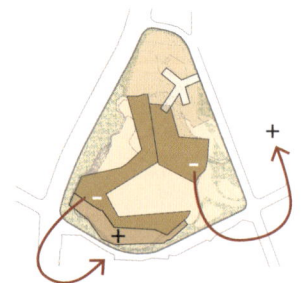

VEGETATED BUFFER

3. CUT AND COLLECT

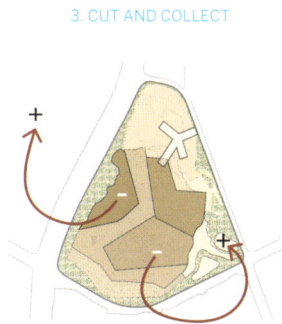

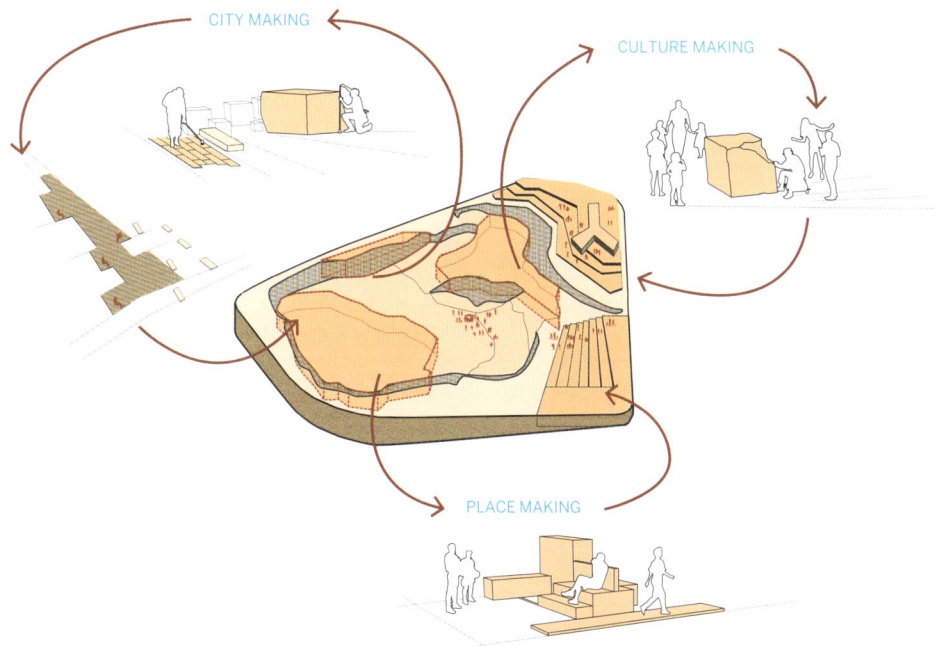

CITY MAKING

CULTURE MAKING

PLACE MAKING

Connective Ground

Over the past century highway and civil engineering projects have severed communities from their waterfronts and environs. Connective ground is a sectional landscape strategy to reweave connections above, over, and through infrastructures to create contiguous public space.

—

Water Works
Minneapolis, Minnesota

For 12,000 years, the Mississippi River has powered through Minnesota, cascading over St. Anthony Falls and scrawling a deep gorge, like a signature through limestone and prairie. It was along the banks of this gorge and around the power source of the falls that the city of Minneapolis was built. Later, roadways, rail lines, and dam infrastructure further severed downtown from the Mississippi riverfront. This project uses a stepped section and repurposes old railway trestles to transform the former West Side Milling District into a public space that reconnects the city with its historic waterfront. Water has literally shaped the natural and man-made landscapes of the site, and consequently, the Water Works design seeks to embrace, reveal, and interpret the historical narrative set in motion by the mighty waters of the Mississippi and its industrial use. The new park excavates Mill Ruins from sediment and gravel and juxtaposes these historic industrial artifacts with a contemporary water landscape infrastructure that includes a wet-dry scrim foundation and a year-round weep wall fed by stormwater. By improving public access to the riverfront site, exposing its history, and enhancing its ecology, Water Works invites the public to reconnect with and remember a site of tremendous cultural and historic significance.

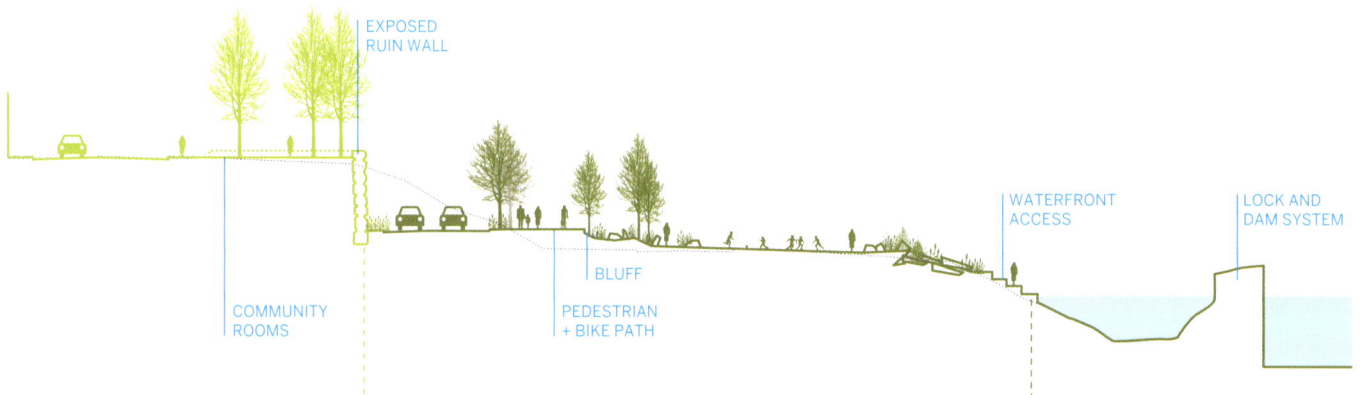

CANAL RUINS PLAZA

EXPOSED RUIN WALL

WATERFRONT ACCESS

LOCK AND DAM SYSTEM

COMMUNITY ROOMS

BLUFF

PEDESTRIAN + BIKE PATH

BLUFF

MISSISSIPPI RIVER

WATER WORKS

Urban Manager

Cities are drivers of design innovation. Urban managers are on the front lines of change, bringing the tools of urban design, economics, and policy together to make equitable, sustainable places that foster civic life.

—

Interview with Mayor Jim Gray

Jim Gray is currently in his second term as mayor of Lexington, Kentucky, a vibrant university city surrounded by rolling bluegrass pasture and world-famous horse farms. As the former CEO of Gray Inc., an international engineering and construction firm, Mayor Gray has brought an executive's approach to city government and is committed to building Lexington into a great American city through sustainable urban development. Over the past several years, Gray and his administration have worked in close collaboration with SCAPE and the Lexington Downtown Development Authority on Town Branch Commons, a long-range plan to develop a new linear park along the path of a buried stream that runs through the city's downtown.

SCAPE
What was the origin of the Town Branch Commons idea? How did it emerge?

Mayor Gray
I wish I could claim private authorship, but I can't. Many others—citizens and leaders in the community over the past ten to twenty years—have been inspired by Town Branch: the history, the ecology, the environmental influence and impact, and the economic potential in reviving it. And fortunately SCAPE's proposal illuminated and revealed opportunities that we had not imagined.

S
Town Branch is very hidden. Do you think there's a collective understanding about the waterway?

MG
No, there's no shared understanding. I would say that today, maybe 3 percent of citizens are aware of it. The absence of that collective understanding actually illustrates how much potential we have. SCAPE's design stimulates the imagination that much more. People say: "Really? There's a river buried underground?" And then we get to explain that it's not exactly a big river, but a small perennial stream, a wet-weather stream that historically has flooded Lexington. That was one of the reasons that Town Branch was taken underground: to prevent this flooding of the downtown, which was the prolific economic engine of the city at the turn of the twentieth century.
Part of what we see with SCAPE's proposal is the potential to really reveal this remarkable

history—Lexington's original water source—and through it to have a teaching influence on kids, young people, the whole culture of the city. That's what really inspires, stimulates, and encourages the project, despite the usual challenges and ups-and-downs of a major public work such as this.

S
You've spent some time traveling to other cities to look at how they use water systems as catalytic neighborhood agents for change. Have those experiences informed your sense of what Lexington can offer and how it can progress?

MG
Annually the Lexington Chamber of Commerce takes a tour of another city and brings back ideas. When the chamber went to visit Providence, Rhode Island, and Oklahoma City, they saw those cities' water features and both times came back saying, "We need something like this." Well, now's the time, we've got the plan: here it is! And it's not a canal, as in those cities; it's a living stream and hopefully a much greater step forward. Are we going to have to manufacture a little bit of water in some places? Perhaps. Pump it? Yes, right? But not to the extent that it is in these other urban plans. In that way it's much more convincing. Since it's authentic, it's going to get more currency, more traction culturally and economically.

S
That's what's inspiring for us about it: that the project was really conceived and built around the idea of the regional karst geology.

MG
Full confession: I love hiking, and I love the Red River Gorge, just southeast of Lexington. I grew up about twenty miles from Mammoth Cave, so I am very familiar with this karst deposit and its caves, its caverns, its crevices, and its waterfalls. When SCAPE came up to do a site visit and hike, it was so fantastic.
Every other proposal in the competition was a canal project. Would those have the potential to create the personal attachment that this does? I would say no. This model is very inspirational, I can't think of anything more appropriate. It connects what we know is an extraordinary rural landscape through an ecologically, environmentally, and economically aspirational approach that takes into account the history and culture of Lexington.

S
That really highlights the ways in which a mayor can be an urban designer. A mayor can have an enormous impact on the relationship of a city's inhabitants to their home.

MG

I've discovered that the significance and responsibility of the mayoral position is even greater than I had imagined. The city is the place where every citizen's heart can sing, and anything that's built should add to the beauty of the city. The mayor has the responsibility to be an advocate for good city design. Cities over time have demonstrated that when they think, create, and build imaginatively, they improve the culture quotient, which improves the economic vitality. It's all very holistically, symbiotically integrated. But getting there is really hard. There are a lot of moving parts to public projects, especially one like this, and it requires a lot of persuasion for the public to buy into a transformative project. But we see it as infrastructure for the next generation.

Over time the cost of these projects that are so transformative is nominal, but it looks enormous and overwhelming at first. Everything is to scale: New York City has a $60 billion budget; Lexington has around $600 million. But as former New York Mayor Bloomberg said when I met him, "We've got the same opportunities and challenges, it's all a matter of decimal points."

So despite adversities, despite what are perceived as the inefficiencies of government, we muddle along. And over that arc of time, over that history, very special characteristics emerge and develop. America was a pioneer settlement, so each of us has something special in America—an attachment to the land, in one way or another, where these settlements occurred. Usually they were around water, an essential natural resource—ours happens to be a smaller body of water than most. What I think is so remarkable about this project is that SCAPE really peeled the onion and revealed what is unique and authentic and special and original about Lexington, and that is worth so much.

S

You were talking about the time scale of 200 or 300 years, but we also have to work on the time scale of four years—the mayoral term. How do we think about scaling up these projects into initiatives that can happen within a reasonable time frame but also impact the next 100 or 200 years of Lexington's future?

MG

I've learned that unlike private sector busi-nesses, which operate on the micro scale and are very susceptible to the ups-and-downs of an economy, in the macro-economy where cities and governments are positioned we're enormously sustainable. In 2009, at the bottom of the recession, the city's revenues only dropped 3 percent. The real challenge is the allocation of those resources and the political will to take on projects that will fundamentally alter the city. It's particularly

challenging in a democracy—it takes a lot of persuasion to make change. We have to get the private and public sectors engaged. But when you do get both, it really works.

One of the challenges now with the Town Branch project is to stoke up the quiet phase of the campaign, to get the private sector commitments. All of the real money in Kentucky is in Louisville. Louisville was an industrial town; Lexington, an agrarian and university town. If you look historically at university cities and agrarian cities or populations, they rarely had that institutional wealth over time.

S

Another aspect of the project is connecting the downtown and the more rural countryside, where Lexington's agrarian and academic economies are largely intact. That's what's amazing about the place.

MG

It's true. The project will create these larger connections, but the region really centers on Lexington. These initiatives don't bring in a lot of philanthropy, which is why the work that SCAPE is doing now—the education and outreach initiatives like the Town Branch Water Walk—is so important. Folks need to know about it!

S

To follow up on this idea of education: in some of these smaller projects, like the Town Branch Water Walk, where we're creating a tour and listening posts along the length of Town Branch in collaboration with students and educators, the aim is to build on the idea that youth engagement and persuasion play a role in the design process. From your perspective, what role does education play in this project?

MG

Oh, it's huge! When I talk about the project to an elementary school group, for example, the kids' eyes just get as wide as silver dollars and they're excited about it. That's my barometer, always. If you can excite the kids about a project then you've got a great chance of exciting the parents and citizens.

I'll never forget when the daughter of a friend heard about the underground river. Lily was then six or seven, and she was just so excited about the river that she collected nickels and pennies and dimes and quarters and gave them to me as a contribution to the project. That pretty well sums it up. The future Town Branch Park ties together so many aspects of the his-tory of Lexington—from the water system to the karst, to bourbon production, and even the legacy of horse farms—and I've found that the more people know about it the more they are inspired to get involved in making it happen.

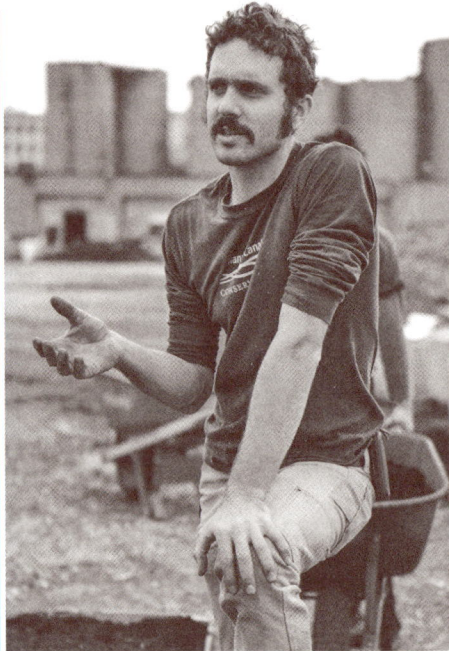

SCAPE
How has the Gowanus Canal become such a locus for community building? Do you think it has to do partly with the nature of the canal as a site?

Hans Hesselein
I would say what has influenced the growth and direction of the canal most is its physical place, its geologic history. It was a creek that was dredged to create a canal, really to drain farmland around it, but also to create an industrial waterway that could be used for importing and exporting goods from Brooklyn. That it is still an open body of water today continues to be the primary thing that draws people to it. Because it was an industrial canal, it was for a long time a center of commerce and important culturally to Brooklyn for that reason. It provided a significant number of jobs back when Brooklyn was part of America's industrial heartland. The Gowanus was the center of that, and it's also the southern—or eastern—terminus of the Erie Canal system.

I want to say it's always been loved by the community—although I can't say that from personal experience because I've only been a resident for seven years. But it certainly has always had a reputation, especially for the way it smells: it's clearly been very polluted and abused. There are a lot of rumors, too—urban legends about bodies and mafia dumping. So it's always had a legendary place in the local psyche and for a long time it was a no-man's land. A lot of the locals look at its renaissance now and kind of shake their heads like, "I never would have seen this day coming!" But the Gowanus always held an important place in their minds and hearts. It's ugly and beautiful at the same time.

S
Can you give us a little background on the Gowanus Canal Conservancy? How did you get involved?

HH
A volunteer program called Clean & Green was initiated in 2009 by two board members. They would gather groups of people, go out, and work in the community. They were intended for picking up trash—and there was plenty around the canal, a lot of illegal dumping at the time—removing invasive species, and maintaining green streets and street trees. I'd been looking for ways to get my hands dirty and satisfy my need to plant and work in the soil. So on a whim I attended one of these events and had a wonderful time. It was really empowering, working in public space, using it—or treating it—as though it was my own personal garden. It actually was an experience that made New York livable for me, as an outlet and a release. I became very engaged in working with Clean & Green. Eventually the Conservancy, which didn't have any staff at the time, got one of the early NYC Department of Environmental Protection Green Infrastructure grants, and put together some federal money as well as some city money, and they needed somebody to manage the initiatives—so I was hired.

S
It seems as if the DIY mindset is growing culturally across the country. Is this work part of that?

HH
I'd say do-it-yourself culture is very Brooklyn. It's certainly something that I've always liked. It was the culture of the organization before I arrived, and I think it's been infectious and attracted a lot of other people to the cause. It becomes a self-reinforcing culture. DIY activi-ties like guerilla greening, building gardens, composting, etcetera—what made all that possible in Gowanus was the fact that it had been neglected for so long, had such a bad reputation, and nobody was paying attention. I think we were allowed to do work without being bothered by officials or public agents because we were working to improve public space down there, so folks were willing to turn a blind eye. We've demonstrated that we can manage not only volunteers but also a landscape in a responsible way and improve it. Now that Gowanus has gentrified in a lot of ways, we're allowed to continue operating and formalizing our partnerships with private businesses and the city because we've demonstrated our level of responsibility and that we do good work.

S
This idea of responsibility seems central to the work of the Conservancy. Part of what you're

doing is rethinking what public infrastructure is: how it operates, who's responsible for it, who maintains it.

HH

We call it Community-Based Stewardship. It's a scalable model, and the volunteer program has grown every year. There are probably about fifty volunteer coordinators now who help organize events, and we have a compost subcommittee that is focused on composting food wastes and organic wastes that we use as a potting soil, a soil amendment, and a mulch for all of the open space work we do. We've got a garden stewardship subcommittee that's working on developing maintenance standards and recruiting people to adopt and care for the open spaces that we create. We've got a design and planning subcommittee of folks who develop project concepts and drawings. And now we're working to develop—formally develop—a bioswale maintenance certification program that will train and certify community members to provide stewardship for city-owned bioswales.

If it works, it's a program that can be packaged and shared with any municipality across the country. Stormwater management and the reduction of combined sewer over-flows is a major issue that a lot of cities are now dealing with: Philadelphia, Portland, Chicago, just to name the big ones. We can't keep dumping sewage in our waterways, so we're going to have to build green infras-tructure and somebody's got to maintain it. It's a really relevant and important program —and it's DIY!

S

How do you imagine the canal playing a role in community development in the future—how do we get there?

HH

Right now the canal is a public body of water. All the property around it is private, and the only opportunity to access and experience the canal is when you're crossing a bridge or at a street that dead-ends into the canal. As the canal gets developed and properties become rezoned, developers are required to set aside a forty-foot esplanade for public access to the canal—that is the mechanism by which a park will ultimately be developed. I don't think we'll ever see a contiguous green band, and I hope that actually the southern third or so of the canal will remain industrial and commercial. But for the northern two-thirds I think we'll see residential redevelopment, and as a result we'll get public open space, brownfields will be cleaned up, the canal will be improved. I'd love to see oyster habitat, wetlands, salt marshes—and more wild space, supportive of diverse species. After Superfund, some of the small spurs and turning basins

will hopefully be restored as salt marshes and wetlands. Once those become functioning ecosystems, they'll provide services that will further improve water quality in the canal and attract more wildlife, make it more beautiful. So in the medium and long-term future I hope to see more habitat, more open space. And I'd love to see people working out there on a daily basis, gardening, maintaining, and really living and working with the Gowanus.

S

This up-close-and-personal view of the Gowanus is key, both in the short and long term. This communal view of infrastructure and the building of our public spaces, how do you see it playing out?

HH

You encourage people to go out, get their hands dirty, commune with nature. Working in green spaces, in gardens, is rewarding—it's important, it's healthy, and people just don't have opportunities to do it in New York. A bioswale could be somebody's garden! I really like the idea of people using public open space as their front or back yard. And you know that as such an empowering experience—it was really an important experience for me as it is for a lot of the people that come participate in our volunteer programs—so why not create parkland and open space that function in that same way? In fact, our vision ultimately for a park around the Gowanus Canal is not a static green space that is designed and then you work against—what's the word I'm looking for, when things tend toward chaos?

S
Entropy!

HH
Entropy, yes. So in a "normal" park you're constantly battling entropy—you're just

trying to keep it going in the state that it was drawn on paper. I like green spaces that evolve and change. This doesn't work; let's look at that. It evolves, it's dynamic, and it's really a true public space in the sense that people are operating it and not just passing through.

MAKING ROCKS PUBLIC
Jane Hutton

Liquor, the savory and delectable elixir that surrounds an oyster on a half shell, is, anatomically speaking, its blood. Rather than flowing through tubes, an oyster's blood circulates openly between its organs and shell cavity; this blood is primarily seawater and its flavor reflects the mineral composition of the water that the oyster grows in—its so-called *meroir*. Oysters concentrate large amounts of zinc, copper, and iron from the sea into their bodies, offering to the human who tastes it an addictive *umami* flavor and deep mineral satisfaction.[1] As it matures, an oyster accumulates and organizes calcium carbonate into its shell, building layer upon layer of refuge from the sea that becomes the elegant, palm-sized stoneware dish from which humans slurp. In its humble bivalve lifetime, an oyster gathers minerals from afar and produces a sturdy, rock-like shell that far outlasts its life; if anything, it illustrates the uncanny dependencies of organisms on their abiotic environments. The oyster is a soft animal in a hard mineral world, and serves as a reminder that we are too.

Oysters have been the featured protagonists in two of SCAPE's widely acclaimed projects. Oyster-tecture (at the *Rising Currents* exhibition at MoMA in 2010 [see pp. 88–107]) and, more recently, the Living Breakwaters project of 2015 for the south shore of Staten Island, introduced the notion of constructed oyster reefs as critical ecological infrastructure for New York City (see pp. 236–59). In oyster-like fashion, SCAPE proposed a rope-and-landform framework, attractive to thumbtack-sized oyster spats as a place to settle down. Individual oyster shells are small, but at the scale of the breakwater, their collective mass roughens water flow, creating hydrological drag and slowing the water's movement—they have the power to mitigate storm surges and the slew of hydrological dynamics that come with climate change. These projects have brought the formidable ecological role of oysters and oyster reefs in filtering water and providing storm surge protection to the public's mind. They approach overwhelming challenges of climate change with ecological intelligence and modest means, in contrast to the defensive engineering strategies that prevail. They have helped us to envision what lies beneath the water surrounding New York City's islands, and to appreciate that the mineral cycles and processes of their invisible world are fundamentally connected to our life on land. Furthermore, our interests in the success of the oyster reefs are doubly piqued because we want to eat the oysters that grow on them; Living Breakwaters makes us imagine and work toward a future in which that might be possible.

SCAPE brings mineral cycles and geological processes to the forefront of their projects in order to construct both public landscapes and public discourse. In Town Branch Commons, Lexington, Kentucky's own karst landscape inspired the project's public space strategy and materials palette (see pp. 26–45). Otherwise invisible hydrogeological processes and their inherent cultural relationships (from the flavor of bourbon to the settlement of the city) are brought to Lexington's main streets. Along the Mississippi River in Minneapolis, Water Works is a new public space alongside a waterfall and an obsolete mill (see pp. 64–65). The project makes people consider the geologic timescale of the river's formation and its relationship to industrial evolution. Likewise, in the proposal for Be'er Sheva Quarry Park in the Negev region of Israel, a decommissioned quarry would be reopened; workers are slated to transform the landscape into a working quarry while constructing the park through subtraction (see pp. 62–63). In each of these projects, mineral or geological elements are not seen as static, passive contexts to be manipulated to serve human needs; instead, SCAPE foregrounds mineral and geological cycles as active components of their work. Mineral and geological processes are conceptually, programmatically, and materially incorporated into the physical projects and their narratives. The result is that processes that are otherwise too small or big to see and that occur on vast timescales are made knowable and palpable. As a field, landscape architecture is founded on an intricate understanding of geological context—for purposes of aesthetic effect, construction technology, and notions of ecological fit. And while SCAPE's practice certainly builds upon this tradition, their approach extends far beyond responsible contextualization and compelling tectonics. Instead, SCAPE's work offers a thought-provoking and ecstatic engagement with rocks and minerals in ways that engage the public.

In other words: They make rocks public.

To say that SCAPE is making rocks public is to borrow from sociologist and philosopher Bruno Latour's provocation *Making Things Public*, launched as a catalog and exhibition curated with Peter Weibel at the ZKM Center for Art and Media in Karlsruhe, Germany, in 2005.[2] In it, Latour revisits the etymological origin of the term *res publica*, or "republic"—as the *res* (things, causes, concerns) that the *publicus* debates. Latour argues that we have lost the *res*, or the "thing-ness" of politics, and we need to get it back. "Thing-politic" is important because we can gather around things to debate them; they are open-ended, heterogeneous, material, and complicated, and give us something to agree and disagree on; they are human and nonhuman, and importantly, don't distinguish between them. They might be rivers, rising carbon dioxide data, land grabbing, wetlands, or schools. "Thing," or *ding*, Latour traces, was not only the name of the issues that people circled around, but the physical assembly space for debate. Examples of ancient parliaments, not surprisingly, involve rocks: from the stone circles of German *Thingstatten* to the Icelandic *Althing*, situated on geologically charged terrain.[3] At Thingvellir, just outside Reykjavik, Norse settlers convened the world's first parliament along the fault line produced by the spreading of the North American and Eurasian tectonic plates. What better place to debate the union and fractures of society and the nonhuman world, Latour suggests, than where the bedrock does the same? SCAPE continues this tradition by bringing rocks again to the spaces of public debate.

SUSPENDED IN GROUNDWATER

On a research trip for their Town Branch Commons proposal, the SCAPE team traveled around the Bluegrass Region to study the elusive karst limestone landscape. They came across a site where erosion had rendered a perfectly legible cross section of the karst. Like a geological diagram that you find in a national park, the dynamics of this rock's formation were evident. Horizontal strata showed how vast numbers of microscopic marine organism skeletons had settled and solidified into matte calcium carbonate limestone. A network of cavities, channels, and fissures, all interrupting or slipping between the limestone layers, showed paths of water moving and carving through the rock. Calcite and aragonite, the minerals that limestone is made of, can withstand all kinds of pressures, but are defeated by any weak acid—rain and groundwater are acidic enough to erode them. A sectional view easily allows the eye to trace a couple of interconnected channels, but in three dimensions the complexity of the underground network is mind-boggling. From the limited human perspective, water merely appears and disappears from the earth's surface; we can't easily identify the direction in which the water is moving.

Like most cities, Lexington's specific urban history can be linked to its geophysical context. Lexington's settlers began near a limestone spring, drawing water for milling, farming, quarrying, and manufacturing. Early bourbon distillers established their shops close to limestone springs.[4] Limestone water, with its suspended calcium carbonate, both facilitated fermentation with its high pH level, and precipitated iron, which removed the bitter flavor associated with that mineral.[5] SCAPE's project for Town Branch—the creek that runs, channelized, under current-day Lexington's central business district—foregrounds the foundational role of karst for Lexington, and learns from karst itself.

The proposal translates the nonlinear, episodic appearance of water on the surface in the karst landscape into a public space strategy. Rather than make a generic river-like form, Town Branch Commons draws from the specific hydrogeological processes of karst itself: a sequence of different water-focused areas are linked along the site, each communicating a different type of water movement above and below ground. Sometimes water is pooled on the surface; sometimes it sinks quickly from the street into filtration gardens or through permeable paving; sometimes it moves in a thin sheet across rock surfaces. As a guiding principle for the project, the karst landscape solved several pragmatic problems at once: overall site organization, a programming logic, and an idea about animating the city.

On daily routes through the city, visitors conjure the region's complex three-dimensional underground landscape. Previously obscure karst vocabulary becomes commonplace. While the diligent landscape architect thinks of the "below-ground" as contiguous with a project, the work is usually all about the "above-ground." In this case, while people stay on the street level, efforts are made to connect them to the movements of water below them. We are paradoxically disconnected from "below-ground" despite the fact that it is the very thing we stand on. By drawing attention to the karst landscape as part of daily urban life, we are reminded of the connection between the water flowing down Vine Street's storm sewers, kitchen faucets, and even our blood.

At stake is being able to link urban life with regional groundwater dynamics; this, for example, raises the public controversy of the implications of fracking in Kentucky. In the book *Petrochemical America*, Kate Orff drew our attention to the underground storage facilities where tons of hazardous petrochemicals are deposited out of sight, but close enough to harm nearby residents' drinking water—residents with the least political power to fight back because of class and racial bias. *Petrochemical America* reminds us irresponsible toxic dumping isn't democratic, as the symptoms of climate change disproportionately afflict the world's least powerful and least culpable. Town Branch Commons, through a relatively benign play of water, provokes a tougher discussion about the relationship between the surface and the "below-ground." By helping visitors to hone their underground vision, they become better equipped to gather around the issue of utmost importance: the ground itself.

COLLAPSING INTO THE MISSISSIPPI

St. Anthony Falls, today lodged just east of Minneapolis in the Mississippi River, has been moving upriver for years. They likely formed 12,000 years ago, somewhere near current-day St. Paul, as coursing torrents drained from the massive glacial Lake Agassiz. Platteville limestone covers the region; it lies on top of a thin layer of mud slate and a thick deposit of St. Peter sandstone.[6] The limestone is hard and the sandstone is soft, so water pouring over the falls quickly undercut the sandstone below. As the underlying sandstone was carved away, mammoth-sized blocks of overhanging limestone ledges tenuously extended until they catastrophically collapsed into the pool below. As they collapsed, the falls—the location of greatest height difference—migrated up the river, bringing the potential energy of gravity with them. We're used to thinking of erosion as a subtle process that occurs incrementally over time, but these falls moved spectacularly fast.

SCAPE's promotional video for Water Works, a new public space along the St. Anthony Falls Historic District, instructs us that the falls advanced up the Mississippi by roughly a mile every millennium. By the time the falls had reached the current location of the Minneapolis airport, they were a significant portage site for the Dakota Native Americans who lived nearby. By the time the falls entered what is now downtown Minneapolis, cutting forests and grasslands, transformed into wheat fields far from the city, brought in lucrative commodities; sawmills and flour mills harnessed the energy of the falls, fueling the city's industries. Despite the city's investment in mill infrastructure and milling as its economic base, the falls wanted to keep moving. With extraordinary efforts, some unsuccessful, the falls were braced in place with lumber and concrete in 1869 and then again, more robustly, in the 1950s and 1960s. Minneapolis's social and industrial history is entwined with its geological history and the specific rock types and natural processes that have propelled St. Anthony Falls—now temporarily paused—upriver. SCAPE explicitly situates Water Works within this long history.

A collapse at the Falls

Rather than commemorate the rise and fall of the milling industry alone, the project foregrounds the entanglement of Minneapolis's urbanization with geological change and places visitors squarely within it. In this way, the falls are understood beyond their momentary—even if instrumental—role as power generator, and instead as an ongoing phenomenon-in-motion that preceded and will succeed current patterns of settlement. SCAPE made two major site moves: first, the excavation of industrial ruins, and second, the construction of terraces in reference to the limestone ledges and sandstone bluffs that were shaped by the retreating falls. Together, these human and nonhuman landscape typologies provoke an understanding of their inter-connectedness. We are left to consider the dependence of modernizing Minneapolis on the power produced by the migrating falls, and the dependence of contemporary Minneapolis on power coming from elsewhere.

Workers build an apron at the Falls

The Water Works "bluff," a central organizing element, references the geologic section of the falls with overhanging bedrock and loose sand-gravel underlay. On top of the bluff, visitors peer out from cantilevered ledges to St. Anthony Falls, arrested beyond; below the bluff, people driving through the site are faced with a massive stone wall, confronting the underside of the geologic section. By making these geologic landforms and processes present in the park and emphasizing the site's geological and industrial formation, the project enables the public to imagine and even to embody environmental change: the mammoth falls in motion, the cascade of falling limestone blocks, the delicate dependence of industry on the river. Although the St. Anthony Falls haven't moved for fifty years, Water Works suggests their past and future movement, and more specifically, our relationship to large-scale natural processes that are otherwise outside the scope of our usual contemplation.

EXTRACTING AND BUILDING IN THE QUARRY

An aerial photograph of the landscape around Be'er Sheva pictures a sea of yellow-tinged beige, reflecting bright light in the Negev Desert. The hue comes from the ubiquitous red hammer stone that forms the basis of the land itself and has sustained generations of masonry construction. In the center of the city, you can see the now-defunct quarry from which stone was first extracted during the Ottoman-era. The quarry grew wider and deeper as stone was displaced to grow the city wider and taller. Once on the outskirts of the current "old city," the quarry became engulfed by the city during the twentieth century as it modernized with steel and concrete construction and expanded.

Rather than seeing the quarry as a site for historical preservation or a postindustrial leisure landscape, SCAPE—together with LOLA Landscape Architects and TOPOTEK1—proposed instead to make it functional again. Today, landscape architects routinely have the opportunity to work on postindustrial and brownfield sites: closed-down ports, steel mills, and factories. These signal the global migration of industry and jobs from developed to less-developed countries and regions. While such projects have offered the discipline some of its most interesting and experimental contemporary work, they rarely critique or comment on the local evacuation of employment and industry. In contrast, the design team of Be'er Sheva Quarry Park takes a firm position on labor and industry by emphasizing their place in the city. Not only do they recognize the value of the working quarry, they insist that there is something to be gained from the proximity of the rock operation to the public. For example, new smaller-scaled quarry operations reinstate a fading cultural practice of working with stone, employ and train local residents, and champion local industry—all under public view and with public access. The public is always able to peer into the construction zones—like the tempting peephole in a construction fence—and watch the site develop over time.

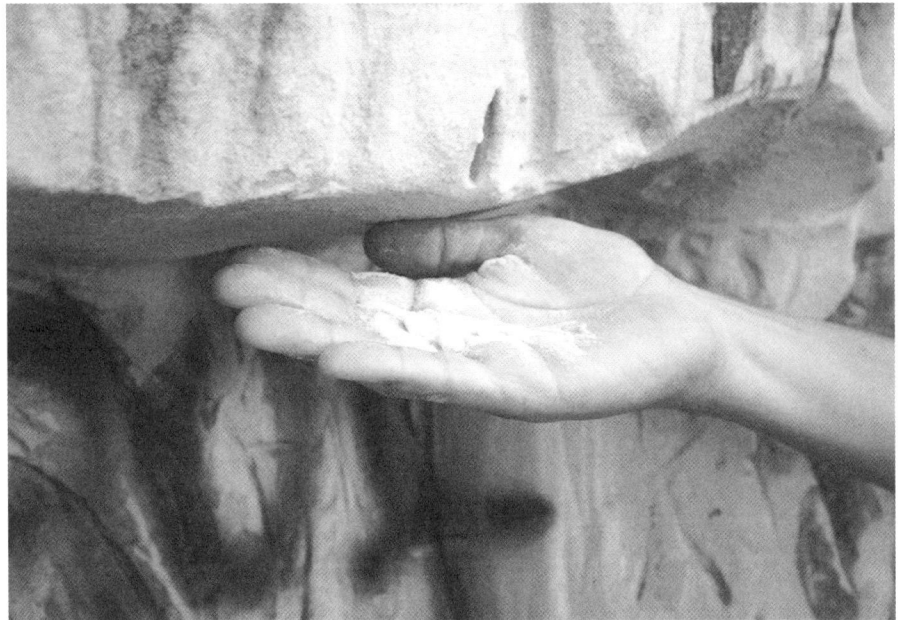

Sandstone at Be'er Sheva Quarry

Be'er Sheva reminds us of the 1:1 relationship that always exists between the stone cut out of a quarry or landscape and the building site where it is eventually installed; in this case, however, these are one and the same space. Extraction sites are typically out of sight and mind to those who use the materials, as is the labor. But here stonework is not only visible, it is conceived as integral to the activity of the park and the public sphere. Visitors are able to inhabit the sheer faces, deep plunges, and overscaled ledges and ramps of the quarry landscape. While people are accustomed to visiting geological sites outside of the city, here the mammoth cliffs, located within the city limits, were fashioned by humans. Furthermore, while the design team proposes workshops to maintain and value traditions of stoneworking, they do not exclude other traditions and voices: visitors are able to climb and carve their own personal messages into a wall of red hammer stone. Be'er Sheva Quarry Park makes rocks public by bringing people into a sublime rock landscape produced entirely through human labor, by foregrounding the quarry as a site of work and cultural activity, and by drawing attention to rock extraction happening squarely within the city's center. In global material production, uneven development means that those with the least power bear the riskiest working conditions and greatest exploitation. While material production sites are always far away and invisible, Be'er Sheva Quary Park enables people to understand the work of cutting stone, and perhaps therefore, to have a stake in labor conditions.

ROCK-POLITICS

Landscape architects have long been interested in "revealing" geological processes; this type of often-didactic work aims to educate disconnected urbanites about their natural contexts. In contrast, SCAPE doesn't simply teach us about geology—instead, they reassert how human activities are founded on and remain inseparable from geological processes. Rocks are not, they argue, archaic material stocks or inert site contexts; they are the very contemporary matter that we feed on, build with, fight over, and survive by. They are of political consequence. SCAPE brings geology into public discourse, whether it be by bringing an understanding of the underground karst landscape to the streets of Lexington, Kentucky, by expanding our sense of the present to include geologic processes of the last glacial retreat, or by drawing attention to the labor of extraction and material production. Instead of merely warning of climate change, emphasizing physical and phenomenological geologic presence helps people to experience and grasp environmental change firsthand. These projects comment on critical controversies and raise difficult questions: for example, how does understanding groundwater dynamics impact the debate about fracking for shale gas? How does considering our place within geological timescales reframe the criteria for decisions about dumping chemicals underground that will persist for generations beyond our own? And how does paying attention to labor practices in the construction industry inflect our tolerance for exploitation that we can't see?

Public landscapes, like the Icelandic *Althing* that Latour recalls, are powerful fault lines around which to gather today. Because of this, landscape architecture must do more than simply provide amenities to ameliorate urban life in cities like Lexington, Minneapolis, and Be'er Sheva. Instead, as the makers of public parks, which remain symbolic sites of public discourse where human and nonhuman elements come together, landscape architects have great potential to "make things public," to make work that provokes the public imagination and prompts discourse about how we relate to other species, minerals, and rivers, for example. Landscape architecture offers the potential to help us think differently about our actions in the world—particularly a world whose climate is changing in front of, in spite of, and because of us—and the problems that will be disproportionately borne by the world's poorest. Rather than evaluating landscape architecture for its successful programmatic elements and smart design details alone, perhaps we should also qualify a project as a success by gauging the kinds of ideas and debates it helps to raise with the public that gathers in it. By making rocks public, SCAPE shows us how landscape architecture, rather than being an end in itself, might prompt an alternate future.

1. Rowan Jacobsen, *A Geography of Oysters* (New York: Bloomsbury, 2007), 53.
2. Bruno Latour, "From Realpolitik to Dingpolitik: or How to Make Things Public," in Latour and Peter Weibel, eds., *Making Things Public: Atmospheres of Democracy* (Cambridge, Mass.: MIT Press; Karlsruhe, Germany: ZKM Center for Art and Media, 2005), 2–33.
3. Ibid, 13.
4. University of Kentucky, Kentucky Geological Survey, Geology of Fayette County, http://www.uky.edu/KGS/geoky/county/fayette.htm
5. Alan E. Fryar, "Springs and the Origin of Bourbon," *Ground Water* 47, no. 4. (July–August 2009): 605–10.
6. John O. Anfinson, "Spiritual Power to Industrial Might: 12,000 Years at St. Anthony Falls," *Minnesota History* (Spring/Summer 2003): 253–68.

Cohabit

"... nature is the place to rebuild public culture."[1]
—Donna Haraway

To cohabit is to live together in an intimate relationship, to dwell with one another, and share the same place. But to date, Homo sapiens has not done exceedingly well in sharing the planet. We've remade the earth to support human life at the expense of other life-forms. The historically recent avicide of the North American passenger pigeon, which was once so numerous its flocks were recounted as darkening the skies, stands as an emblem of our unmitigated predatory instincts and a key lesson in human-caused population collapse: we ate them and shot them for sport so enthusiastically that the last confirmed sighting of a passenger pigeon in the wild took place in 1900. The first landscape architecture program notably opened its doors to students that same year, so the profession can regrettably be held as accountable as the rest of our species for presiding over the precipitous decline of other life-forms as well.

What does this mean for design? What does it mean for health, comfort, food, spirituality? How can we expand the traditional notion of working for a "client" to include perceived human and animal needs? Whether dominant or not, "humans depend on ecosystem properties and on the network of interactions among organisms and within and among ecosystems for sustenance, just like all other species."[2] Cohabit as a concept frames a new scope of advocacy and responsibility for the urban designer of the twenty-first century.

We're living in the sixth wave of mass extinction. But rather than meteorites hitting the earth and triggering a collapse of interdependent species, as Elizabeth Kolbert writes, "this time the cataclysm is us."[3] Just as our understanding of the stresses that humans place on the planet become clearer and we begin to shift our design goals, the cycles—terrestrial, aquatic, and biogeochemical—that provide life support are nearing dangerous thresholds. As Homo sapiens expand in population and our resource footprint proliferates around the globe, most other species are being obliterated, diminishing the biodiversity on the planet and paving the way for a series of quiet extinction events.

Not only does this portend a future that must contend with the economic, moral, and ethical horror of extinction, it completely changes the concept of aesthetics in the here and now. Rachel Carson wrote in Silent Spring (1962) about not only the health disaster of chemicals in the environment, but the resultant eerie silence. "Over increasingly large areas of the United States, spring now comes unheralded by the return of the birds, and the early mornings are strangely silent where once they were filled with the beauty of bird song."[4] An increasingly homogenous biosphere, with silent forests, empty seas, a world with less diversity of sound, layers, textures, living colors, and perceptible differences, could be the landscape of the future.[5] In 1757, philosopher Edmund Burke categorized the landscape experience into the picturesque, the sublime, and the beautiful, based on degrees of emotion and awe. But where do silent and empty fit into the aesthetics of his landscapes? And how late is too late to act?

When we think about urban fauna, mostly what come to mind are cockroaches, rats, and pigeons. These species thrive by default in the city when we design exclusively for humans, just as highly adaptive white-tailed deer and scavenging raccoons come by default with the suburbs. Urban species interactions are complex and often fraught with unintended consequences; some of their stories are told in our Safari 7 project. For example, the Metropolitan Transit Authority (MTA) aims to reduce the number of rats in subway tunnels and so, in a seemingly logical response, distributes rat poison. Raptors like falcons and red-tailed hawks unfortunately prey upon the tainted rats, with disastrous consequences. In 2011, a beloved male red-tailed hawk in Riverside Park was killed by rat poison during nesting season. Toxicology showed significant amounts of rodenticide in its body.[6] However, U Thant Island, an artificial island made of dredge spoils from the Number 7 train excavation in the East River served as a kind of accidental habitat lifeline for double-breasted cormorants, which have made a comeback in New York Harbor since pesticides have been banned. The needs of humans and the needs of other species often seem to be in direct conflict in cities—but there are a few beacons pointing to how the scenarios can be mediated by design or behavior change.

INVASIVES

When Hurricane Andrew blew through Florida in 1992, pet Burmese pythons—along with monkeys, mountain lions, and other captive animals—were released into the Everglades. Since these apex predator reptiles gained this newfound freedom in the vast wetland, the balance of the food chain has changed dramatically, with 99 percent of the swamp's small mammal population, including bobcats, raccoons, and opossums, presumed to be mostly eaten. Rabbits and foxes have not been seen in the Everglades for years. It's hard to turn away from a YouTube sensation like "Python versus Alligator, Episode I" (spoiler alert: alligator wins) and even harder to turn away from Episode II, where python swallows alligator whole, then bursts. But the real issues of sudden extinction over just a few years in a US National Park confirm that there are no actual boundaries to the urban landscape and that, abandoning passive "conservation," humans need to actively deal with and manage animal populations.[7] Just as we have cultivated plants for millennia, we must similarly be stewards for fauna in what is now a contiguous, planet-sized, open zoo with no keepers. Pursuing and euthanizing invasive species like the fifteen-foot python or the white deer—or any other, for that matter—create varying ethical dilemmas, relative to weighing degrees of suffering and effect. But without immediate action, there will be nothing to talk about. We need to advance a rational conversation about dealing with the most aggressive invasive species in order to be able to manage what little biodiversity is left in America's critical habitat zones.

The concept of "novel ecosystems" is defined by Richard Hobbs as "a system of abiotic, biotic, and social components that, by virtue of human influence, differ from those that prevailed historically, having a tendency to self-organize and manifest novel qualities without intensive human management."[8] This one concept can bring normally congenial scientists to blows, so varied are its interpretations and perceived repercussions. We all acknowledge that we have profoundly and inalterably changed the environment, but we can still adopt an ethical stance and a pragmatist approach toward giving animals a foothold in the world that we have made, to do them the most good with the least harm and actively manage the zone formerly known as "the natural world." Perhaps philosopher of animal rights Peter Singer has a more refined theory of justice about these issues, and certainly industrial agriculture, ocean acidification, and deforestation have caused unimaginable "silent" loss of life, but for the purposes of this essay I'll put forward a humble proposal that landscape architects will need to tread into these thorny ethical and moral issues in the decades ahead.

MUTUALISM BY DESIGN

The notion of a sustainable future is inseparable from robust habitats and the fostering of global biodiversity. It is also inseparable from economic justice and local needs. This is an opportunity. The field of conservation is evolving from a philosophy of solely protecting "wild areas" to engaging local community programs and economies, to include the concept of "conservation-reliant species," which require active management to survive. This mutual approach requires collaboration across the fields of architecture, landscape, biology, sociology, and economics to lead toward a syncretic understanding of environmental and developmental issues, with an understanding that humanity and the animal world share a common fate on a crowded planet.

Mutualism in biology describes a relationship between two species in which both benefit from the association. Designing for mutualism means recognizing and fostering the links between environment, organisms, and land-use practices—both human and animal—and identifying the complex cycles that tie together different species and systems. Two principles that can operate at all scales, in all contexts of design are: first, do no harm; second, design for mutual benefit. An immediate example of "do no harm" are the Bird-Safe Building Guidelines created by SCAPE and the Columbia Urban Landscape Lab (see pp. 118–9). These guidelines aim to reduce bird strikes in cities and improve urban design standards to supplant the building of towers and public spaces that actually disrupt or harm other species, and instead, at the very least, offer instructions to build ones that do no harm. But is that enough? The concept of *cohabit* reaches further: in order to begin reversing the trends of extinction and creating an obverse trend, we need to start designing in a way that actively benefits a diversity of species and fosters a regenerative context that makes room for nonhuman animals, shaping urban spaces to support more biodiversity.

SCAPE's Oyster-tecture project aims to do just that (see pp. 88–107). Like the passenger pigeon population, once-bountiful oysters collapsed around 1910 in the New York area, and beds were formally closed in the 1920s. 85 percent of reefs have been lost globally.[9] As documented in Mark Kurlansky's book *The Big Oyster* (2006), New York once had about 350 square miles of oyster beds. Oysters were a food source for both rich and poor and generated a robust economy. We won't be recreating that old relationship, and diminished water quality (although improving!) means that we can't eat the oysters anytime soon. But what could a new relationship look like? With the loss of the oysters, we have also lost a visceral cultural connection to the watery geography that laid the foundation for a world-class city, Manhattan, to emerge from the muck of the Hudson Estuary.

OYSTER-TECTURE AS COHABITAT

SCAPE's concept for Oyster-tecture for the *Rising Currents* exhibition at the Museum of Modern Art in 2010 was to develop an influencing strategy toward change aimed at resetting this broader relationship between New Yorkers and their harbor. We proposed a community-based reef-building project in the Gowanus Bay that would slow waves and filter water, generating a new waterfront context for New Yorkers to productively work on as well as celebrate. This sets into motion a regenerative cycle of cleaner water, engaged citizenry, and safer shores.

Oyster-tecture envisions the whole of New York Harbor as an intensively managed cohabitat. Recognizing the essential ecosystem services our waterways once performed—and could perform again—Oyster-tecture moves away from a harbor defined by human dominance.[10] The massive engineering efforts of dredging, dumping, bridging, infilling, and walling off would yield to processes of interspecies engagement with reef-building, oyster cultivation, and FLUPSYs (FLoating UPwelling SYstems, or oyster nurseries). The new processes would create the contexts for a landscape that truly fosters multispecies habitation.

Just as biology defines "mutualism" as a state in which both organisms benefit, the field of sociology refers to "the cooperative as opposed to the competitive factors operating in the development of society." Key to Oyster-tecture was aligning the oyster regenerative life cycle with social patterns and gatherings on shore. We worked with biologists, community groups, teachers, and high school students from the New York Harbor School to understand what is happening now. Rather than speculate on a futuristic waterfront and necessarily scale down, the idea was to scale up the discourse, think across disciplines, and make connections. The goal is to generate change over the long term by synthesizing and visualizing a larger strategy while deploying urban ecology toolkits, like oyster gardening, on a small scale.

Oyster-tecture model

A key embedded concept is that addressing climate change can't be the sole purview of older, "experienced" engineers and architects, but rather can be engaged more successfully through informed intergenerational exchange and broad-based coordinated actions within communities. Industrial accidents like the BP oil spill, the Dan River coal ash spill, and the Fukushima nuclear plant disaster have revealed the limits of technology in engaging the physical world. This project focuses on people and behavior as a way forward—a way to remake the relationship between nature and city through determination and hard work. Oyster-tecture calls for a recalibration of the harbor estuary in a larger sense and builds upon existing pilot projects, incorporating a coordinated design vision with the techniques of the self-built.

Ultimately, Oyster-tecture is about trying to create a physical scaffolding system on which mussels and oysters and the web of creatures dependent upon them (such as horseshoe crabs and wading birds) could survive in an urban environment: by raising them above the silt line. It intended to create an infrastructure that would help animals persist; that's where the term "oyster-tecture" came from—literally creating an ecological structure for a species that is presently not supported by what exists.

SCALES OF MUTUALISM

Cohabit defines a place or an environment that is supportive of life and growth—both for *Homo sapiens* and for other plant and animal species—

and in which a diversity of species can live together and prosper on mutually beneficial terms. It is vital to expand architecture beyond the idea of it being just "design for us," beyond a built environment conceived exclusively for human consumption and comfort, and to address the wider global ecosystem as a shared space for all species. Urban design can be recast as a form of new, activist, joint urban-and-environmental stewardship whose "project" is to create footholds for biodiversity.

Global climate change presents a challenge to define and apply our technical and visionary expertise. There are clear directives we can embrace: reduce greenhouse gas emissions; consume fewer resources and drive less; increase the viability of threatened ecosystems that serve as carbon sinks, such as the forests, peat swamps, and salt marshes that frequently exist alongside robust cities. Can we imagine a global cohabitat? At the very least we can pause to consider the bird, slow down for the turtle, make room for the osprey, and maybe one day in the distant future, cultivate the oyster in New York Harbor.

1. Donna Haraway, "Otherworldly Conversations, Terran Topics, Local Terms" in Vandana Shiva and Ingunn Moser, eds., *Biopolitics: A Feminist and Ecological Reader on Biotechnology* (London: Atlantic Highlands, 1995), 71.
2. United Nations Environment Programme, "Ecosystems and their Services," http://www.unep.org/maweb/documents/document.300.aspx.pdf
3. Elizabeth Kolbert, "The Sixth Extinction?" *The New Yorker* (May 29, 2009).
4. Rachel Carson, *Silent Spring* (Boston: Houghton Mifflin, 1962), 103.
5. A German landscape architect and good friend once asked me, "Kate why do you waste your time on this marine stuff, nobody can even see it!" After an obligatory correction—that the Living Breakwaters reef will be visible at low tide and reduce risk for people on shore—I replied that its sedimentation effects will also be visible, the increased fish population will be visible, wading birds will come back, and clam diggers will return to the shallows: an enlivened section versus a rational plan.
6. New York City Audubon Society, "Protecting Raptors," http://www.nycaudubon.org/issues-of-concern/protecting-raptors.
7. A good example is the Everglades Python Patrol, which trains citizens to respond to and in some cases capture pythons.
8. Richard Hobbs, Eric S. Higgs, and Carol M. Hall, eds., *Novel Ecosystems: Intervening in the New World Order* (Hoboken: Wiley-Blackwell, 2013).
9. M. W. Beck, R. D. Brumbaugh, L. Airoldi, et. al., *Shellfish Reefs at Risk: A Global Analysis of Problems and Solutions* (Arlington, VA: The Nature Conservancy, 2009).
10. "Ecosystem services are the benefits people obtain from ecosystems. These include provisioning services such as food and water; regulating services such as flood and disease control; cultural services such as spiritual, recreational, and cultural benefits; and supporting services, such as nutrient cycling, that maintain the conditions for life on Earth." United Nations Environment Programme, "Ecosystems and their Services."

Oyster-tecture

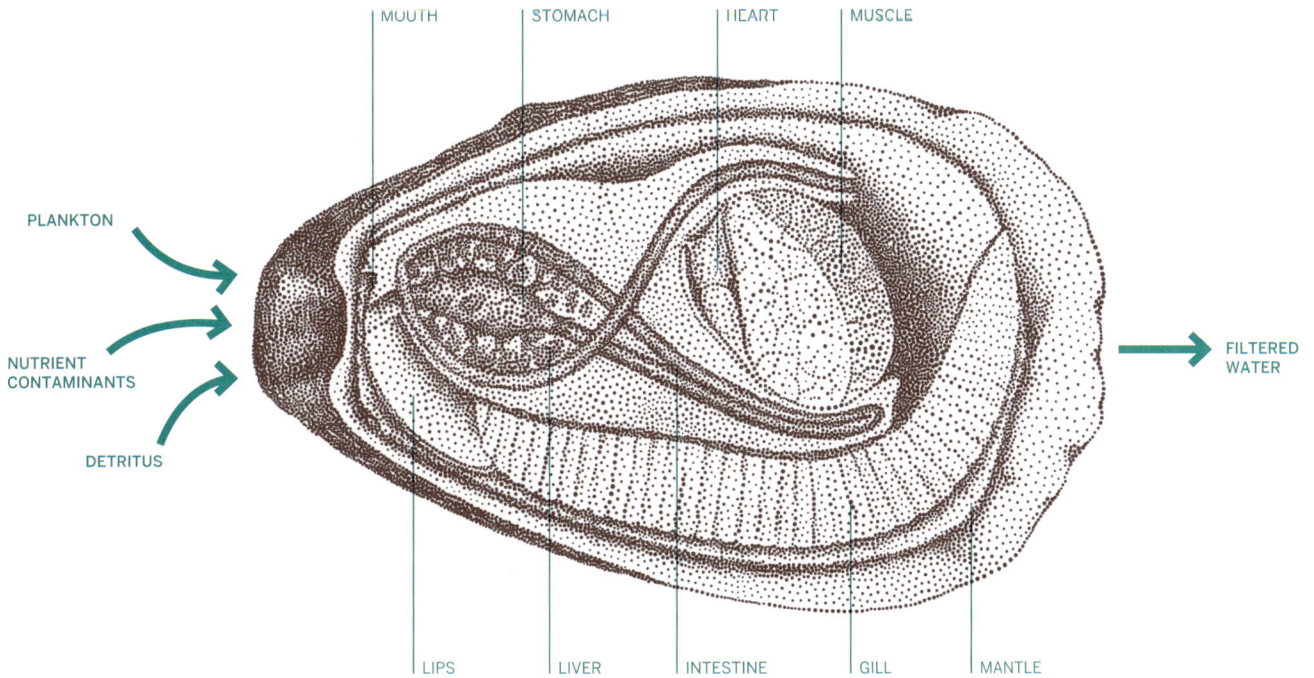

MOUTH STOMACH HEART MUSCLE

PLANKTON

NUTRIENT
CONTAMINANTS

DETRITUS

FILTERED
WATER

LIPS LIVER INTESTINE GILL MANTLE

EASTERN OYSTER: *CRASSOSTREA VIRGINICA*

Oyster-tecture is a proposal for rethinking the watery edges of Brooklyn's Gowanus Canal, Red Hook, and Manhattan's Governors Island in the context of changing climates and extreme storm events. Engaging issues of water quality, sea level rise, and community-based action, the project builds on an already developing revitalization of long-lost oyster reefs in New York Harbor and the economies that surrounded them, and aims to restart a "reef culture" that fosters public life near the water's edge while mitigating future storm events.

The proposal shown here was developed for the Museum of Modern Art's *Rising Currents* exhibition in 2010, addressing climate change and rising sea levels in New York City.

Facing page: New York Harbor

Brooklyn 1776

Why the oyster? It is an ecosystem engineer,
a unit of multipurpose infrastructure that
filters nutrient contaminants from the water,
provides aquatic habitat, and attenuates waves
through the buildup of reef systems over time.
Oyster beds once covered nearly 25 percent
of the harbor and were capable of filtering
nutrient contaminants from all of the harbor's
water in a matter of days. What is now the Red
Hook Gowanus area was an archipelago of
small islands interconnected by shallow tidal
flats and meandering waterways that teemed
with bivalves and other aquatic life. Reefs,
shoals, and marshlands protected upland areas
and were part of a thriving maritime economy.
Through centuries of cutting and filling, these
flats were shaped into a uniform channels and
hard edges that could no longer support the
same diversity of life.

Lenape fishing method

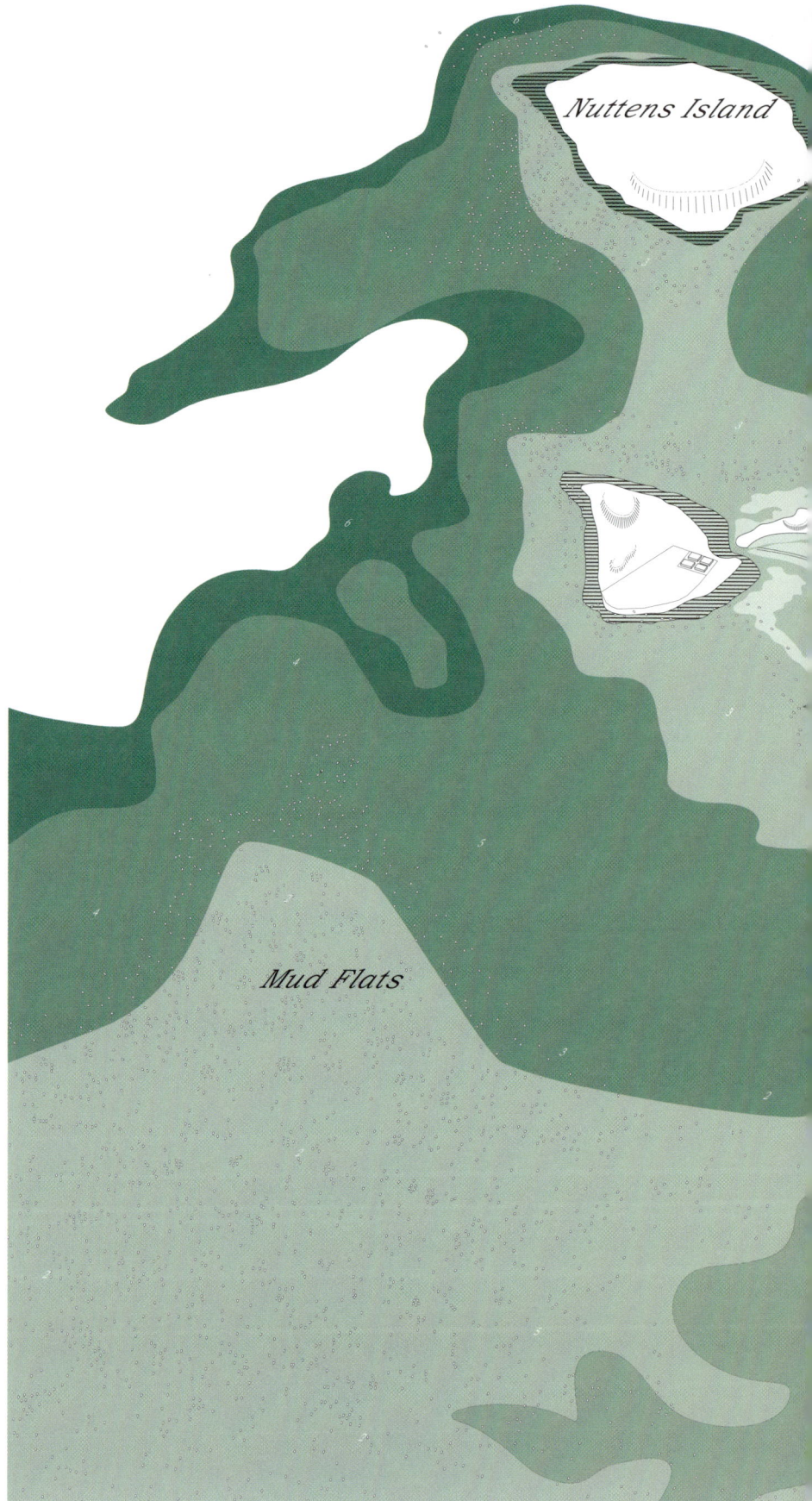

Nuttens Island

Mud Flats

TOWARD AN URBAN ECOLOGY

Dimond Reef

Brockland

Red Hook

Gouwanes

Gouwanes Cove

Back to the Future

SCAPE looked to the past to envision the future of this place. The project inserts a new Oyster-tecture to support oyster regeneration and community involvement, rebuilding a rich three-dimensional mosaic landscape both out in the bay and along the inland shores. The two-part proposal includes an oyster-culture strategy for remaking the Gowanus Canal and a constructed Palisades Reef offshore, which reduces wave action and provides new forms of water-based recreation.

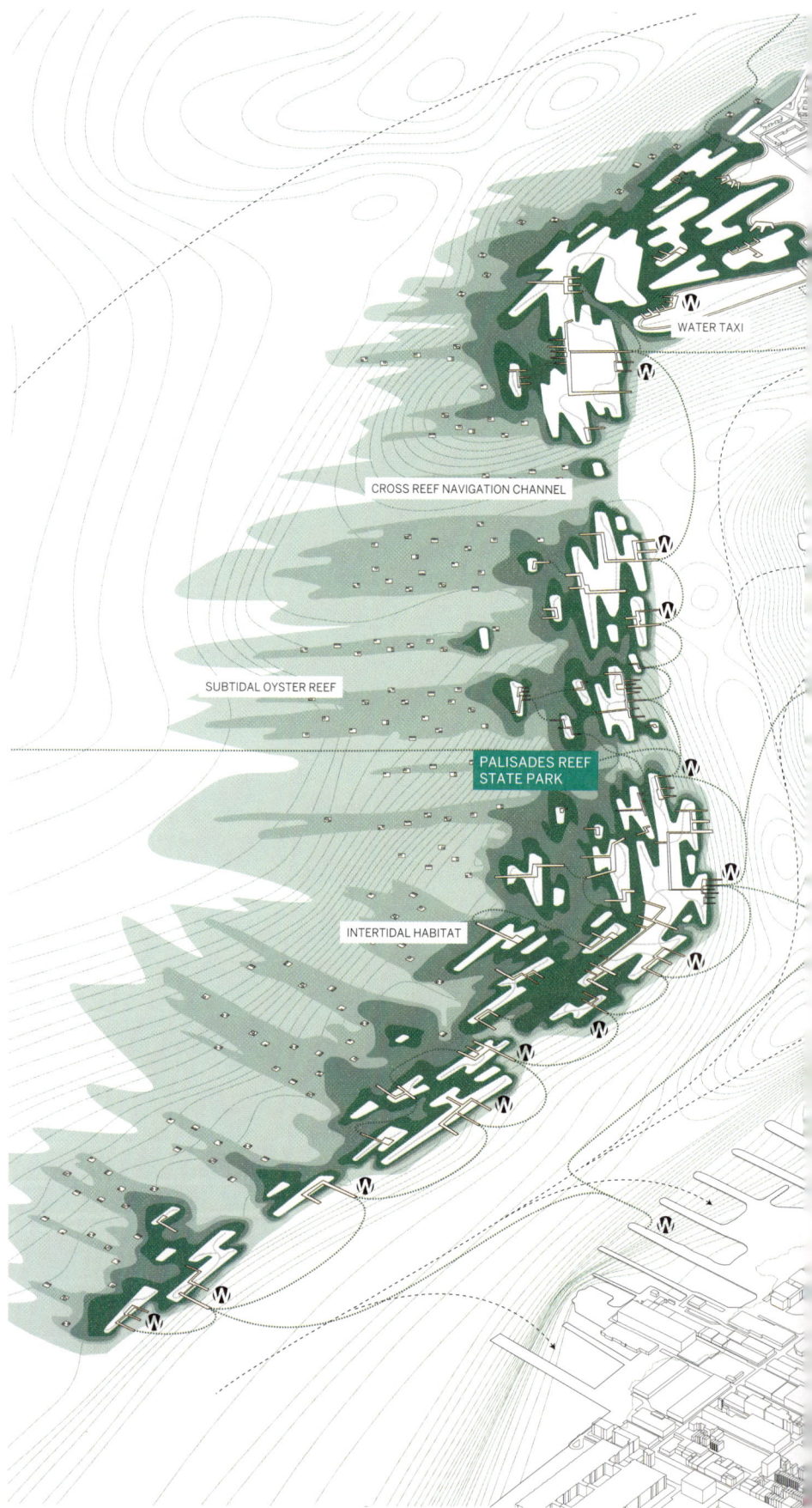

WATER TAXI

CROSS REEF NAVIGATION CHANNEL

SUBTIDAL OYSTER REEF

PALISADES REEF STATE PARK

INTERTIDAL HABITAT

GOVERNORS ISLAND

FERRY TO MANHATTAN

BUTTERMILK CHANNEL

FLUSHING TUNNEL INLET

RED HOOK

ERIE BASIN

FLUPSY PUBLIC PATH

NEW GOWANUS

OYSTER NURSERY

SOFTENED EDGE

SUNSET PARK

CAT 4

MAGNETIC

Life Cycle Design

Oyster-tecture adopts the oyster life cycle as a model for change. The cycle begins in the Gowanus Canal, where the Superfund cleanup process is removing heavy metals from the water column, but nutrient contamination remains. Here, oyster larvae (or spat) are raised in floating upwelling system nursery rafts (FLUPSY rafts), along the canal's edges, taking advantage of the nutrient-rich waters. Over time, as oysters grow, the young specimens are transported down the canal to the Bay Ridge Flats and seeded on an armature of fuzzy rope, where they mature and aggregate over time into wave-attenuating reef structures.

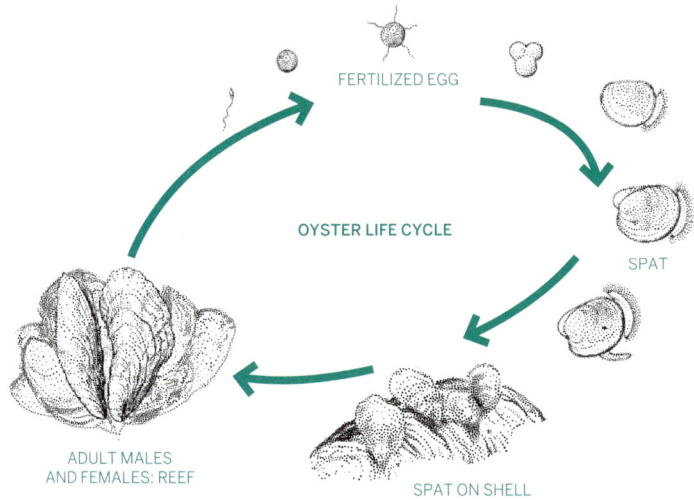

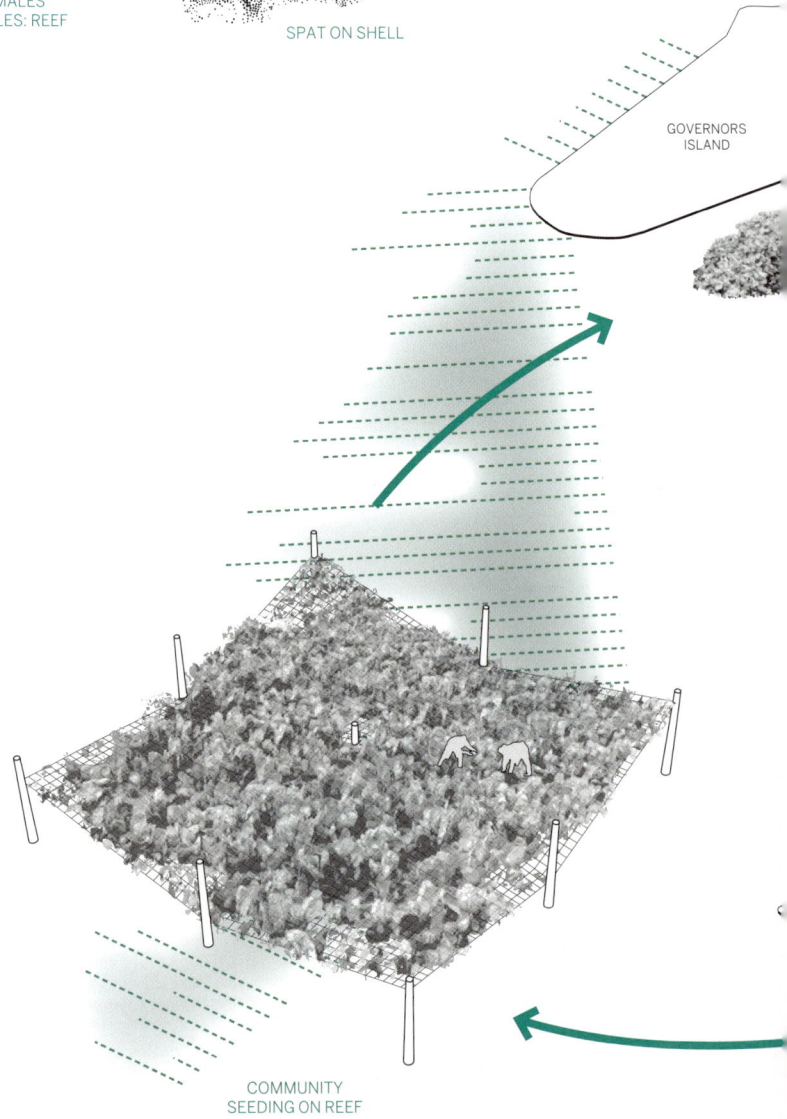

FERTILIZED EGG

OYSTER LIFE CYCLE

SPAT

SPAT ON SHELL

ADULT MALES
AND FEMALES: REEF

GOVERNORS
ISLAND

COMMUNITY
SEEDING ON REEF

OYSTER-TECTURE LIFE CYCLE

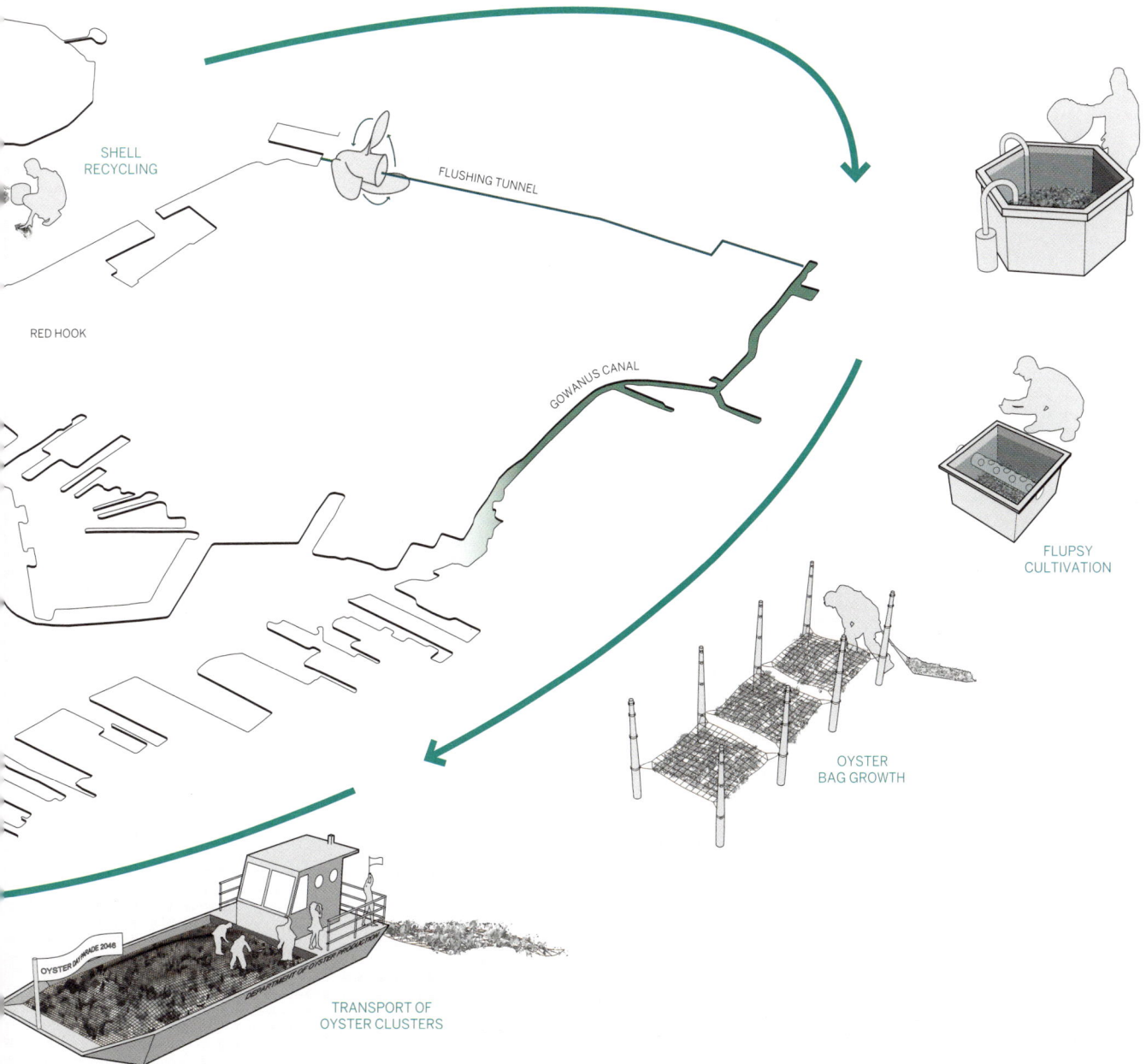

SHELL
RECYCLING

FLUSHING TUNNEL

RED HOOK

GOWANUS CANAL

FLUPSY
CULTIVATION

OYSTER
BAG GROWTH

OYSTER DAYMADE 2046

DEPARTMENT OF OYSTER PRODUCTION

TRANSPORT OF
OYSTER CLUSTERS

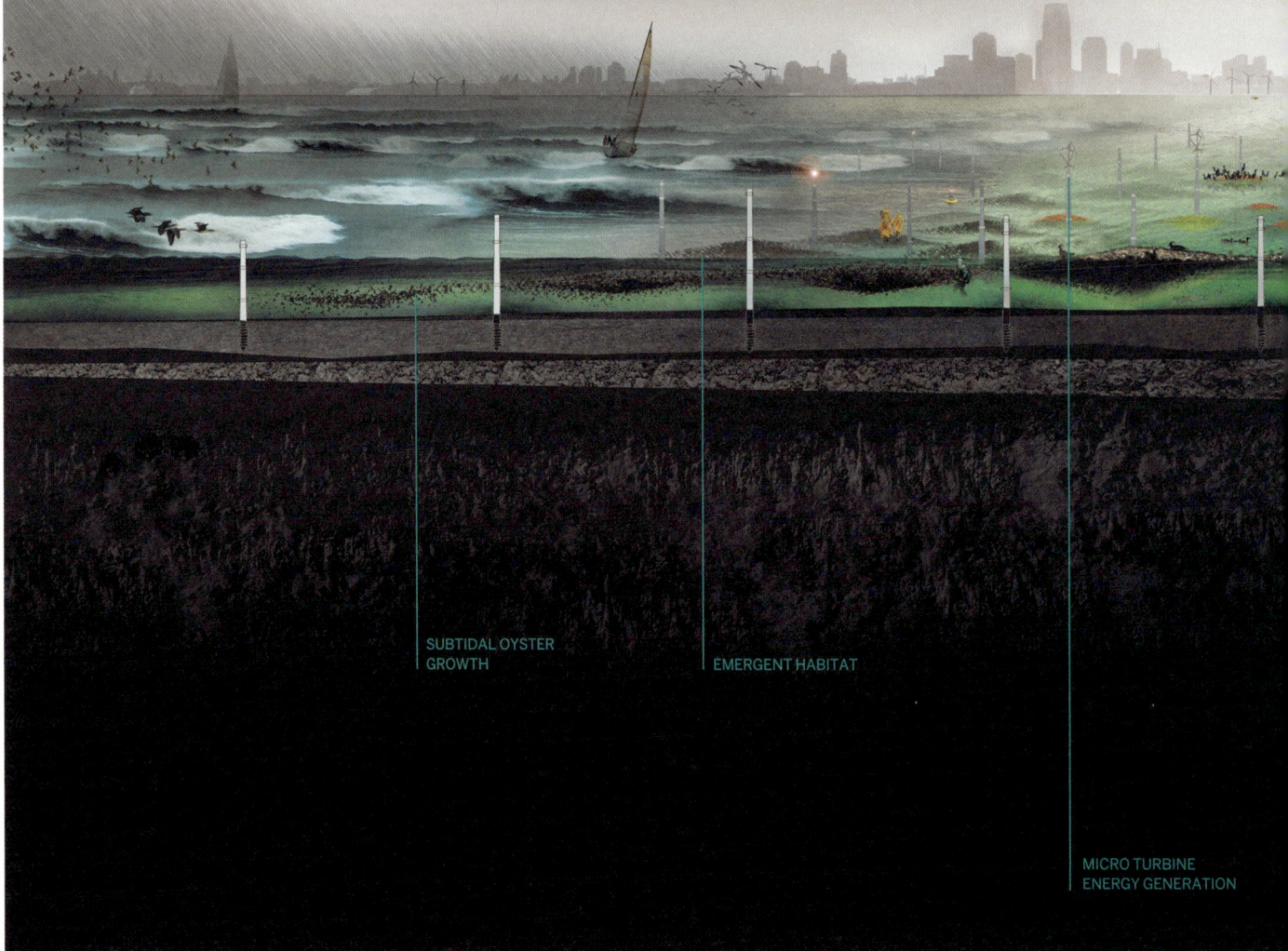

Palisades Reef

Built from a woven matrix of fuzzy rope and pylons, the subtidal and intertidal reef armature in the Bay Ridge Flats dissipates wave energy from storm surge while supporting oysters and other filter-feeding shellfish above the sediment. This inhabitable archipelago emerges about the high water line, forming new watery public space within New York's harbor.

SUBTIDAL OYSTER
GROWTH

EMERGENT HABITAT

MICRO TURBINE
ENERGY GENERATION

1. WAVE ATTENUATION

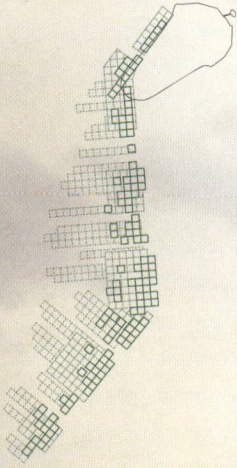

2. HABITAT DEVELOPMENT

3. WATER-BASED RECREATION

SUBTIDAL OYSTER RACKS

OYSTER GROWTH AND
EELGRASS RESTORATION

REEF AND NAVIGATION
CHANNEL ESTABLISHMENT

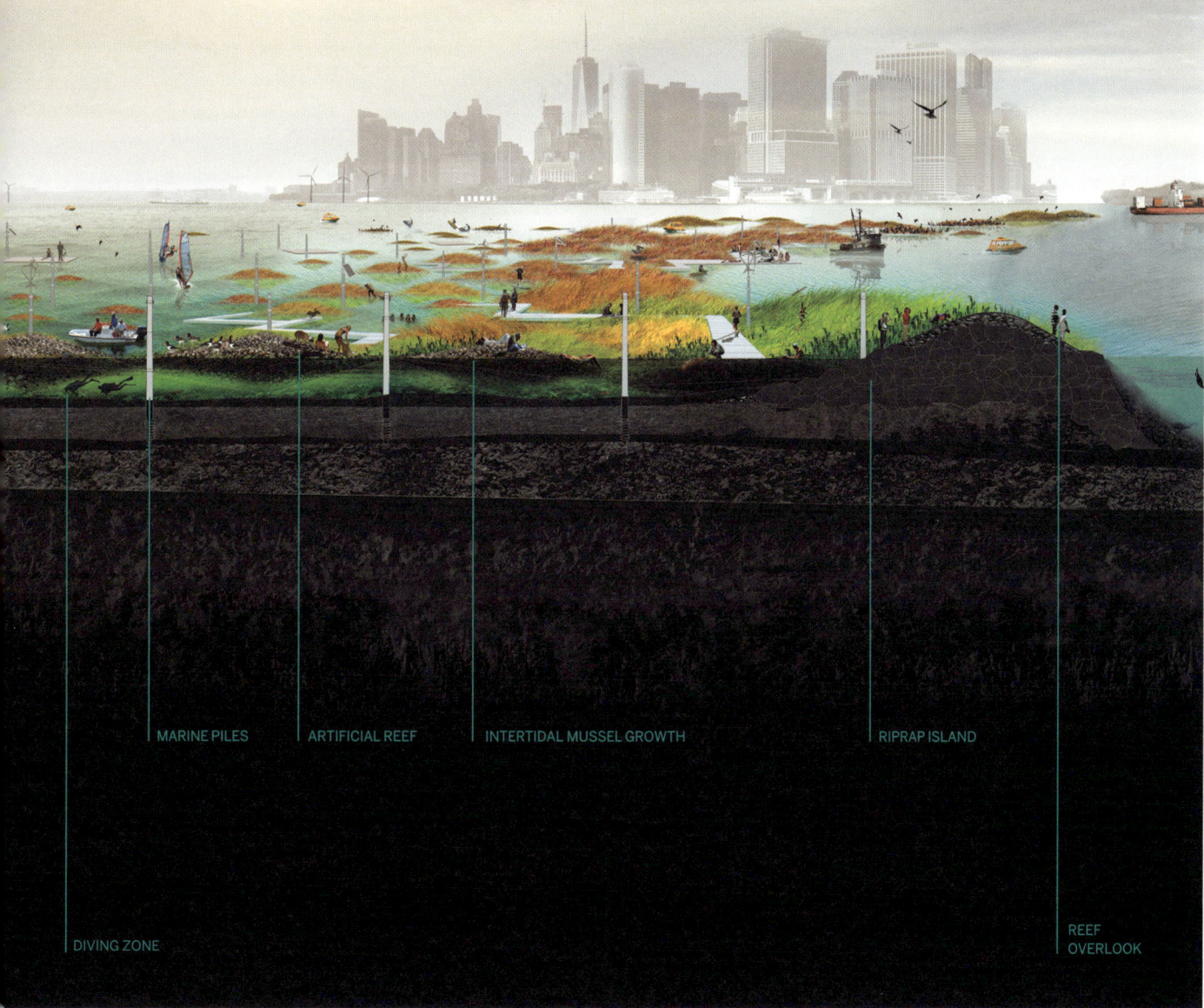

MARINE PILES   ARTIFICIAL REEF   INTERTIDAL MUSSEL GROWTH   RIPRAP ISLAND

DIVING ZONE

REEF
OVERLOOK

Blue Park

Emergent and constructed reef islands in the bay slow and clean the harbor's water while providing sanctuary for oysters, mussels, marine birds, and the occasional seal. Amenities for human visitors include boat anchor poles and slips, BBQ grills, diving platforms, and amphibious trails. This inhabitable archipelago emerges at the high water line, forming a signature new regional "blue" park that returns New York City to its harbor city origins.

PALISADES REEF PARK: RECREATION

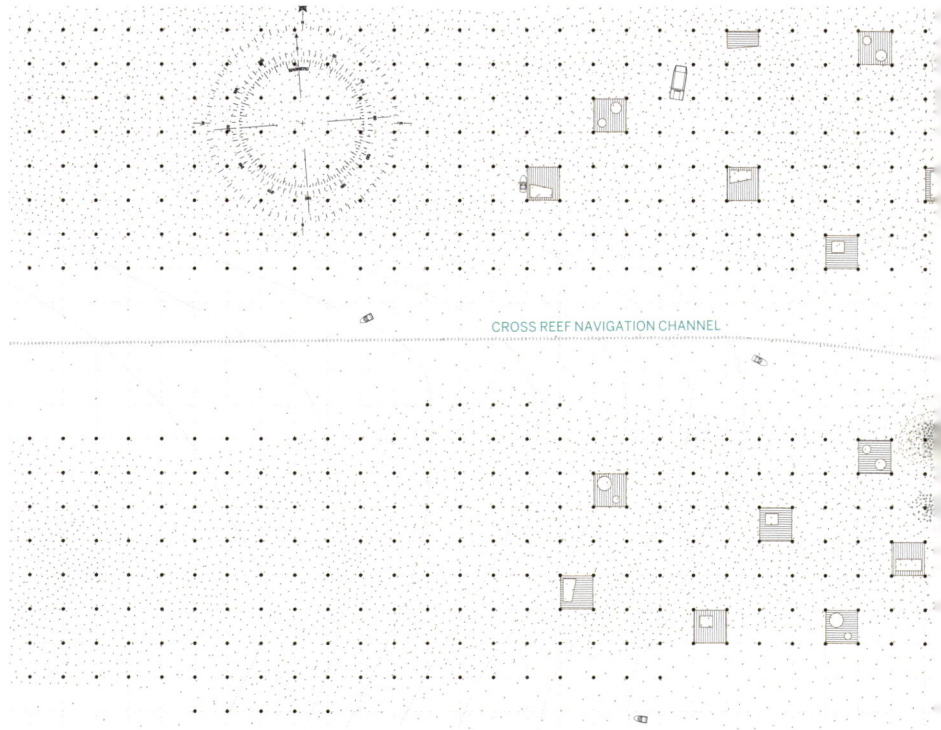

CROSS REEF NAVIGATION CHANNEL

PALISADES REEF PARK: RISK REDUCTION

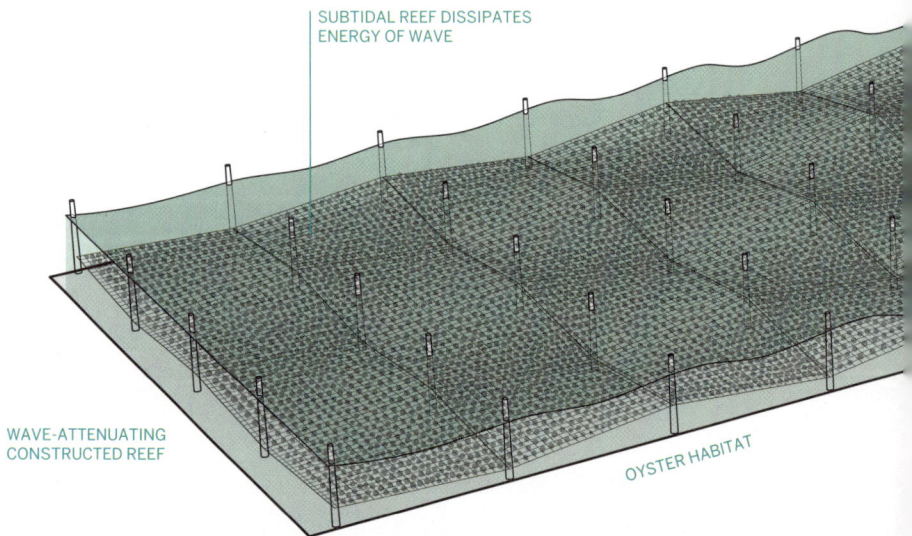

SUBTIDAL REEF DISSIPATES ENERGY OF WAVE

WAVE-ATTENUATING CONSTRUCTED REEF

OYSTER HABITAT

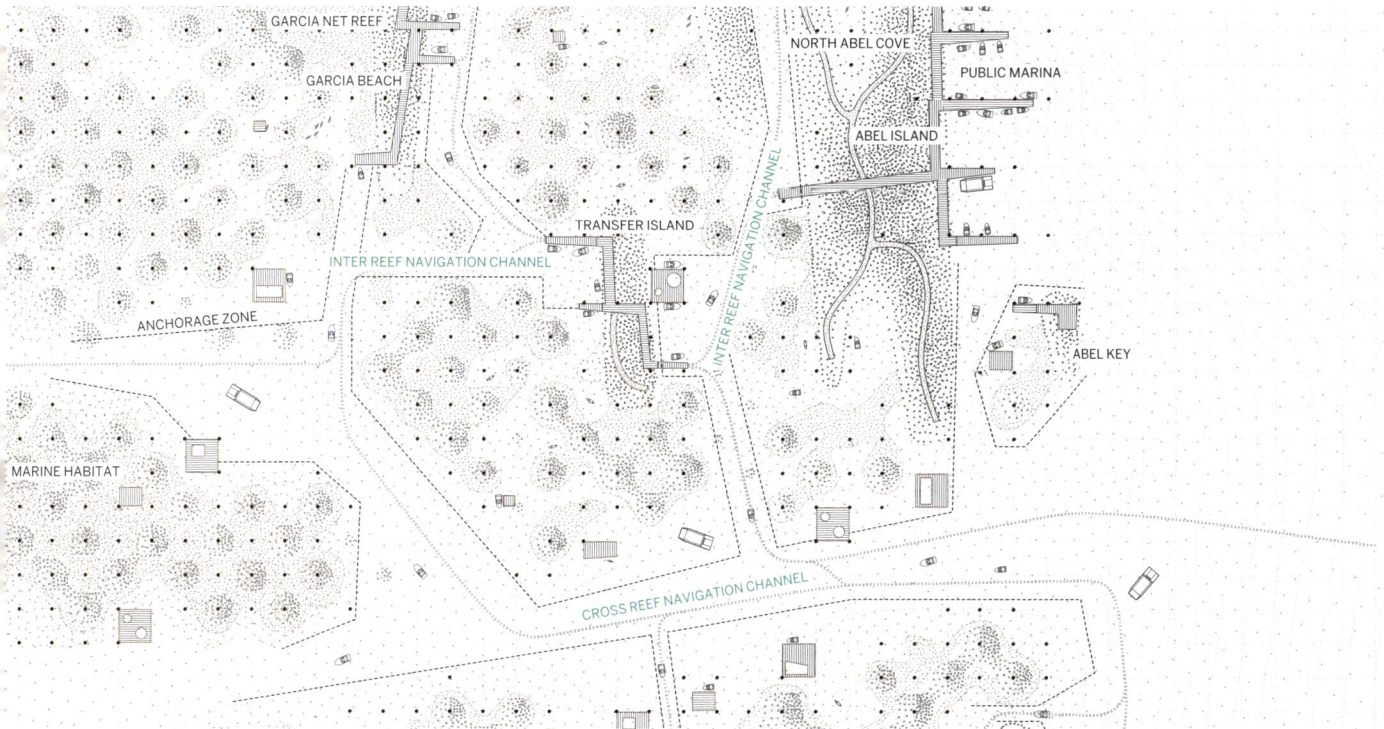

GARCIA NET REEF
GARCIA BEACH
NORTH ABEL COVE
PUBLIC MARINA
ABEL ISLAND
TRANSFER ISLAND
INTER REEF NAVIGATION CHANNEL
INTER REEF NAVIGATION CHANNEL
ANCHORAGE ZONE
ABEL KEY
MARINE HABITAT
CROSS REEF NAVIGATION CHANNEL

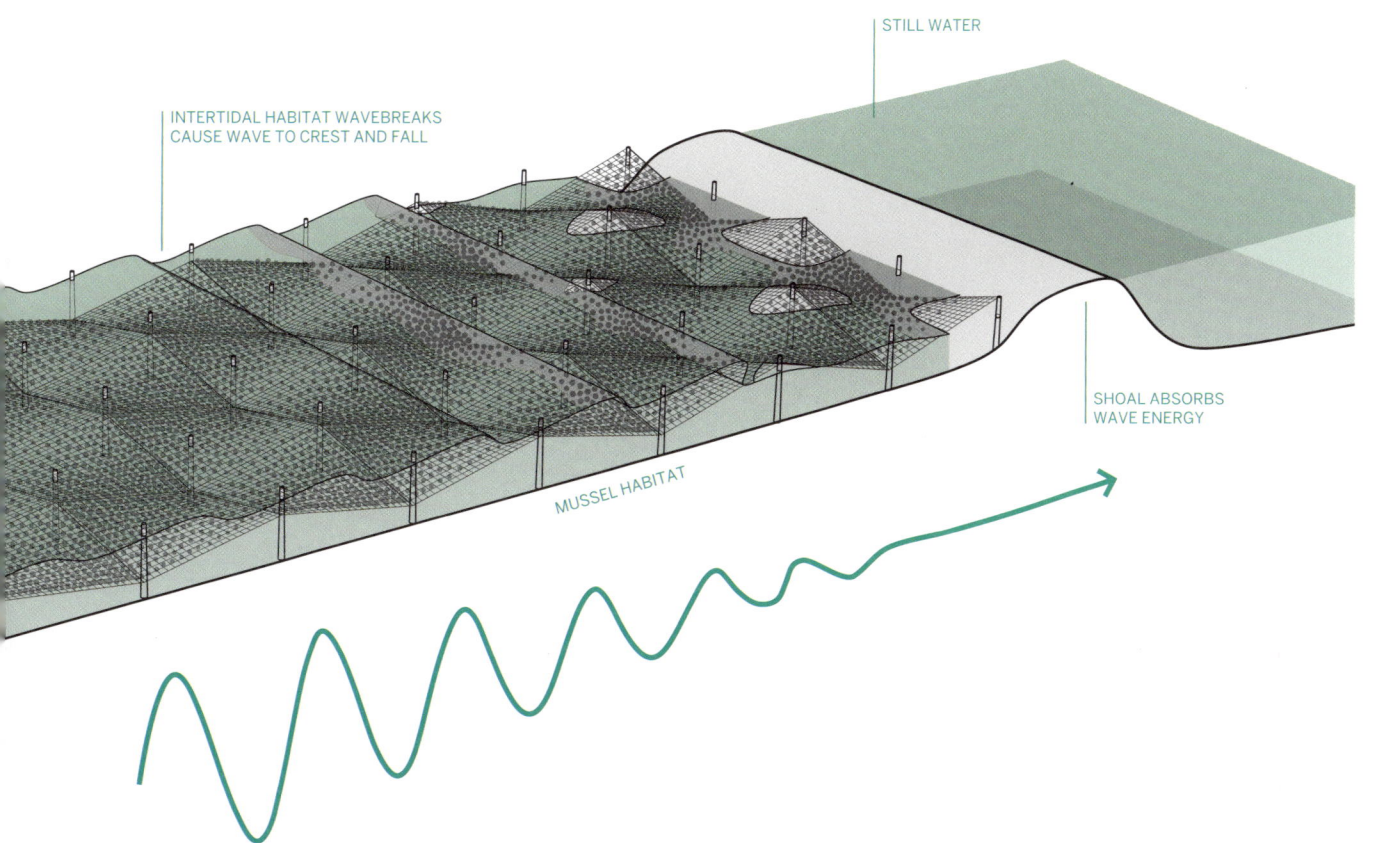

STILL WATER
INTERTIDAL HABITAT WAVEBREAKS
CAUSE WAVE TO CREST AND FALL
SHOAL ABSORBS
WAVE ENERGY
MUSSEL HABITAT

Reef Building

The reef grows over time, keeping pace with sea level rise, as the natural processes of oyster agglomeration combine with community-driven oyster gardening and aquaculture. A joint recreational and working landscape, the space is at once a park, a living experiment, and a piece of climate change infrastructure.

The Oyster-tecture model embodies the community approach. The model was created using materials and means that mimic the proposal, with fuzzy rope panels knitted and woven by volunteers and assembled incrementally on-site over time. This community weaving event influenced the creation of the fuzzy rope test panels at the Sims Habitat Pilot Pier, a later evolution of the Oyster-tecture project (see pp. 212–3).

Oyster-tecture model knitting

Gowanus Nursery

Gowanus's oyster-centric working waterfront acts as the catalyst for a larger urban transformation. Combined Sewer Overflow (CSO) gardens, stick-culture beds, and the continuous FLUPSY path are the first steps towards a thriving live/work community centered around water-based transit, aquatic education, and new models for living on the water.

CAPPED
CONTAMINATION

STICK
CULTURE

OYSTER
BAGS

FLUPSY
PATH

1. CSO MITIGATION GARDENS AND CONTAMINANT REMOVAL

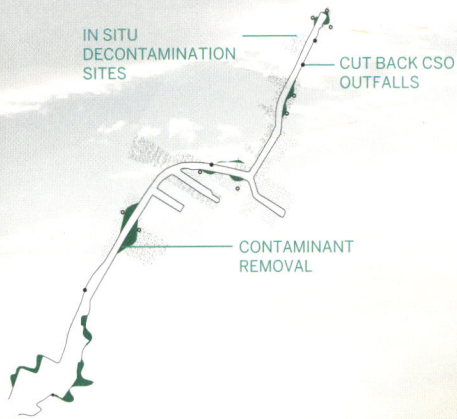

IN SITU DECONTAMINATION SITES

CUT BACK CSO OUTFALLS

CONTAMINANT REMOVAL

2. OYSTER CULTURE + FLUPSY DECKS

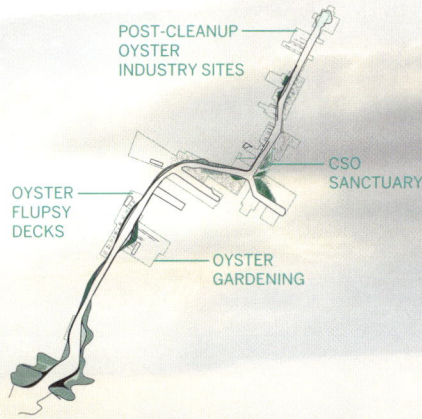

POST-CLEANUP OYSTER INDUSTRY SITES

OYSTER FLUPSY DECKS

CSO SANCTUARY

OYSTER GARDENING

3. PUBLIC ACCESS + NEIGHBORHOOD CONNECTIONS

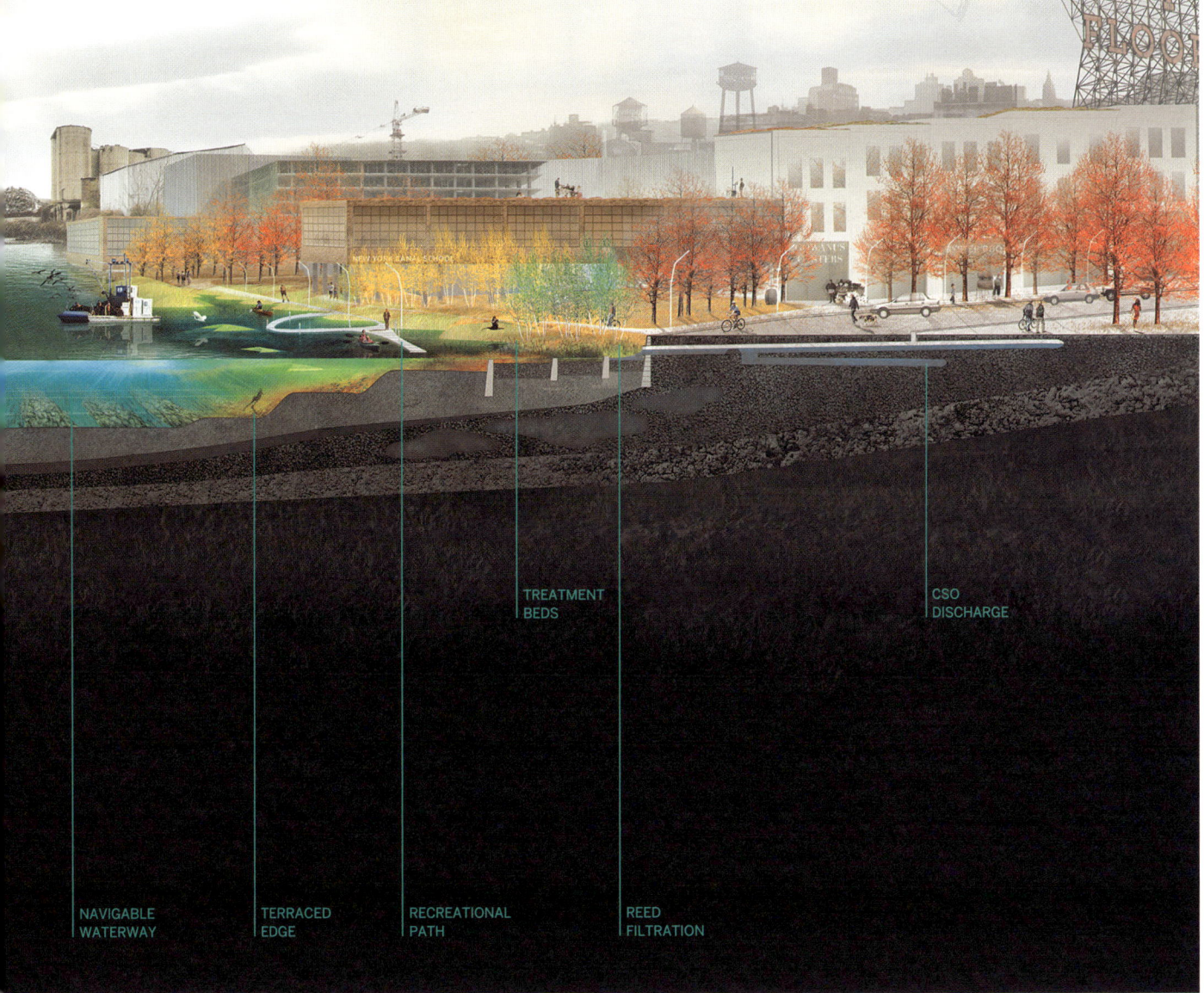

FLUSHING TUNNEL

PUBLIC WAY

NEIGHBORHOOD ACCESS

TREATMENT BEDS

CSO DISCHARGE

NAVIGABLE WATERWAY

TERRACED EDGE

RECREATIONAL PATH

REED FILTRATION

FLUPSification

A FLUPSY is a floating oyster nursery that increases organism growth rate by drawing nourishing nutrient-rich water through chambers filled with spat. The canal's existing infrastructure, the Flushing Tunnel, draws in water from the Buttermilk Channel out towards the Bay Ridge Flats, and creates the perfect conditions for the Gowanus Canal itself to become an urban-scale FLUPSY.

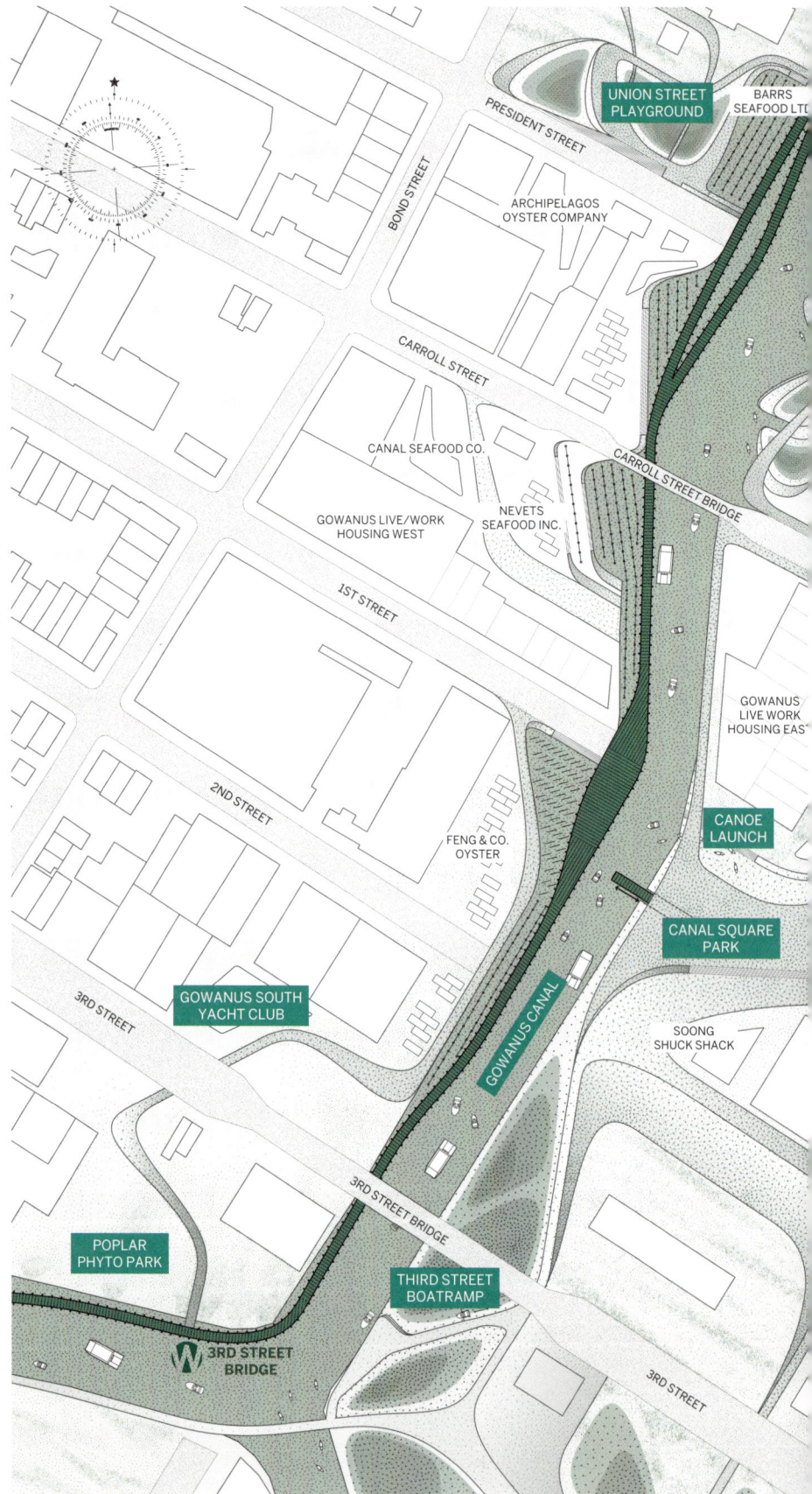

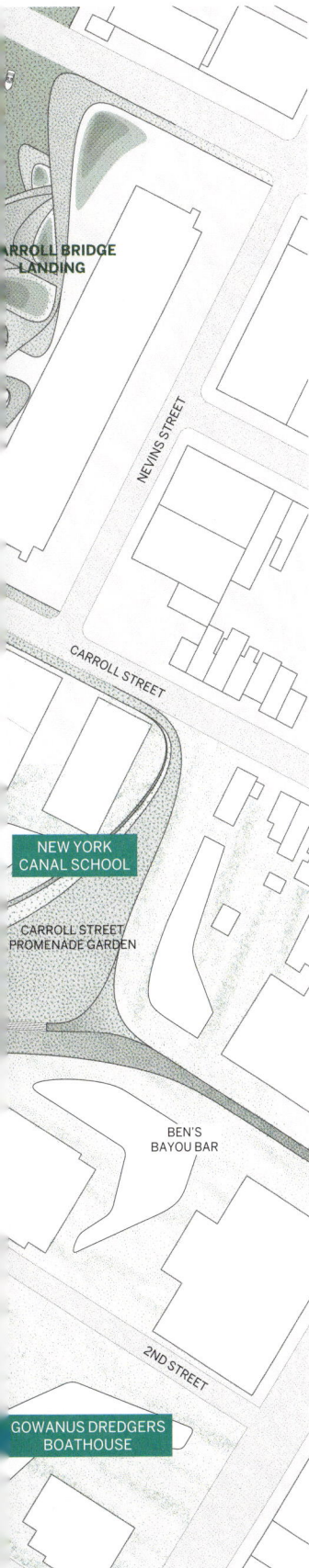

FLOATING UPWELLING SYSTEM (FLUPSY)

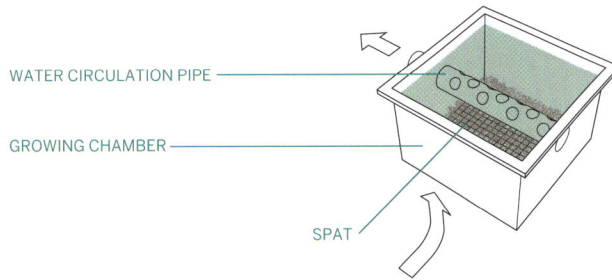

WATER CIRCULATION PIPE

GROWING CHAMBER

SPAT

FLUPSY PATH

PUBLIC ACCESS PATH

WATER IS DRAWN
THROUGH CHAMBERS
BY CIRCULATION FAN

NUTRIENT-RICH WATER
FLOWS THROUGH OYSTERS
IN CHAMBER

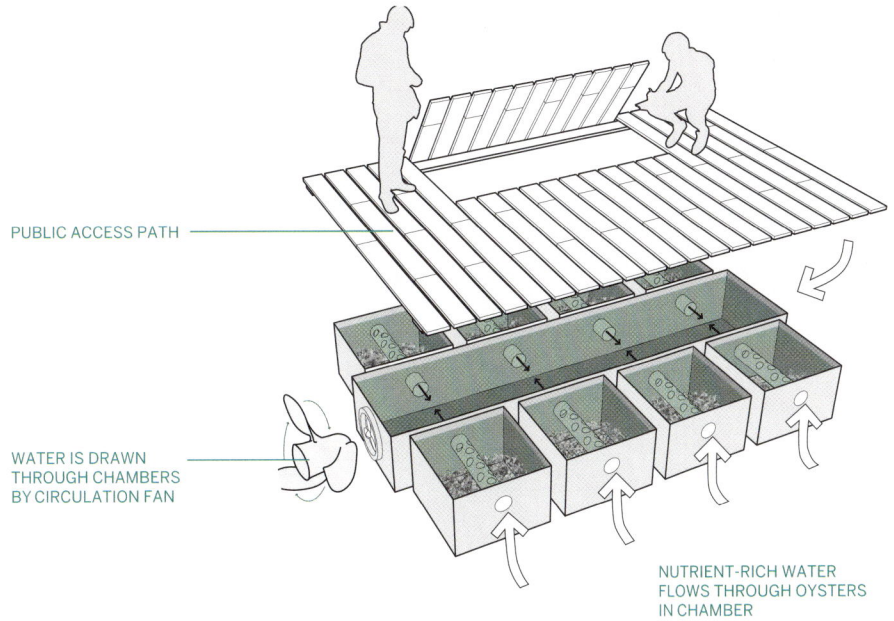

OYSTER FARMING TECHNIQUES

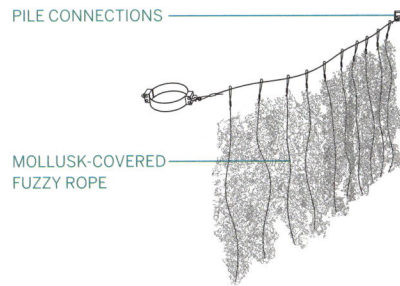

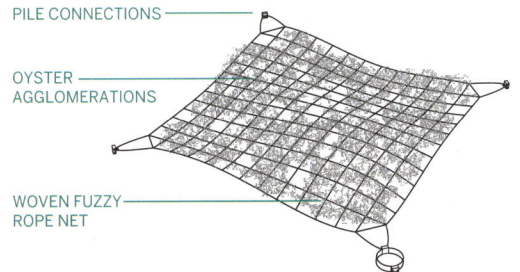

PILE CONNECTIONS

MOLLUSK-COVERED
FUZZY ROPE

PILE CONNECTIONS

OYSTER
AGGLOMERATIONS

WOVEN FUZZY
ROPE NET

CARROLL BRIDGE
LANDING

NEVINS STREET

CARROLL STREET

NEW YORK
CANAL SCHOOL

CARROLL STREET
PROMENADE GARDEN

BEN'S
BAYOU BAR

2ND STREET

GOWANUS DREDGERS
BOATHOUSE

Oyster-tecture 2050?

At the heart of the proposal is an attitude about the potential of our collective waterfront as a site of ecological health and climate-resilient development. In the near term, oysters are "working here" and not fit for consumption, as they are inundated with CSO contamination from nearby outfall pipes and contaminants not contained in the Superfund cleanup process.

But if our shores and waters were reconceived as ecosystems, rather than as waste conduits, what potentials exist for the future? While it is not possible today to safely consume a NYC-grown oyster, Oyster-tecture outlines a conceptual trajectory for this potentially delicious future.

Urban Flyway
Artificial Habitat
Shifting Baselines
Forestation
Adaptive Management
Citizen Scientist
Aquaculture Teacher

Urban Flyway

New York City provides vital habitat stopovers along the Atlantic Flyway—the migratory path for birds and insects along the Atlantic Coast. These urban sites have become even more critical as global warming shifts migratory patterns and threatens habitats worldwide.

—

Bird-Safe Building Guidelines

Birds traversing North America via the Atlantic Flyway make stops in waterfront, coastal, wetland, wooded, and weedy environments, and many of these are in or near America's most densely populated urban areas. Scientists estimate that migrating birds have a 70-percent chance of encountering at least one major metropolitan area during migration from breeding to wintering grounds, and an estimated 100 million birds are killed every year in the United States due to collisions with buildings. The Bird-Safe Building Guidelines, a freely downloadable publication produced in conjunction with the New York City Audubon Society in 2006, examines the causes of bird mortality in the built environment, and advocates for a series of preventative and rehabilitative strategies while describing precedents for regulatory initiatives such as LEED™. Bird injury and death are largely attributable to two factors: transparency and reflection of glass facades. Birds are unable to detect or avoid glass, either during the daytime or night. One of SCAPE's early, orienting projects, these guidelines inform architects, building managers, and public officials about the issues and provide clear, achievable solutions. They demonstrate how operative toolkits can initiate widespread urban ecological repair with ramifications beyond the scope of a bounded site or single project.

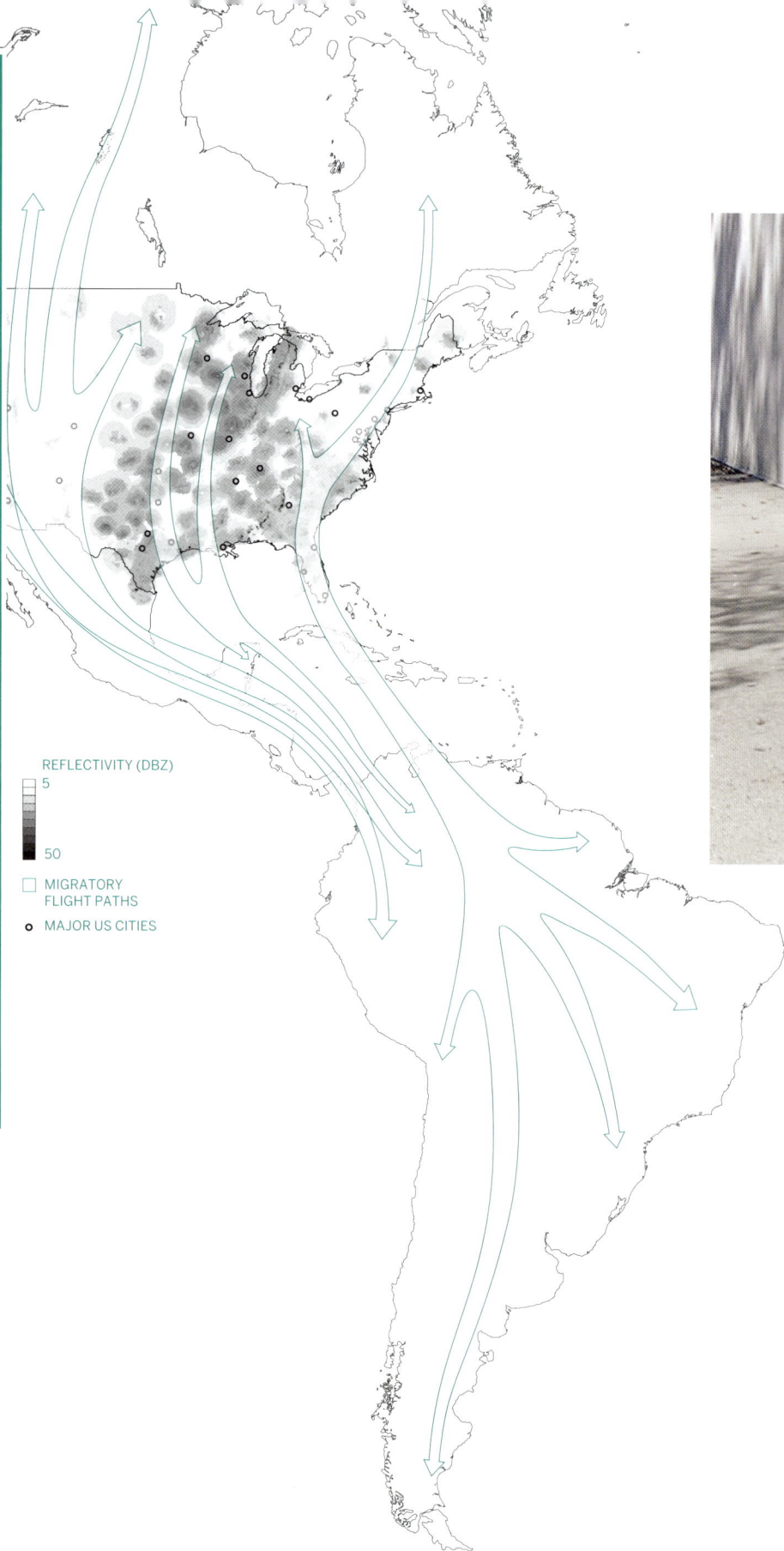

REFLECTIVITY (DBZ)
5
50

MIGRATORY FLIGHT PATHS
MAJOR US CITIES

PROBLEM

TRANSPARENCY

REFLECTION

FLY-THROUGH

BEACON EFFECT

SOLUTION

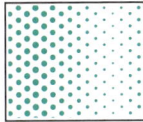

SCREEN / FRIT

VEGETATION NEAR
BUILDING

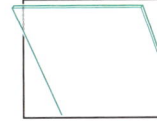

GLASS TILTED
DOWNWARDS

LIGHTS OUT

VISUAL NOISE

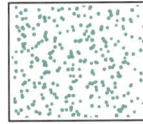

NONREFLECTIVE
MATERIAL

NONREFLECTIVE
GLASS

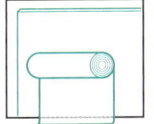

PLASTIC FILMS
+ DICHROIC COATING

Artificial Habitat

Nature doesn't just come back into cities or rewild them without an invitation: artificial habitat mimics lost habitat niches and fosters the return of wildlife to areas inalterably changed by urbanization.

—

Osprey Nest Structures
Brooklyn, New York

Ospreys were once dominant, apex predators in the Northeast, when fish populations were stable and healthy. In the past century fish populations have severely declined and the waterfront has been cleared of the large, dead trees where ospreys traditionally nested. The loss of food sources, nesting sites, and the introduction of DDT and other chemicals have severely impacted osprey populations. However, people can play a role in expanding the birds' options for available nesting sites in order to reintegrate and reestablish the species in the urban realm. The osprey nest site shown here is located along Bush Terminal Park in Brooklyn, where an artificial platform was constructed to encourage nesting activity. SCAPE worked with Bart Chezar (see interview pp. 128–9) to design a nest structure and solar-powered "osprey cam" system to transmit information about the birds to a monitoring website and to engage the public.

BROOKLYN BRIDGE PARK
OSPREY PLATFORM

THE NEW YORK HARBOR SCHOOL
OSPREY PLATFORM

BUSH TERMINAL PARK
OSPREY PLATFORM

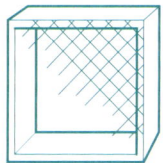 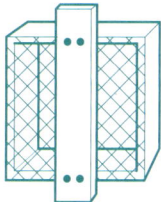 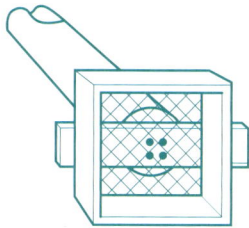 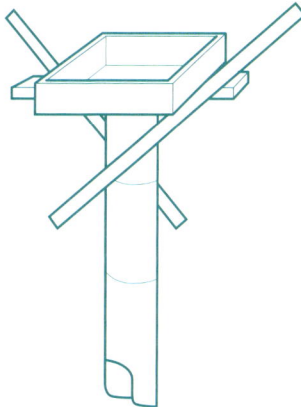 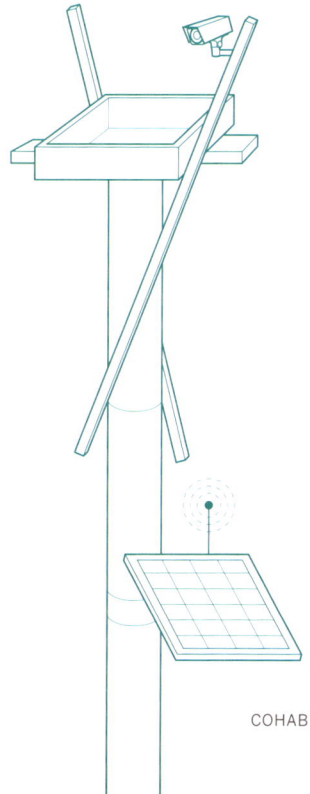

our

very life-sup-

stock - could

CHICORY A European plant, Chicory is now abundant in the United States, growing in pastures, roadsides, and waste places. The light blue flowers (rarely pinkish or white) grow close along stiff-branching stems 1 to 5 feet high. The flowers soon wither in the sunlight. Millions of pounds of Chicory root, imported or grown locally, are roasted as a coffee substitute. — *Summer and fall. Composite Family.*

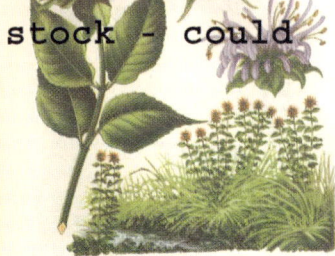

1 species

BEEBALMS These tall, coarse, aromatic mints are also called Wild Bergamot, Oswego Tea, Horsemint. They vary in color from scarlet red to pale lavender. The brilliant red-flowered Oswego Tea grows in moist places, but the other Beebalms prefer dry waysides and fencerows. Some are native; others, brought from Europe, have gone wild. Indians and early settlers brewed medicinal tea from the leaves.—*Summer and early fall. Mint Family.*

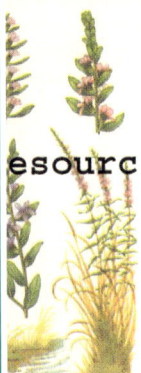

12 species

... are low, spreading plants ... ratively large, attractive ... singly on slender stems. ... ast, where about a dozen ... n hillsides in light shade. ... lue to purple, 5-petaled ... white in the center. Some ... ow under cultivation. — ... aterleaf Family.

esourc-

es has led us

are no pollinat

MILKWEEDS Stout-stemmed Milkweeds are tall plants that grow 2 to 5 feet high. Their broad flower clusters are red to pink, lilac, and cream-white. All parts of the plant contain a milky juice, latex, which gives Milkweed its name. Milkweeds are abundant in old fields, meadows, marshes, and moist roadsides. The seeds, with their familiar "parachutes," sail off in the wind.—*Summer and fall. Milkweed Family.*

60 species

GILIAS About 100 of the 120 kinds of Gilia gro... this country, mainly in western deserts and mount... Dwarfed species are typical of both these habitats. ... commonly, Gilias grow on open slopes and dry hills... They are variable and not easily distinguished from ... another. All have tubular, funnel- or bell-shaped, 5-... aled flowers. On some the flowers cluster at the top o... plant; in others they scatter along the vertical stem. ... vary in color from scarlet to pink, blue, purple, ye... and white.

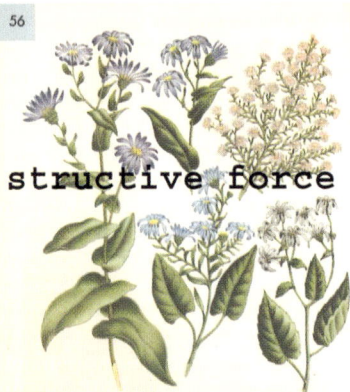

... e slender, colorful plants ... meadows, and swamps. ... uatic. Our tallest, most ... turalized from Europe. ... aller, pink or lavender ... wing in a loose spike or ... -sided stems. The long, ... toothless leaves usually grow opposite one another.— *Summer to fall. Loosestrife Family.*

10 species

53

20

structive force

on Earth for the

to become the

ASTERS Asters number some 150 species in the United States. Most occur in the East where, with Goldenrod, they fill spangled fields in late summer and fall. Each star-like, multipetaled flower is actually a compact cluster, called a "flowerhead." The center (disk) flowers are bright yellow; the outer (ray) flowers, often mistaken for petals, vary from blue and purple to white. When studying Asters, look at the basal leaves as well as those near the top of the plant, since they help in identification.

Asters are typical plants of open fields and roadsides, but there are woodland, swamp, and seaside species too.

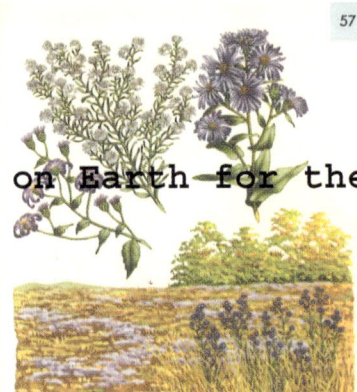

They grow and spread from perennial rootstocks. Best-known Asters include the New England Aster (tall, with deep purple flowers), sometimes cultivated; the New York Aster (blue-violet flowers: thin, smooth leaves); the Heart-leaved Aster (heart-shaped leaves at the base of the stem, and small lilac flowers). The White Woodland Aster has a zig-zag stem, small white flowers, and smooth, heart-shaped leaves.—*Late summer to late fall. Composite Family.*

150 species

The following plants are covered in other sections of th... book because they are predominantly of some othe... colors, but they include one or more species that do ... into the RED, PINK, AND MAGENTA color group:

56

57

54

lie off if there

TRILLIUMS Trilliums are handsome spring plants of moist eastern woodlands and western mountains. As their name implies, they are constructed on a threefold plan: 3 leaflets, 3 green sepals, and 3 petals which vary in color from the deep, purple-red of the common Wake-robin through pink to pure white. There are about 15 species—most grow a foot or so high, usually in rich soil. The flowers ripen into reddish or purple berries.—*Spring. Lily Family.*

15 species

21

ng insects left.

imes of London
bruary 1st, 2009

Gilias grow from 5 inches to 2 feet tall, with rough or cky stems. The thin leaves generally alternate along em. The seeds are also sticky when wet. Some are eaten y gamebirds and by desert rodents. One of the best-own Gilias is the Scarlet Gilia or Skyrocket, a plant that vers western hillsides and has a her disagreeable odor. Other com-on Gilias include Blue Desert Gilia, rds Eyes, Downy Gilia, and Prickly ilia.—*Spring to fall. Phlox Family.*

100 species

55

hingle most de-

IRONWEEDS The flowerheads of Ironweeds resemble small, dark purple Thistles, but the plants are free of spines. The leaves, long and closely toothed, are different too. Ironweeds (3 to 8 feet) grow in moist meadows and roadsides in the eastern and middle states. Some 10 species occur, all purple in color, rarely white. The best known are Tall Ironweed and New York Ironweed. —*Early fall. Composite Family.*

10 species

$1.00

FLOWERS

134 PAINTINGS IN FULL COLOR

A GUIDE TO FAMILIAR AMERICAN WILDFLOWERS
THAT ARE STILL HERE

A GOLDEN NATURE GUIDE

NEW

Forestation

Forestation is the process of actively establishing a mixed forest community within habitat gaps to reduce landscape fragmentation. Once a technique used to create hunting grounds, it is now a tool for increasing biodiversity and ground cover in previously degraded areas.

—

Blue Wall Center
Cleveland, South Carolina

The Blue Wall Center sits within the mixed hardwood forest of the Blue Ridge Mountains. The original site was cleared and used as a camp, and its soils became compacted so severely that they had the physical properties of concrete. SCAPE is reestablishing a rich and biotic soil matrix and foresting the site so that it will grow over time to reveal specific habitat "rooms" and set the stage for the development of a regional environmental education center. In this long-term project, soil regeneration and tree planting supersede site development and building construction by a matter of years, allowing for the long-term recovery of a landscape before the introduction of people. The site is planned to be a forest preserve, art park, education center, eco-retreat, and rural event space. Each program-driven outdoor "room" focuses on an individual microclimate and reveals details about the Blue Ridge Mountains' unique flora, fauna, geology, or hydrology while emphasizing the surroundings' historical, cultural, and ecological influences. Today, native meadow seed mixes and small caliper trees are growing to regenerate the landscape section, and will be thinned in the future to create garden rooms that amplify regional ecological interactions often invisible or inaudible in the forest.

LOGGING ROOM

BAT ROOM

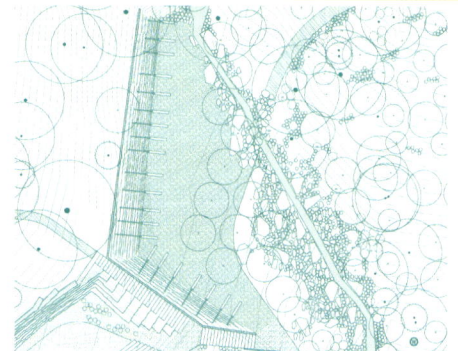

HEMLOCK ROOM

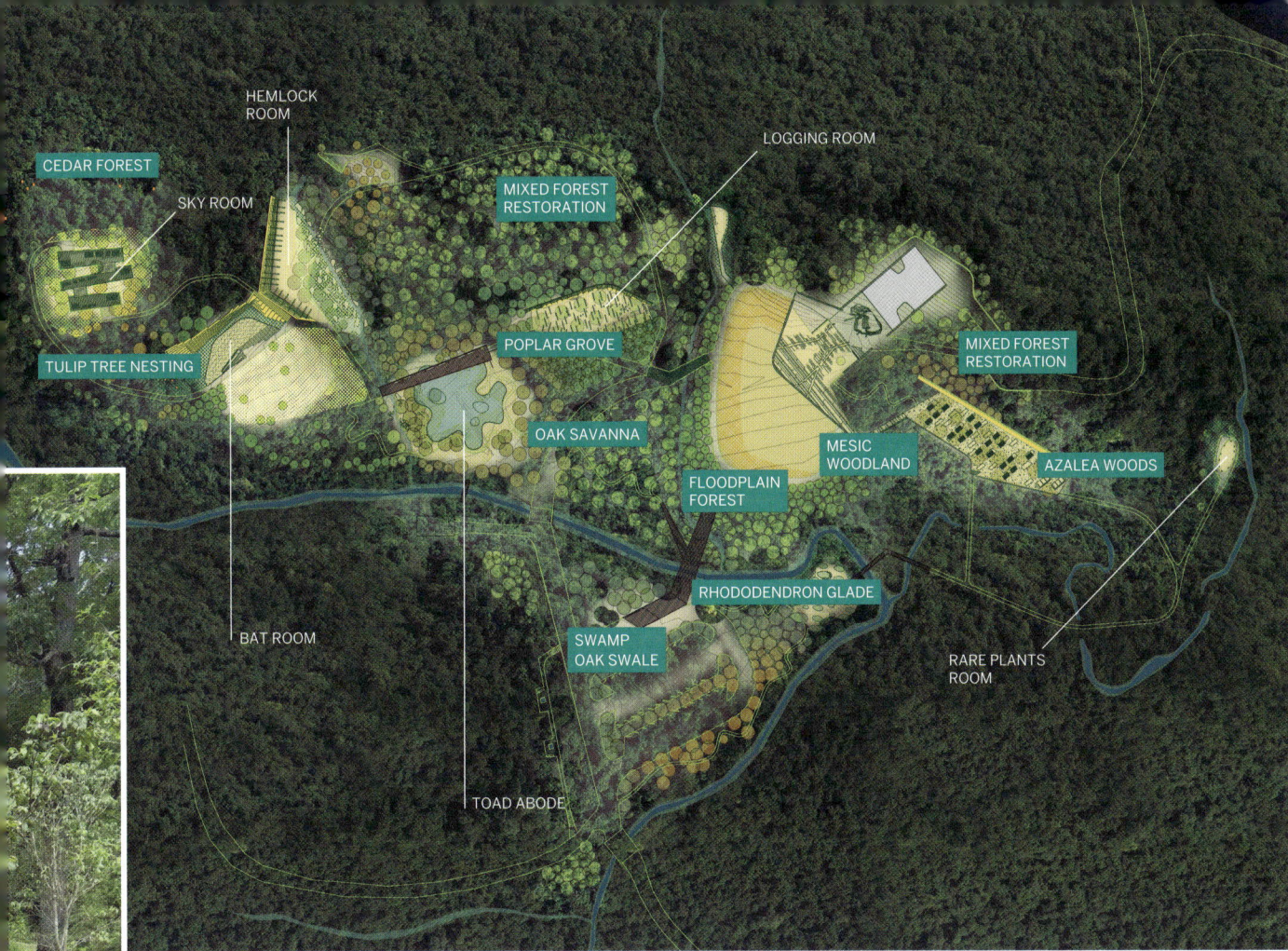

CEDAR FOREST

SKY ROOM

HEMLOCK ROOM

LOGGING ROOM

MIXED FOREST RESTORATION

TULIP TREE NESTING

POPLAR GROVE

MIXED FOREST RESTORATION

OAK SAVANNA

MESIC WOODLAND

AZALEA WOODS

FLOODPLAIN FOREST

BAT ROOM

RHODODENDRON GLADE

SWAMP OAK SWALE

RARE PLANTS ROOM

TOAD ABODE

TOAD ABODE

SKY ROOM

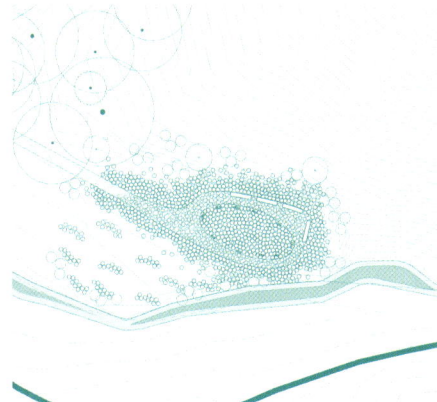

RARE PLANTS ROOM

Adaptive Management

A systematic approach for improving resource management by learning from previous mistakes and linking policy directly with implementation, adaptive management is an iterative process for decision making in the face of uncertainty.

—

Cove Co-Habitat
Sag Harbor, New York

This residential landscape departs from the typical Hamptons vernacular in favor of an ecological vision that integrates native plants and wildlife habitat together with spaces for human use. At the outset, the site was overgrown with invasive plant species such as phragmites reeds and ailanthus trees—all typical of disturbed lands in the region. SCAPE worked to develop an invasive plant management plan, to reintroduce native plantings, and to reconnect the site with the ecosystems of the Long Island Sound. Spaces are reorganized to reveal the beauty of intertidal ecology and to carve out functional zones for relaxing, entertaining, and engaging with nature. The restored coastal landscape is not a static system and requires adaptive management over time. Native junipers have been planted to outcompete exotic invasives along the site's edges, while phragmites remains present in the landscape not as an impenetrable monoculture, but as a part of a diverse mix of estuarine shrubs such as groundsel and bayberry. The strategic management of this landscape by people is essential to preserving biodiversity, through invasive removal, pruning, and selective clearing. Expanded shorebird habitat has been a result, along with the growth of mussels along the shoreline gradient.

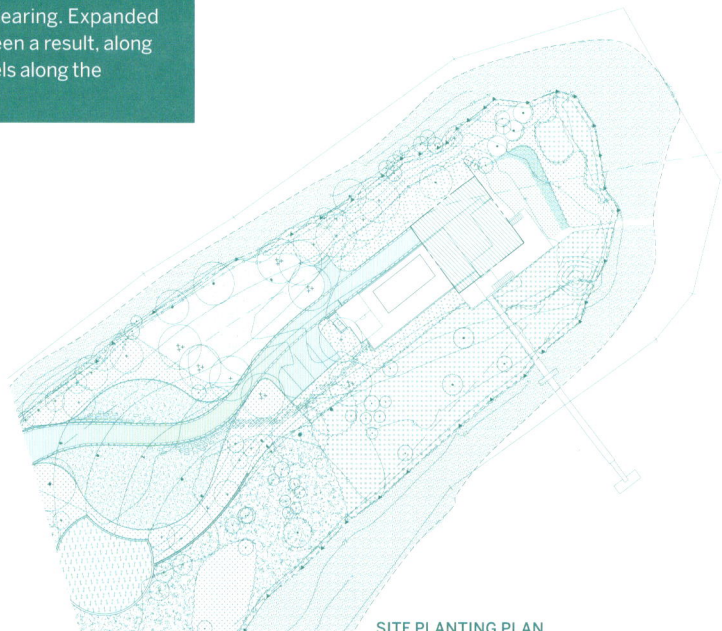

SITE PLANTING PLAN

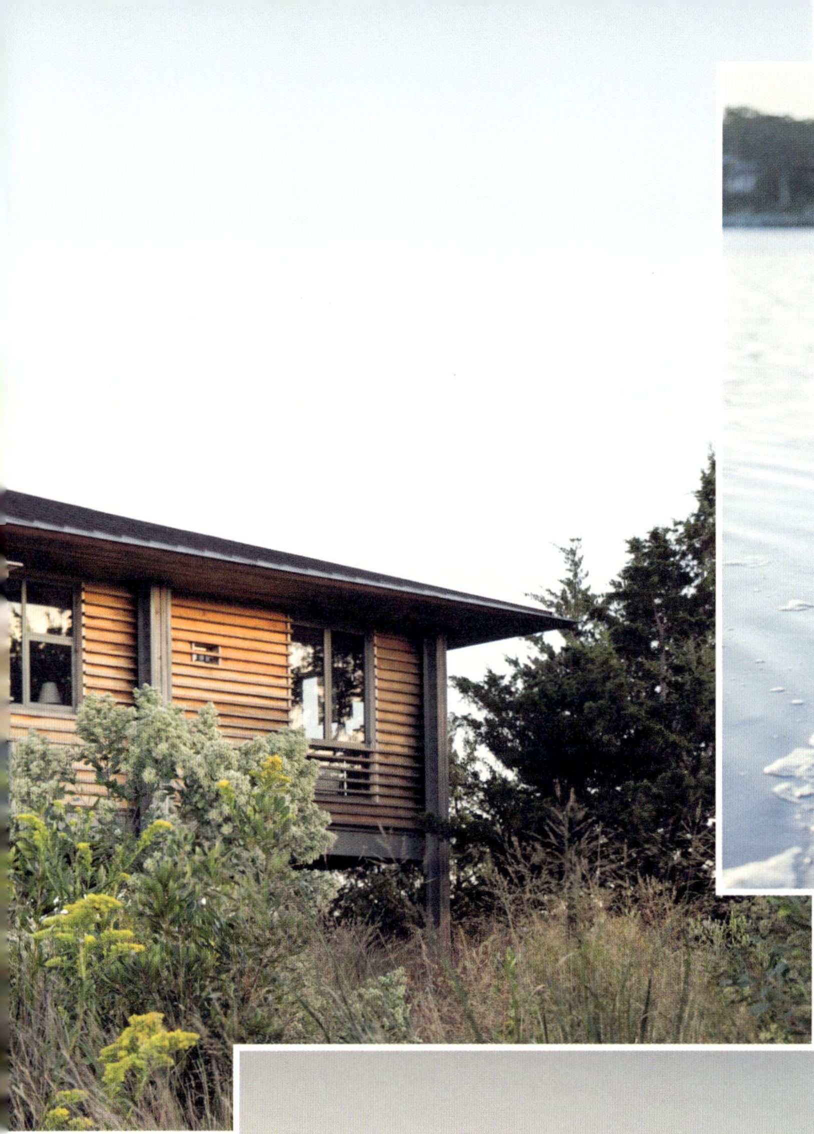

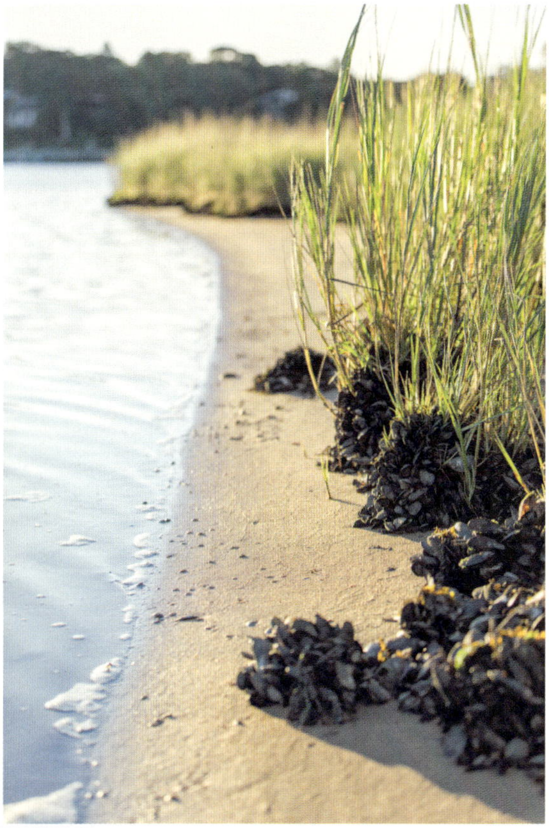

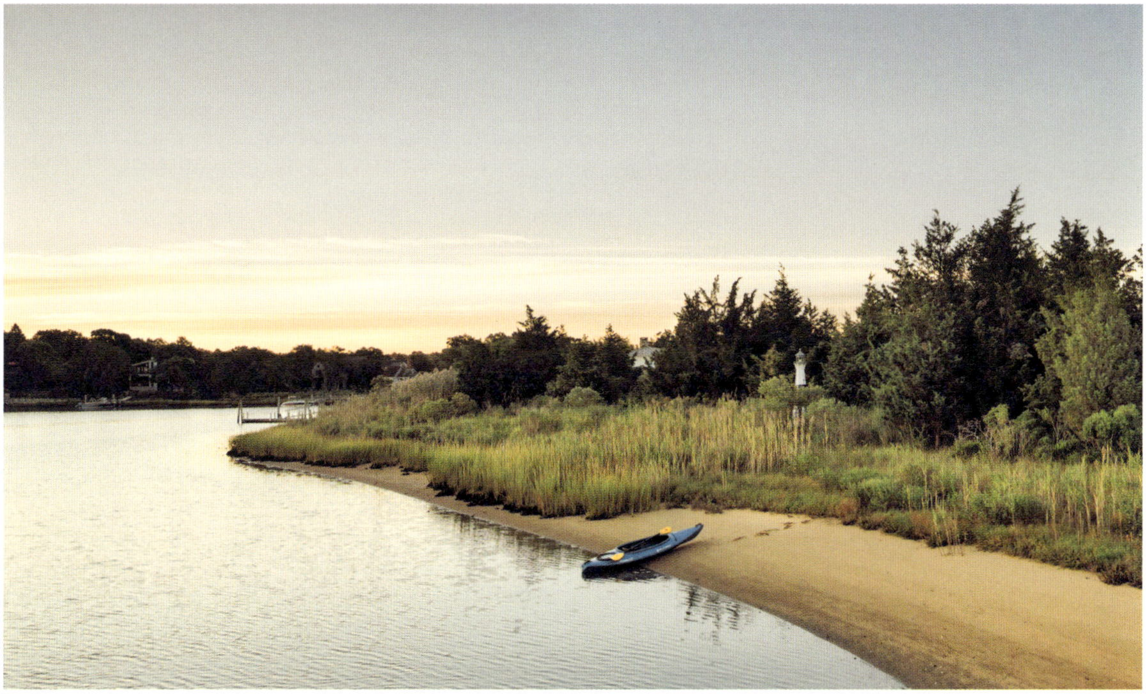

Science conducted by nonprofessionals allows for larger public participation. Part activist, part organizer, and part ecologist, a citizen scientist can help bring global issues down to the personal scale, often communicating the need for change more effectively than those certified as professionals.

—

Interview with Bart Chezar

Bart Chezar was a research and development engineer and manager of electric transportation at the New York Power Authority for most of his professional career. Since retiring in 2002, he has initiated ecological restoration projects around New York City and collaborated with community and environmental organizations, schools, private companies, and volunteers. He received an Environmental Quality Award from the US Environmental Protection Agency in 2014 in recognition of his environmental stewardship efforts. He and SCAPE have collaborated on many projects, including the Pier 5 Deconstructed Salt Marsh conceptual plan, winner of a 2014 American Society of Landscape Architects NY Merit Award.

SCAPE
Bart, you're retired, but also one of the busiest—and one of the most effective—people we know. So, what keeps you motivated?

Bart Chezar
I like what I'm doing. I like to see things that are positive, that can be built on, and that people can understand and feel good about. A lot of the time everything we hear, especially in the environmental area, is negative—and believe me, I understand. But if we just accept that, then that's our future. I'm basically an optimist. I think most problems have solutions, but only if people are willing to move toward them. If we can show people what's possible—whether it's eelgrass or osprey—they brighten up, and they say, "Those species used to be here and we could bring them back—that's cool!" It's that good message that motivates me.

S
It's very interesting too that you find projects that are doable yet simultaneously need a massive leap to succeed. You're not just doing studies, you're trying to do literal interventions that people can see.

BC
I work with nostalgia a lot. The whole idea of some of the plant and animal species I'm dealing with is that they were here before, and we can help to bring them back to our cities—oyster reefs, an osprey, chestnuts trees, eelgrass beds. In and of themselves they each do well, but they may be more important in terms of the message that they're telling—whether reintroduction is a success or not. Failure is a message too, in that it indicates that we've got to get the water a little cleaner or do some more research.

S
Failure is still learning!

BC
Yes. There are all sorts of levels of success. Just getting out there and doing something is a success in my book.

S
What was the trigger for you to shift from your work with the New York Power Authority toward working with specific species?

BC
Well, my background is in marine biology, though I never practiced it professionally. What initially happened was that a friend of mine was participating in an oyster restoration project near the Gowanus Canal, and I saw what she was doing and got interested in trying to get oysters back in their natural habitat. And then meeting other people, be it at the Harbor School or universities or just interested citizens, kept me going. I've never had a problem getting volunteers. We would have boats going out to one of our sites in the harbor and people who had nothing to do with oysters wanted to go out and see it. So that's what got me out there—that and it's fun to get your hands dirty and feel the work.

S
To pick up on the fieldwork concept: one of the things that is characteristic of big cities is that nothing ever seems to get done. There's red tape and layers upon layers of government and formal approvals. So how do you get things done? You seem to be somebody who is working on the ground and pushing up.

BC
I think of it as working on the edge. If I were a big corporation, trying to do some of these things, it'd be very difficult; I'd have to get a bid for this and permits for that. But my projects are all very small and personal. It's just me—call me a citizen scientist or a crazy, whatever. I do it, and I get whatever permits I need, but I would bet that half the time agencies say, "Just let him do his little eelgrass work. It's not such a big project." And they pretty much give me the go-ahead. What's been great is seeing bigger projects develop, like with the oysters, where I've been able to step back and the project goes forward.

S
This metaphor of working on the edge rather than top and bottom is really interesting

because your work actually trickles up and down. For example, people working in agencies look to the Pier 5 project as an example of things happening.

BC
Here's another good example: the osprey. One of the problems is that you have to put the work somewhere. I was familiar with Bush Terminal Park and there was a section that I thought would be a good place for an eco-pier. So I went to NYC Economic Development Corporation, and they kind of said "I don't know, speak to AECOM, the construction managers there." Now it just so happens there were environmental engineers at AECOM who said, "That's cool." So they went ahead and put the ten-foot metal shaft into the concrete. Nobody got paid for that, they just did it. And then Phoenix Marine Company came over one day and erected the whole thing for us. Now if I had had to contract out all these things—

S
They'd say "Forget it!"

BC
Right, but it all captured their imagination and it wasn't too big a deal. They bought into the idea that it would be cool if we could get an osprey here; so it happened.

S
Could you talk a little bit about Pier 5, the project we've been collaborating on? Was that an outgrowth of the work with the Osprey Platform, looking over at the pier and saying "Look at that thing! What's that?!"

BC
Almost exactly. I didn't know much about that part of Brooklyn, I don't even recall exactly how I learned about the park. Something got me over to that area and somehow I came upon Bush Terminal Park and saw what was there— Pier 5 just flooded, collapsed. That's where the whole idea for the eco-pier came up. And then we went over there—

S
And it was this incredible inventory of intertidal, subtidal, upland, just in this one space. All these things that we'd been trying to design into landscapes were already there . . .

BC
Right. And with my marine biology background, I understood the importance of marshes. The whole idea of ecological islands—that's an area where I think cities could fit into the larger picture in a way we don't appreciate enough. New York was great back when Henry Hudson came here and the whole shoreline was intertidal and marshes, but that's not going to happen any-more—and really you don't always need that.

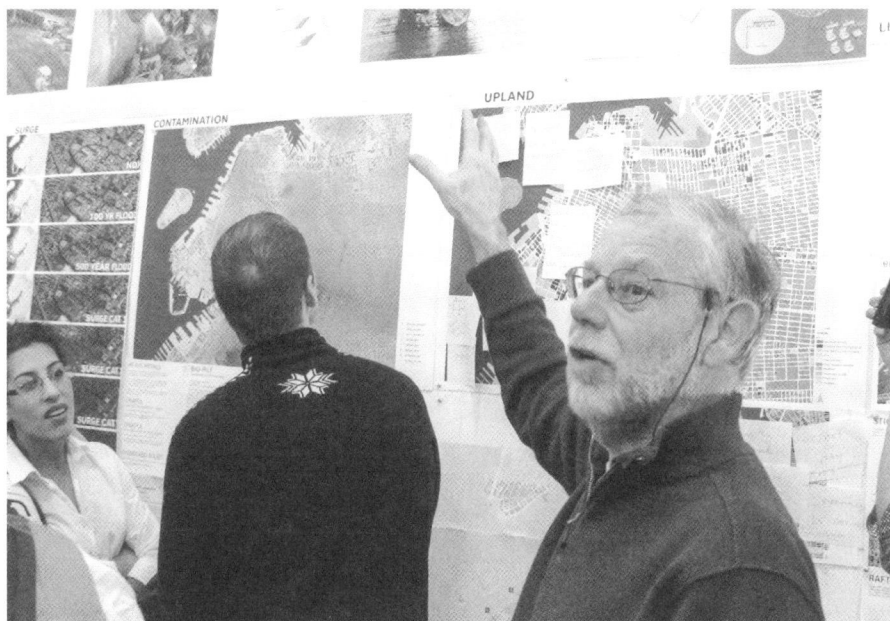

You just need places along the way—oases of habitat. For birds those places are Central Park and Prospect Park and the Jamaica Bay Wildlife Refuge. But it's really just as important in the marine environment to have these oases. If we could have those along the urban, New York City shoreline—pockets of salt marshes, or at least some of the biomes associated with salt marshes—it would be really valuable.

S
One last question for you: we've described you in the past as a kind of "radical retiree." Does that description fit?

BC
Well I don't know that I'm radical. But you know, when I retired I had to figure out what I was going to do. I knew golf wasn't in my future. I love the city, and I love all the cultural things in the city, but I like the natural aspect of it too. This work fit in with that. And again, ecologically it's important, but it's equally important for people to see that there are fish in the harbor, that the light penetrates enough to allow plants to grow underwater, and that the chestnuts that were here a hundred years ago are growing again in the city.

SCAPE
What was the genesis of the Billion Oyster Project?

Pete Malinowski
Murray Fisher [founder of the New York Harbor School] and I came up with the idea six or seven years ago, when we tried to pitch it to the city as a citywide initiative. We modeled it after Million Trees NYC, so when we first came up with the name, it was Billion Oysters NYC. A billion is a nice big round number, and at a density of two million per acre, a billion oysters works out to 500 acres. Also, just coincidentally, the standing volume of New York Harbor from the Verrazano-Narrows Bridge to the Goethals to the George Washington to the Triboro is 74 billion gallons, so a billion oysters can filter that amount of water once every three days—that's only if all the water in New York Harbor stood still, which it never does, but it's tangible. We spent three or four years selling the idea to the Mayor's Office of Sustainability, and they were always really excited about it, but we didn't have the data to say whether or not it was possible. Everyone understands trees: you plant them and they grow, for the most part. But with oysters, we don't know how it will go. So we've been working toward answering that, and still it's an open question.

S
That's what you do every day out in the harbor, isn't it? Testing, modifying, moving things forward—in that way, we see you as a designer. Have you ever thought about yourself as that?

PM
I mostly think of myself as a farmer. But I do think that design is the proving ground of whether or not any of this stuff actually works.

You can do all the modeling in the world, but unless you put something in the water and see what happens, you don't really know what's going on. So, yes, there's a lot of design in what I do—designing aquaculture systems, designing tanks, trying to get the most out of our space in the hatchery—it's all related. And I certainly take pride in the fact that everything we do supports what we're doing in the water and what we're doing with the students at the Harbor School.

S
How did you make that shift from growing up farming oysters with your family on Fishers Island to teaching about oysters and oyster restoration?

PM
I made the shift in college, when I left home. I wanted to become a science teacher, so I majored in biology, applied for the NYC Teaching Fellows, and didn't get in. And then I met Murray Fisher. They were looking for someone to teach oyster farming, so I said, "Okay!"

Growing up working with oysters was a major influence on me in pursuing science education. I worked with my dad all the time while I was growing up: before school, after school, on weekends, all summer vacation. I worked in all the different aspects of the business and just loved it. I really enjoyed trying to create environments that were conducive to oyster growth—using a microscope, feeding, working with algae—and that experience is part of what we're trying to create at the Harbor School. You're required to learn the background biology and math if you're trying to keep something like oysters alive. In order to succeed, you need that knowledge, so we teach it all.

S
How does the Billion Oyster Project dovetail with those teaching goals?

PM
The argument is that a large-scale restoration project can make all our Tech-Ed programs more interesting, and also make math, science, history, and English more interesting. We're building a harbor literacy program, and we're empowering students to know that they can do something, that they are important, and that what they do—even in high school—is valuable.

S
Do you think it's replicable in other cities? How can this model be expanded?

PM
There are a couple of big unknowns. One is whether the oysters can reproduce effectively in New York Harbor. The other is: can the New York City public school system take our model? Can it handle the shift we're trying to apply

to it? But I think that system of developing classes to meet local standards around ecological restoration projects is absolutely replicable. I don't think there are many other places where the Billion Oyster Project is replicable, but it could be a thousand acres of salt marsh, or a hundred acres of Douglas fir. It doesn't even have to be an environmental restoration project. You could imagine a career and Tech-Ed school that was a forestry school, where some students were learning how to log responsibly and some were learning how to plant trees. Instead of having that exist outside of what was happening in their classrooms, it could be part of what's happening in the classrooms.

S

We've been working together for many years now, but more recently, during the Rebuild by Design process, you explained to us that while there were some oyster larvae surviving in the harbor, they didn't have a lot of places to latch onto. All of a sudden, we realized that what we need to do as landscape architects is to get the right substrate in the right place with the right texture and materiality, and integrate this into larger-scale planning initiatives. Now, with Living Breakwaters, we're getting to do that at a scale that can really be tested—13,000 linear feet of reef! Do you feel the scale of that substrate is a game-changer for the harbor?

PM

The scale is absolutely a game-changer, especially if we're able to monitor the whole thing. A big part of the problem is that nobody's looking at the shoreline of the city. All of the riprap in New York Harbor is suitable substrate for oysters, but there are very few eyes on any of that, especially subtidally. There are six hundred miles of shoreline in New York City and so little of it is accessible to people.

S

Scale is one important issue; scalability is another. It seems to us that the work you're doing is also scalable: teaching people, seeding oysters. Even the unit of the oyster scales outward: it's an individual organism that clusters up and grows into a reef. That's a real phenomenon, but it's also a metaphor for a model of change that is accumulative and gradual.

PM

Well that's critical. That's what the billion is: an attempt to get to that point where the project is scaling itself. The whole thing is about a tipping point, from the educational aspect to the biology of it. The Living Breakwaters project is a totally different scale than what's come before it, but you couldn't say with any certainty that it's big enough. At the end of the day, in five or ten years, we could realize that it's got to be bigger!

Our hatchery, when we build it out, is going to be at a new scale for us—the goal is a hundred million oysters a year being produced on Governors Island at our school. At the Horn Point Laboratory at the University of Maryland they're doing a billion oysters a year. They're trying to get to the tipping point in the Chesapeake Bay, which is much bigger than the New York Harbor, but it's not entirely clear whether they're even at the scale that they need to be at. So I think it's just a matter of trying to get to the next size all the time and seeing if you've reached it. It's all about reaching that tipping point, finding reasons to scale up. If Living Breakwaters needs a hundred million oysters, then that provides us with the motivation and the capital to get to that scale. And then it's just stepping up and up and up.

S

What does it look like if we get there? What is your vision for the New York Harbor in twenty years?

PM

If you look at places where there is a vibrant oyster population, like Tampa Bay or Mobile Bay, every square inch of hard substrate that's in the water is covered with oysters. If we could get enough oysters so that had happened, it would be awesome. But I'd like to be at a point where we've caught up and can use substrate to build oyster reefs instead of using live oysters to build oyster reefs. I hope that in twenty years there is a growing oyster population in the harbor and everything that goes with it: more fish, more birds.

Everything that happens on the water in New York is very optimistic. It's not a friendly place to oyster farm. But everyone is really hopeful, just wanting to get there. I think that goes along with the twenty-year vision: New York City turning back to the harbor, realizing that it has this incredible resource here, and making it safer.

S

Do you feel optimistic that the regulatory environment can evolve enough to let this kind of work happen?

PM

The regulatory environment in New York always exists on the edge of what's happening. They need to do their jobs, and that means creating limits and working within them. But they've never said no to anything we've tried to do. They always say, "These are our concerns, this is what you have to do to satisfy them, and then we'll give you a permit." It's a long process and there's a back and forth, but ultimately we make some changes and then they approve them. We've always felt like we've gotten something that we shouldn't have gotten—like

we've won something. So what we're asking for always gets bigger!

We've had great success with partnering with different agencies and nonprofits. We've worked with the Port Authority, the EPA, National Oceanic and Atmospheric Administration, Hudson River Foundation, Baykeeper, the Army Corps of Engineers. A collection of thirty nonprofit governmental partners worked together to build five tiny oyster reefs in the harbor. We have tons of partners doing a lot of work to make these feasibility studies happen, which is how I would qualify everything that we've done. We're trying to see if something works. We just need to do it enough so that New York City or the federal government is invested in it and realizes that we cannot continue to ignore our waterways—that just as we need to preserve, protect, and recreate parkland in cities, we need to do the same thing in the water. If we get that type of investment, then we can really effect a lot of change.

URBAN ECOLOGICAL DESIGN AS FEMINIST PRACTICE
Thaïsa Way

Urban ecological design defines a practice of landscape architecture grounded in the intersections and relationships of social and natural systems. As a design framework, it addresses the dynamic character of a city—its cultural and social networks—while simultaneously expanding the concept of urban nature and urban ecology. In intention, it is a practice not bounded by political territories nor limited to ecological habitats, but seeks to envision a broader and more complex environment that is at once of the past and the future. It enlarges our focus to engage a larger systematic thinking, an approach that is the core framework for work by Kate Orff and SCAPE.

As a frame, urban ecological design has emerged and evolved from over a century of practice, shaped by diverse design practices beginning in the nineteenth century. It is also deeply grounded in a feminist perspective on the urban, on nature, and on the role of design in the public realm. SCAPE's work has built on these foundations as a means to radically alter and retool how we see, imagine, experience, and recall the landscapes in and on which we tread our daily lives. Through such a radical approach, SCAPE is confronting the grand challenges of our next century: climate change and urban environmental justice.

Landscape practice has evolved over the centuries in order to claim the potential to reconceive urban landscapes as natural and cultural tapestries that might alter human behavior. Given this potential, it is worth deconstructing and reexploring the emergence of urban ecological design to more fully realize its power and vision and, in turn, to position contemporary practice by firms such as SCAPE within a more radical framework.

And before you ask, "What about landscape urbanism and ecological urbanism?" I suggest that these labels are attempts by those in power to claim urban ecological design as new and as solely generated through their own creative pursuits rather than as having been built on over a century of practice, often by those practitioners the very profession has marginalized. Yes, landscape urbanism and to a lesser extent ecological urbanism have been useful tropes around which to discuss and challenge urban design and landscape architecture. However, in the pursuit of portraying these practices as "new," their advocates have neglected the very foundations on which the ideas emerged. This essay seeks in part to reignite the role of history in practice and theory, and to use it as a viable and enriching lens through which to think and create and imagine.

As the historian Catherine Howett has suggested, ecological values have been a part of landscape design practice since the "primitive fence" defined a zone of human control.[1] They were also clearly described in the mid-nineteenth-century landscape designs of Frederick Law Olmsted, who sought to make natural systems visible within existing social and cultural contexts.[2] Olmsted firmly believed that landscape design should embrace a "delicate balance, a synthesis of aesthetic, environmental, and social goods."[3] An oft-noted example is the Emerald Necklace and its Back Bay Fens, designed with Charles Eliot as artfully conceived, constructed landscapes redirecting natural systems and human environments.[4] Eliot extended the approach into his open-space plans for the Metropolitan Boston region. Taking this thinking to a larger spatial scale, Benton MacKaye in the 1920s and 1930s envisioned the Appalachian Trail and the Tennessee Valley Authority landscapes as new forms of infrastructure that could merge art and contemporary technology. As architect Keller Easterling has described, MacKaye understood the potential of a simple intervention in the landscape to catalyze an alternative or altered organizational system.[5] Jens Jensen, Ruth Bramley Dean, Wilhelm Miller, and Martha Brookes Hutcheson built design practices in the early twentieth century on their understanding of ecology and by merging the knowledge and practice of science and art. Nevertheless, narratives of landscape as it emerged as a profession neglected the agency of nature and scientific studies in design and its stewardship.[6] Such histories have not considered how landscape architecture was informed by the simultaneous rise of the nascent disciplines of both environmental science and ecology, or the practitioners who engaged these areas of knowledge in their design process and production.

Landscape architecture has always been a somewhat porous practice, one that has rarely been limited by a narrow professional definition despite consistent efforts by the majority of its practitioners.[7] Its complex history reveals many threads, not least of which is the contribution of women to the environmental movements, to the progressive-era city-improvement movements, and to the profession of landscape architecture. While the mainstream of design practice has been enriched, expanded, and creatively constructed by diverse men and women, it is in the margins that we identify the nascent approaches that have, over time, served as radical frameworks for practice. This is nowhere more true than in the emergence of urban ecological design over more than a century, which first appeared at the edges of landscape architectural practice. By refocusing on the margins, we are able to position the work of contemporary firms such as SCAPE in a discussion that identifies new ways of seeing and sharing knowledge, which may in turn inform a common human purpose and effort. We can reposition the focus of SCAPE and others on collaboration versus the single gesture in a longer practice of community engagement and collective knowledge-building. And while many narratives could be told, this essay suggests how urban ecological design arose from their collective body of work as women engaged in the study and design of cities through the lenses of human health and ecology as the study of nature, environmental science, and art.

A feminist approach builds on descriptions of complex and dynamic relationships that catalyze new connections and affiliations. A feminist framework does not seek to merely replace a patriarchal hierarchy, but rather to replace a dualistic and hierarchical view with a fluidity of bonds and associations and webs. It is a wickedly democratic structure that is always becoming and without the distinctions between art and science.[8] This view of feminism is deeply embedded in urban ecological design, where the *urban* is defined as a human construct of relationships in the built environment and the *ecological* is described as the natural processes and systems and, finally, design is the act of intentionally bringing these elements into engagement with each another.

Rachel Carson and wildlife artist Bob Hines

Ellen Swallow Richards described the nascent study of human ecology, which has its roots in the late nineteenth century, as "the study of the sur-roundings of human beings in the effects they produce on the lives of men."[9] In this way, she articulated the critical relationship between environment and humanity as the interrelated effects of clean air, pure water, and fertile soil on human health and nutrition. In the twentieth century, feminist scholars such as Carolyn Merchant have explored how, whether biologically or culturally, there is a gender relationship associated with stewarding the environment.[10] They have described how women have approached the population-environ-ment quandary by building on the ways their daily lives intersect with popula-tion policies and global environmental politics. This, in turn, has shaped how we have come to describe feminist approaches to the environment, even eco-feminism as a foundation for practices that expand across professions and disciplines.

Further, the practice of landscape design can be a means of acknowl-edging the body as the primary site by which we come to know the world, sense the environment. In a feminist practice, this acknowledgement of the body is privileged over any technological or political experiences associated with a given place. Such a feminist view of the urban landscape and ecology is manifested in the practice of urban ecological design, which draws on over a century of practice—by both men and women, but by more women than men, as it was a perspective and framework that privileged an accepted-as-feminine view of the world throughout the nineteenth and twentieth century. This view saw the world as an extension of the family home and thus the woman's expanded domestic realm. In these ways, urban ecological design has emerged as a practice grounded in a complex, even wicked, view of an environment as a system that understands and privileges networks and webs and systems over static objects and singular moments.

To provide a history of urban ecological design practice, I engage two histories: of urban studies and planning as a practice, and of landscape architecture as a profession and practice. It is at the intersection of these three domains that we find the feminist practice within urban ecological design. This works within a larger framework of describing feminist practice as challenging established relations of power (critique), exploring alternative possibilities (theory), and advocating for a change in social relations and spatial realities that privileges the dynamism of catalytic relationships.

URBAN DESIGN AND PLANNING

The development of ecology as a discipline was contemporaneous with an increased interest in the study of cities and urban systems. With the rise of the progressive era in the nineteenth century, Jane Addams, Ellen Gates Starr, Julia Lathrop, Florence Kelley, Ida B. Wells, and Mary McLeod Bethune were influential in the efforts to improve the efficiencies, health, and livability of cities, for all citizens but most specifically for families, and for the women as mothers of their children. Addams and Starr collectively founded Hull House as a kindergarten and adult education center while working to campaign for laws to reform child labor regulations. Addams's leadership in the efforts to address issues of public health as well as world peace was accomplished at the scale of the neighborhood as well as in the international sphere. While she is often acknowledged for establishing the profession of social work, it is critical to emphasize that her view was as much about practice as about place. Addams understood and championed the role of spaces that fostered community, including community arts centers and social service facilities. The settlement house was one manifestation of this vision and, as such, included social and gathering spaces, living apartments, and outdoor places while offering adult education in a variety of subjects including art, drama, and music. This integrated view of community building and place-making emerged from a focus on women and children—it was a feminist perspective and practice. It catalyzed alternative connections and affiliations.

However, the legacy of such influential women was deemed insignificant in the 1940s as the fields of urban design and planning were defined and shaped by privileged, educated, white men. Professionals sought to distinguish themselves from earlier social efforts—that is, from the women who had been leaders and advocates. The focus of city planning during the course of the twentieth century was increasingly, although not exclusively, oriented to large-scale planning efforts, quantitative methods of analysis, and on policy rather than on the lived experience of urban dwellers. Women engaged with these issues during this time included Catherine Bauer Wurster and Frances Perkins, who was appointed secretary of labor under Franklin D. Roosevelt. Both offered views grounded in the individual and the family. It is in the work of those at the edges of mainstream practices, again, where we find the radical beginnings of integrated design that sought to address the potential of the ecological and cultural performances possible in the urban landscape.

WOMEN AND LANDSCAPE ARCHITECTURE

It was only in the mid-nineteenth century, with the design of Central Park, that landscape architecture became a recognized profession—it would, however, be formalized in 1899 with the establishment of the American Society of Landscape Architects. The profession was not confined to one typical sort of practice, but engaged people from distinctly diverse backgrounds, and it included women: Beatrix Jones (later Farrand) was a founding member of the ASLA, and was elected as one of the first fellows along with Frederick Olmsted, Jr.[11] Women rose as leaders and mentors in the profession including Florence Yoch, Annette Hoyt Flanders, Ellen Biddle Shipman, Helen Jones, Katherine Bashford, Ruth Shellhorn, and Barbara Fealey.

By the late nineteenth century and well through to the mid-twentieth century, women were attracted to landscape architecture in part because it engaged the knowledge of horticulture, botany, gardening, and the fine arts—all considered appropriately feminine areas of study.[12] Women were not blind to such possibility, and while we will never know truly how many, we do know many, probably thousands of women pursued education in landscape design, landscape gardening, and related fields. By 1940, 19 percent of ASLA members were women.[13] Their practices reflected a broad range of projects typical for contemporary professionals, from the small domestic garden to the city plan, from the intimate neighborhood park to industrial parks, from the bog to hydrological infrastructure. Women explored the same variety of styles and design approaches as their male colleagues.

CATALYTIC CHANGE—CARSON AND JACOBS

These narratives of urban practice and landscape architecture synergized in powerful ways in the 1960s as the environmental movement emerged. And it is no coincidence that two of the most influential books published about the urban environmental movement were by women: *Silent Spring* (1962) by Rachel Carson, and *The Death and Life of Great American Cities* (1961) by Jane Jacobs. These drew on a century of growing interest in ecology, natural systems, and the environment as well as the social and cultural systems of cities by women. In turn, those in landscape architecture built practices centered on alternative approaches to nature, land, and cities. Women were leaders in these catalytic decades. Sally Schauman, for example, served as the leading landscape architect with the USDA Soil Conservation Service and, at the University of Washington in 1980, she was appointed the first woman chair of a department of landscape architecture. Anne Whiston Spirn joined the Harvard faculty in 1979 and served as director of its landscape architecture program from 1984 to 1986. She spearheaded an ecological approach to community-based design, and was later appointed chair of the Department of Landscape Architecture at the University of Pennsylvania. In 1984, Spirn's book *The Granite Garden: Urban Nature and Human Design* revolutionized urban landscape architecture by reframing the city so that it could be viewed as a place of ecological systems and networks. These women advanced the study of plants and ecology within the curricula of landscape architecture pedagogy, despite many practitioners rejecting studies on urban ecology—instead focusing their attention on explorations of minimalist art, choreography, and large-scale planning.

URBAN ECOLOGICAL DESIGN

Throughout the twentieth century, women's design practices had engaged ecology, the environment, and the city. Many female landscape architects sought to create urban environments that nurtured social and environmental health. Their work called out landscape as an active medium for both nature and culture. As Easterling has noted, it is the active form, not the object form: "[not] the pattern printed on the fabric but the way the fabric floats."[14] In this frame, we can describe ecological design as the interplay of active forms always adjusting and responding to the specifics of site and time and culture. The practice has been positioned at the overlapping intersections of domains of knowledge: urban life and ecological design. We identify a feminist practice of integrating the urban and the ecological with the art of design. The women described here, like Kate Orff today, drew on knowledge grounded in the sciences—particularly ecology—to create successful practices at a time when other professionals chose to set such disciplines aside. When science returned to landscape architecture in the 1970s and 1980s as a legitimate framework for practice, these domains of knowledge were revived and reengaged by the larger profession.

Urban ecological design remains a feminist practice in that it seeks to challenge design to engage the lived experience of individuals and communities, and advocates for alternative narratives and futures as we can identify in the work of SCAPE. This approach privileges efforts to steward the future and the long-term view over immediate gratification while simultaneously appealing to the senses. It addresses the scale of the human body, the experience of people in their daily lives, now and tomorrow. It is also a practice that is inherently indeterminate—it acknowledges the primacy of change over time, of the constant dynamism that serves to catalyze new responses and reactions. As such, a practice such as SCAPE is positioned to critically contribute to the future of cities and of urban landscapes across the globe as we address the challenges of climate change and population growth, of decreasing natural resources and increasingly toxic landscapes, and of economic disparities and environmental injustices.

As geographer Nik Heynen writes, "If we take David Harvey's dictum that 'there is nothing unnatural about New York City' seriously, this impels interrogating the failure of twentieth-century urban social theory to take account of physical or ecological processes. Re-naturing urban theory is, therefore, vital to urban analysis as well as to urban political activism."[15] This concern is most richly investigated by the gritty process of working with communities, people, and politics in the effort to get things done. This requires a commitment to make change, to challenge the status quo, to radicalize the practice. To again refer to Easterling, it is understanding the power of knowing *how* rather than knowing *what* that differentiates the radical. Today, SCAPE is catalyzing alternative relationships and systems that foster networks between ecological systems and public infrastructure, between urban nature and urban culture, between the urban, the ecological, and design. They are building a powerful sphere of influence that considers stewardship of the future of our cities as paramount.

1. Catherine Howett, "Ecological Values in Twentieth-Century Landscape Design: A History and Hermeneutics," *Landscape Journal* 17, no. 2 (1998): 80–98.
2. Anne Whiston Spirn, "Constructing Nature: the Legacy of Frederick Law Olmsted," in William Cronon, ed., *Uncommon Ground: Rethinking the Human Place in Nature* (New York: W.W. Norton & Co., 1996).
3. Howett, 80–98.
4. Charles E. Beveridge, Paul Rocheleau, and David Larkin, *Frederick Law Olmsted: Designing the American Landscape* (New York: Rizzoli, 1995); Frederick Law Olmsted, Charles E. Beveridge, and David Schuyler, *Creating Central Park, 1857–1861* (Baltimore: Johns Hopkins University Press, 1983).
5. Keller Easterling, *Organization Space: Landscapes, Highways, and Houses in America* (Cambridge, Mass.: MIT Press, 1999), 25–34.
6. See for example Mariana (Mrs. Schuyler) Van Rensselaer, *Art out-of-doors: Hints on Good Taste in Gardening* (New York: C. Scribner's Sons, 1893).
7. See Thaïsa Way, *Unbounded Practice: Women and Landscape Architecture in the Early Twentieth Century* (Charlottesville: University of Virginia Press, 2009).
8. Among other discussions, see Maurice Merleau-Ponty, *Phénoménologie de la perception* (Paris: Gallimard, 1945) and Judith Butler, "Performative Acts and Gender Constitution: An Essay in Phenomenology and Feminist Theory," *Theatre Journal* 40, no. 4 (December 1988): 519–31.
9. Ellen H. Richards, *Sanitation in Daily Life* (Boston: Whitcomb & Barrows, 1907), v.
10. Janice Jiggins, *Changing the Boundaries: Women-Centered Perspectives on Population and the Environment* (New York: Island Press, 1994).
11. See Way, *Unbounded Practice.*
12. Ibid.
13. By 1972 only 6 percent were women. It would take until 1984 to return to the earlier numbers. See Lamia Doumato, *Architecture and Women: A Bibliography Documenting Women Architects, Landscape Architects, Designers, Architectural Critics and Writers, and Women in Related Fields Working in the United States* (New York: Garland Pub., 1988).
14. Keller Easterling, *Extrastatecraft: The Power of Infrastructure Space* (London and New York: Verso, 2014), 21.
15. Nik Heynen, Maria Kaika, and Erik Swyngedouw, "Urban Political Ecology: Politicizing the Production of Urban Natures," in *In the Nature of Cities: Urban Political Ecology and the Politics of Urban Metabolism* (New York: Routledge, 2006).

Engage

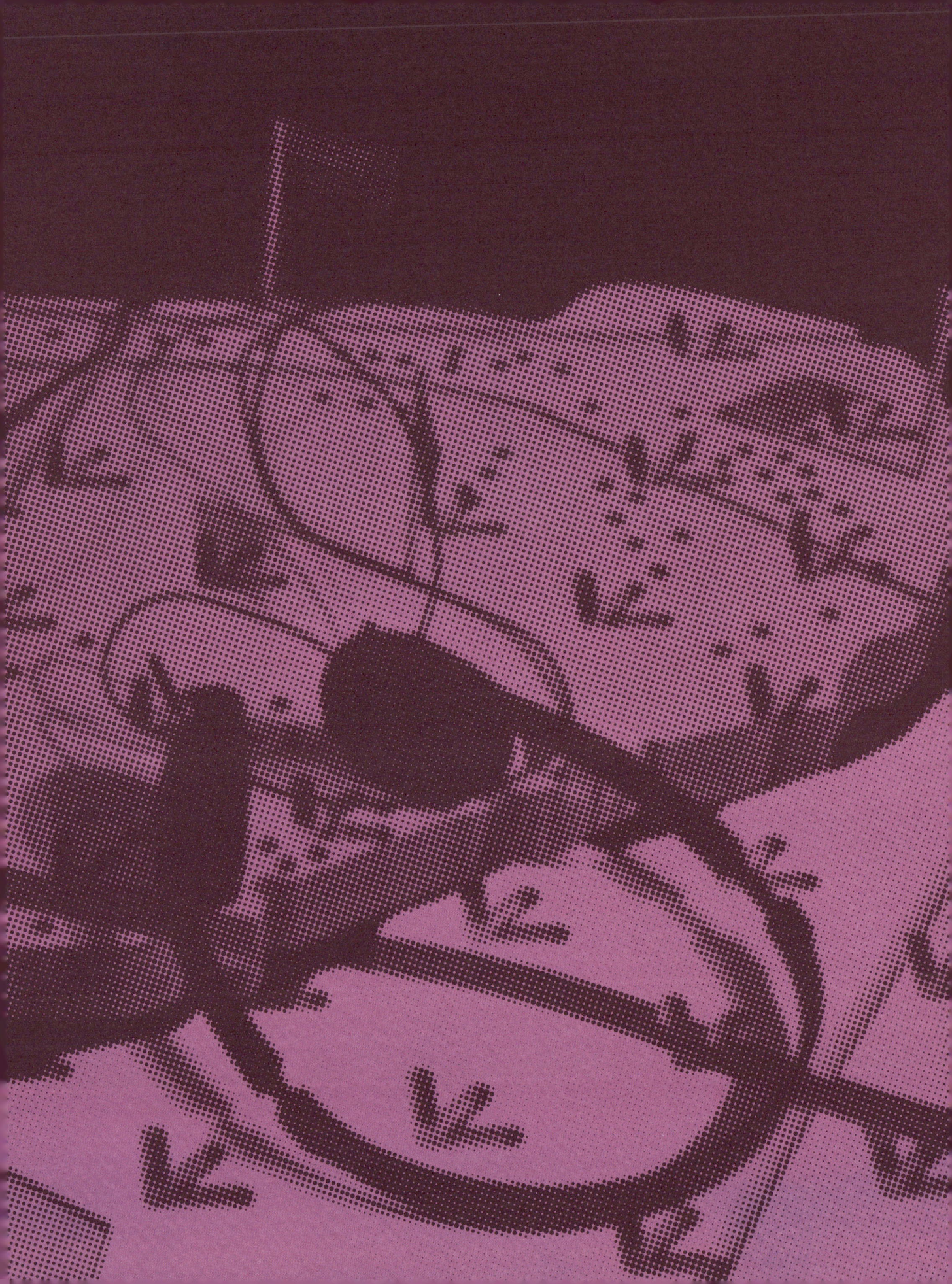

"All actual life is encounter."[1]
—Martin Buber

To *engage* means to occupy the attention or efforts of another person. It also means to interlock, engross, interest, and involve. This chapter describes projects where SCAPE has tested a new model for community process. We've aimed to move away from a one-way relationship between designers as experts and the public as receivers of expertise and toward a two-way dialogue that is mutually productive and that ultimately engenders a joint creative collaboration. Here, to engage is to create spaces of engagement, tools of engagement, and processes of engagement—in sum, an urban culture of engagement.

Social cohesion, a critical yet difficult-to-define factor in robust civil life, is not easy to measure and/or create spatially. Its absence, however, is readily perceived. Eric Klinenberg's book *Heat Wave: A Social Autopsy of Disaster in Chicago* (2002) tracked the death rate due to extreme heat in two adjacent neighborhoods relative to each neighborhood's "social infrastructure: the sidewalks, stores, public facilities and community organizations that bring people into contact with friends and neighbors." Spatial conditions that fostered interaction significantly improved outcomes in disaster conditions, and presumably have a similar beneficial effect in everyday conditions of everyday life. This chapter explores how we can move past the notion of traditional "community input" as a mere legal obligation in the planning process and toward a truly engaged stance, so that design itself serves to strengthen bonds and generate social cohesion.

Community input is a critical aspect of any robust democratic society. Indeed, legal due process is prescribed in a plethora of federal, state, and local land-use laws in the United States, ranging from Environmental Impact Statements to ULURP (Uniform Land Use Review Procedure) to basic local construction permits. However, community input processes in the modern era have evolved mostly as a means of blocking or protesting against projects instead of as a means of truly learning and exchanging information on potential tradeoffs and opportunities. It was a legendary moment in urban planning history when activist and author Jane Jacobs forced "master builder" Robert Moses to stand down over a proposed Lower Manhattan expressway that would have cut through New York's SoHo district in the 1960s. More recently, on the West Coast, the 2006 demolition of the South Central Farm, a fourteen-acre community plot in Los Angeles, reverberates as both a traumatizing memory and a truly defining moment, when common resources were threatened by infrastructure development and private real estate interests. These events, among many others, justifiably fueled a grassroots oppositional stance that still shapes current debate about the built environment. New scenarios of visioning, proactive scenario building, advocacy, shared sacrifice, and comprehensive planning that bridge public- and private-sector actors are needed at multiple scales of governance.

We need to engage in a way that moves beyond balkanized public discourse; this is even more imperative in the age of climate change, where we have a limited time frame to reduce greenhouse gas emissions. As national governments move into an era where even the most modest, non-binding political goals are not easily achievable—closing the gap of average temperature increase from 3–4 degrees Fahrenheit down to 2 degrees Fahrenheit (from catastrophic to mildly catastrophic)—these policies require radical changes to infrastructure and neighborhoods, all of which will manifest locally on coastlines, in deserts, and in backyards. When community review proceeds on a project-by-project basis, the larger picture can be lost for decades in a tangle of viewshed complaints and personal property line encroachments. In many cases, there will only be bad choices. But now is the time to reopen a discussion about how to define the common good and each person's roles and responsibilities in light of the imperatives of global environmental justice. Average global temperatures are increasing, and the related effects of fire, flood, erosion, and drought are becoming increasingly unpredictable. The world's poorest are anticipated to suffer the most greatly, whether on the Bangladeshi coast, in the drought-stricken savannas of Kenya, or in the arid American Southwest. This imperative requires a new approach to public discourse, and urban designers and landscape architects have the tools to lead this discussion and shape the debate.

TOP-DOWN VS. GROUND-UP

Even the knee-jerk impetus to read strong cultural shifts and immediately invert from "top-down" to "ground-up" planning would not be enough to address the real and important challenges we face—we need to pair coordinated policies and incremental methods. Climate change adaptation and resiliency measures expose profound weaknesses relative to solely "ground-up" planning and the need for a comprehensive approach to reducing risk and adapting to uncertainty. SCAPE has experienced this firsthand in our post-Sandy disaster planning efforts with the city and state of New York. Many noble political responses to ground-up community initiatives have resulted, in some cases, in only a smattering of smaller projects that may prove to be largely ineffective in addressing coastal flooding, emergency energy supply, or other future, shared basic needs.

Traditional community meetings present only stark choices—often "for" or "against" a particular initiative or proposal. At times community meetings serve to further polarize already fraying social fabric, pitting neighbor against neighbor relative to loathed "stakeholder priorities." It's dog walkers versus playgrounds, bikers versus pedestrians, history buffs versus developers. We aim to go beyond a check-the-box approach and to integrate education—and fun—into a longer-term process. This is not to say that every challenge has a seamless resolution, but we can reframe issues via a shared educative process and build on the knowledge and experiences of the people who live in the area to be affected.

Park raising at 103rd Street

Our *engage* stance is about having a vision of a better future, but also working with the world as it is and meeting people where they are. Climate change has been called a "wicked problem" on many levels. Excess carbon dioxide in the air is the product not only of large industrial economies, but also an infinite number of small actions. Addressing climate change can't be the sole purview of experts or engineers coming up with technical solutions. Incremental behavior change is the key to an alternative future, so the ability of designers to know how to initiate discussion and frame key issues in the public realm is a critical tool. To engage is to foster intergenerational exchange and strategize smaller, cumulative, coordinated actions.

A CULTURE OF SHARING

SCAPE is trying to chart a path for community engagement centered on education, information, and interaction that can set a broader stage for informed, meaningful dialogue. This stance starts inside the office, where we have developed a culture of sharing—sharing our work with each other at weekly pin-ups, and welcoming school groups and other landscape architects into the office. We also frequently attend and support nonprofit workshops and events around the New York/New Jersey region such as the Raritan Bay Festival, the New York State Marine Education Association conference, workshops on Jamaica Bay at the Stevens Institute of Technology, and more traditional academic panels.

Our culture of sharing extends to the kinds of imagery that we create as well—rather than conventional drawings that are difficult to understand by your average (but not expert) aunt, uncle, or friend, we test out imagery, use big, clear labels, and have developed a range of strategies to gather input. We enable people to comment directly on drawings, we gather small groups to go more in-depth based on topics of interest, and we host broad forums where people can take the microphone and expound upon whatever strikes them as important about a plan or a proposal. At the same time, we explore other nontraditional methods of outreach. For example, while designing Blake Hobbs Park in East Harlem, SCAPE project manager Lanie McKinnon taught a class of seventh graders about landscape architecture at the adjacent school. Gena Wirth, project manager for Living Breakwaters, led an all-ages balloon mapping shore tour on Staten Island in order for families to better understand their eroding and vulnerable coastline, how further degradation could affect them, and the recreational and ecological potential of the landscape.

Choreographing participation itself is imperative to design thinking. Today urban designers not only need to be geo-data interpreters and distributors, but we need to be special events coordinators as well. How can designers move beyond a one-way display of information to involve others and build commitment and understanding? What does this look like in practice? Does the creative integration of activities, education, and information suggest that a project can have catalytic effects beyond its physical boundaries? That it can start on day one, not after years of effort and a multimillion-dollar capital campaign? One example of how this might work was SCAPE's Oyster-tecture knitting party, during which the physical making of the museum-quality model, a quarter-scale mockup of mussel-recruiting fuzzy rope, became essentially a crowd-sourced craft project that was ultimately displayed at the Museum of Modern Art (see pp. 100–1). In a culture marked by fragmented interests, knitting was both an apt metaphor and an easily shared activity. It reached out to people of diverse ages, and brought them together in social and collaborative ways while prodding them to think about water quality and their shared harbor. Every action has the potential to pull together an engaged citizenry. Engagement itself is a process, a project, and a product. Community events—following either conventional or unexpected formats—must be woven into the DNA of the design process itself from now on.

DEMOCRATIZING THE MAP

To engage is not to just propose solutions, but to increase the perception and understanding of place. Lived, direct experience with the physical landscape and its long-term stewardship simply leads to better outcomes. "Like verbal literacy, landscape literacy is a cultural practice that entails both understanding the world and transforming it," Anne Spirn writes. "To be literate is to recognize both the problems in a place and its resources, to understand how they came about, by what means they are sustained, and how they are related."[2] Landscape literacy has catapulted into unprecedented operational territory via new creative mapping tools and crowd-sourced techniques. These technologies, combined with technology platforms that enable information sharing, have sparked new forums for exchange, community input, and education. Public Lab, for example, is an open-source, DIY group that teaches how to access tools and techniques that can allow invested citizens to participate in land-use decisions. Their lessons, which include outfitting balloons with cameras to peer over perimeter fence lines, developing home-based oil-testing kits, and explaining how to collect, map, analyze, and transmit environmental data, give people tools for seeing the boundaries and fluidity of a landscape.[3]

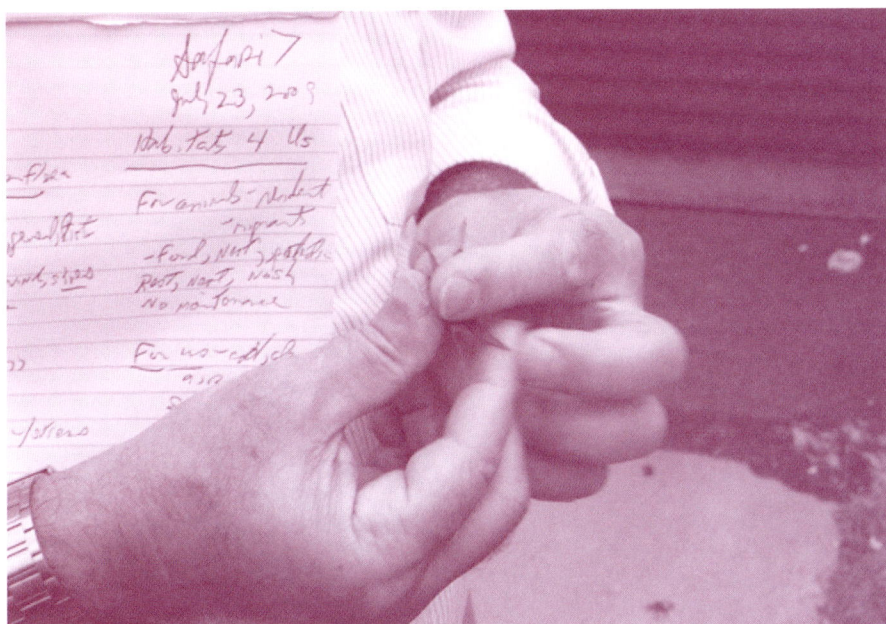

Weedy landscape literacy

Scaling up community engagement means that SCAPE aims to make tools for others to share, which helps a project grow exponentially outward, and build a shared knowledge base. For example, the Bird-Safe Building Guidelines, produced by SCAPE and the Columbia Urban Landscape Lab in 2006 for the NYC Audubon Society, was developed as a freely downloadable and updateable document; the American Bird Council has since edited and adopted it (see pp. 118–9). In many of our projects, we identify a small-scale product that could contribute to the public good and be executed regardless of official projected outcomes. For Reviving Town Branch, we developed a Water Walk (see pp. 180–1). For Living Breakwaters, profiled in the Scale chapter, an oyster-gardening manual for distribution and use in New York City schools sparked oyster-farming projects in New York Harbor through the Billion Oyster Project (see pp. 252–3).

BARN RAISING

As Brian Davis explores in his essay on the pragmatics of public land-scapes, community building is now an essential part of the work of design more broadly (see "Public Sediment," pp. 228–34). Agriculture serves as a metaphor of sorts for this. Landscapes that achieve sustainability in terms of both civilization and ecology are, by necessity and by nature, participatory. They are working landscapes. And if we are to achieve a new kind of working landscape for the twenty-first century—one that, as Peter F. Cannavò writes of the traditional agrarian working landscape, is "characterized by a long-standing balance between human and natural forces," we must build upon the embedded knowledge and collective power of an engaged citizenry. Cannavò continues, a working landscape "is an ongoing, collective project of many individuals and generations."[4] Landscape—and engagement—can be defined by the shared work of learning about and making landscapes.

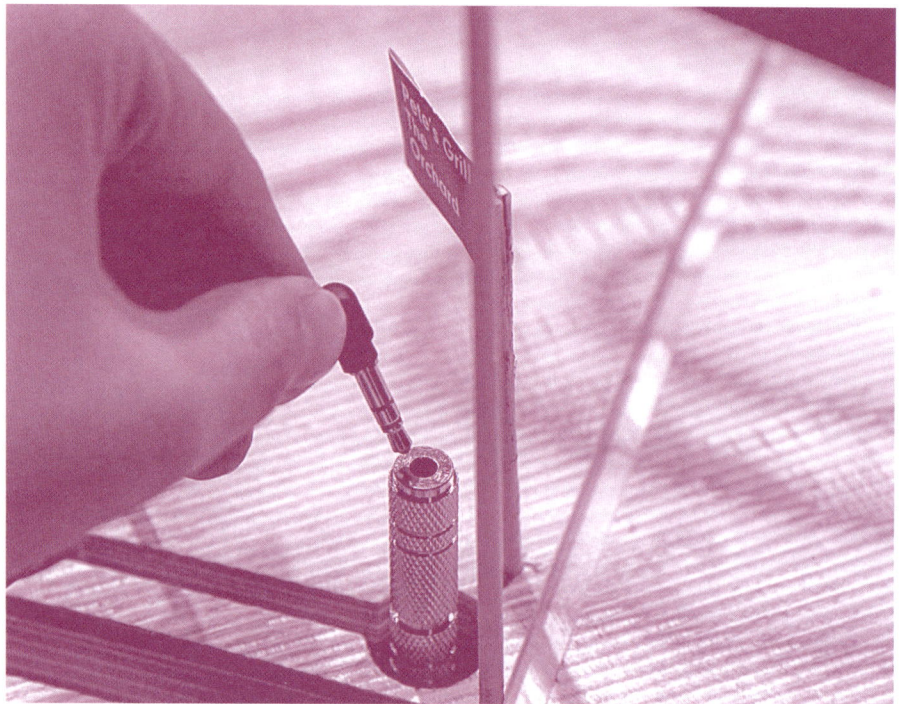

Tools of engagement: plug in

If we hosted a knitting party to raise awareness about marine water quality, our project for the 103rd Street Community Garden resembled yet another community gathering—a traditional barn raising (see pp. 174–5). This project was designed not as a plan but as a template—one with an extremely clear layout and straightforward construction methods so that community members themselves could build the park. Rather than fetishizing the details of construction, we worked to radically simplify the process. Embedded in SCAPE's philosophy is the idea to design by integrating "you-can-do-it" construction techniques. Rather than just thinking about things that could be made, we are also thinking about tools that we can provide to the larger community.

SAFARI 7

A project that democratizes the map, integrates new social technologies, and includes countless fun excursions is the Urban Landscape Lab's Safari 7, a platform from which to view, celebrate, research, and exchange ideas about urban nature.[5] Safari 7 is a self-guided tour of urban animal life along New York City's 7 subway line (see pp. 150–65). At the start, we asked: What is urban nature? How can it be perceived and engaged by a broad cross section of people? How do natural and urban systems coexist within megacities? In doing so, we aimed to redefine and expand the role of landscape in interpreting the urban environment and to move beyond the static media of "reporting" to engage students and the public in dialogue about the built environment through social networking tools.

Safari 7 accomplishes this through a timed series of downloadable podcasts, keyed into subway maps that show animals living along the route so you can listen while you ride and learn about the places you are moving through. We worked with college students and volunteers to develop and share an expandable series of maps, digital uploads, and podcasts that explore the complexity, biodiversity, conflicts, and potentials of New York City's ecosystems.

The interactive plug-in map and posters, keyed into specific urban nature stories along the 7 line, exhibited at Columbia University's Studio-X space in 2009 and in Vanderbilt Hall at Grand Central Terminal as part of MTA Earth Day festivities in 2010. A teaching kit for schoolchildren was distributed in advance, and schools near the 7 line in Queens made field trips to Grand Central to participate in the exhibit and hear a brief lecture on the surprising benefits of urban weeds by Dr. Steven Handel. Safari 7 Metrocard "tickets"—usable and refillable Metrocards—were distributed and subway car advertisements, produced by the Metropolitan Transit Authority, were displayed throughout New York City as part of this event.

By coupling public transportation with learning about the bees, bugs, birds, and nuisance animals that inhabit the cracks and eddies of New York's urban landscape, Safari 7 brings attention to new audiences about sustainability and biodiversity in the region, raising issues of stewardship (as well as ridership!). This is important in that the Audubon Society Report on climate change lists 314 species on the brink of extinction or that were imperiled this century due to shifting habitat ranges and related climate threats.[6] Reducing greenhouse gas emissions, expanding biodiversity, and increasing wonder about the flora and fauna that we share this planet with can go hand in hand. Importantly, Safari 7 creates a framework of engagement that is replicable in other locations—similar experiences have been staged in São Paulo, Beijing, Hong Kong, and other global cities.

A core challenge for design in the next century will be to work with democratic processes that emerged largely in opposition to master-planned construction—like "slum clearance" and the Cross-Bronx Expressway.[7]

Designers must work to advance the positive, comprehensive, and coordinated interventions needed to address climate change and new energy systems.[8] Much of the infrastructure implemented to transport carbon-polluting energy—oil and gas pipes and the highway systems that drove urban and suburban development—was laid before the 1960s. How can we remake an energy and social system of the future? With wind farms, solar arrays, denser development, and neighborhood buyouts? By helping to move neighborhoods to safer, higher ground? Education integrated with the engagement process can help connect people to forces and issues larger than themselves, frame issues in a way that clearly defines what is at stake, and divert the unraveling of the built environment as a commons.

Climate change needs to be an intergenerational conversation, one that can progress through scenario-driven design methods and inclusive processes to build social cohesion through conceptualization, design, and construction. Engaging is about choosing to participate, to opt in. It is choosing to have a dialogue, to enter the fray, to commit oneself to exploration and action. To engage others is to draw them into the conversation, to involve them in the process, and to persuade them to opt in also.

1. Martin Buber, *I and Thou*, trans. Walter Kaufmann (New York: Charles Scribners, 1970), 9.
2. Anne Whiston Spirn, "Restoring Mill Creek: Landscape Literacy, Environmental Justice and City Planning and Design" in *Landscape Research* 30, no. 3 (July 2005): 395–413.
3. The book *Petrochemical America* generated a comprehensive portrait of the ecological impact of the lower Mississippi region's industry, which ultimately served as an engagement tool for the Louisiana Environmental Action Network. By depicting and interpreting data on toxic releases, community displacement, and species loss, our book generated an informed discussion about that landscape, which has served as the launch pad for deeper conversation and political change. Public Lab's work influenced this investigation.
4. Peter Cannavò, *The Working Landscape: Founding, Preservation, and the Politics of Place* (Cambridge, Mass.: MIT Press, 2007), 220.
5. This project is collaboration with Glen Cummings of MTWTF and Janette Kim and Kate Orff of the Urban Landscape Lab at Columbia University GSAPP. For a full list of collaborators, see www.safari7.org
6. National Audubon Society, *Audubon's Birds and Climate Change Report: A Primer for Practitioners*, 2014. http://climate.audubon.org/sites/default/files/Audubon-Birds-Climate-Report-v1.2.pdf.
7. As documented in the biography of Robert Moses: Robert Caro, *The Power Broker: Robert Moses and the Fall of New York* (New York: Vintage Books, 1975).
8. Naomi Oreskes and Erik Conway's sci-fi work *The Collapse of Western Civilization: A View From the Future* (New York: Columbia University Press, 2014) concludes with an epilogue about how nation-states with democratic governments fared poorly and were "without the infrastructure and organizational ability" to deal with the unfolding climate crisis.

Safari 7

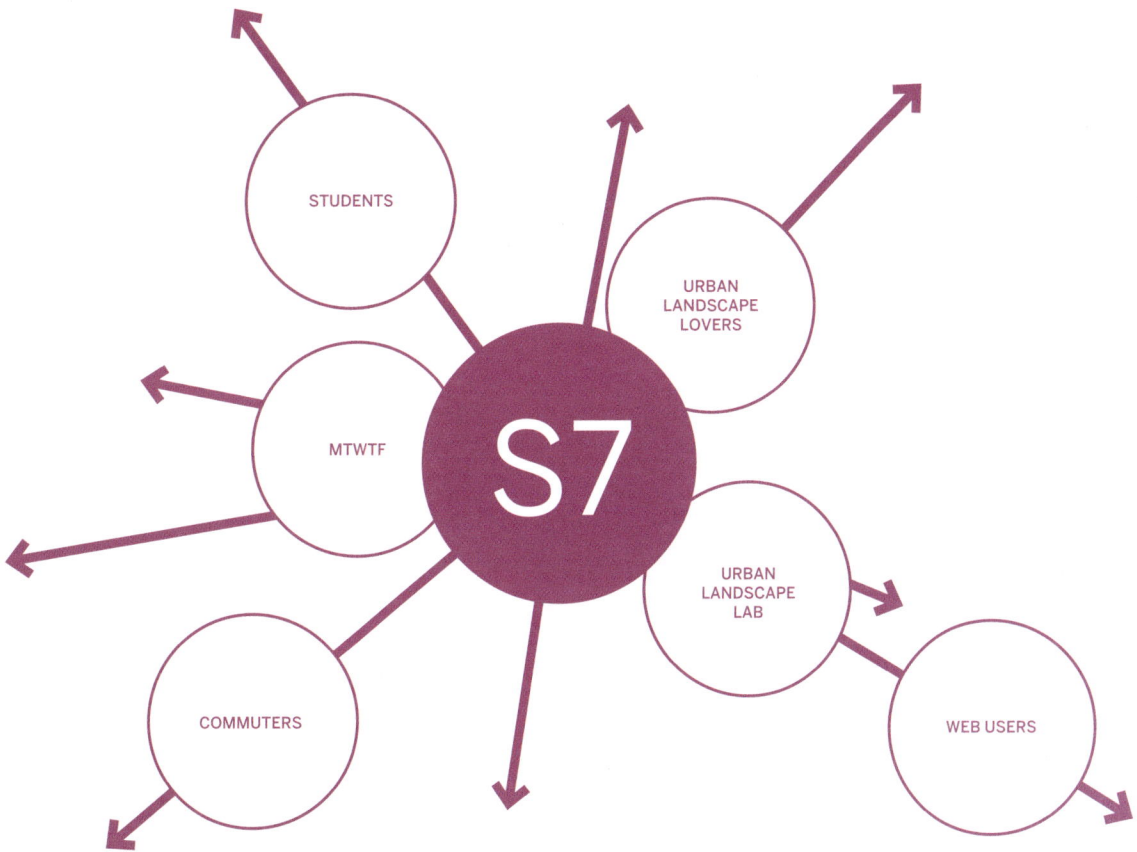

STUDENTS

URBAN
LANDSCAPE
LOVERS

MTWTF

S7

URBAN
LANDSCAPE
LAB

COMMUTERS

WEB USERS

SCALES OF ENGAGEMENT

Safari 7 is a self-guided tour of urban wildlife along New York City's 7 subway line. The 7 line is a physical, urban transect through the city's most diverse range of ecosystems, from Manhattan's dense core to the more widely dispersed residences and parklands of Flushing, Queens. A collection of podcasts, maps, events, and curriculum guides that are freely available on the web aim to engage a broad range of New Yorkers in active exploration of their joint urban/natural environment.

Safari 7 itself is a highly engaged collaboration. Conceived through Columbia's Urban Landscape Lab (ULL), the project is a joint work between Kate Orff, Janette Kim, and Glen Cummings of MTWTF. *www.safari7.org*.

Facing page: Collaborative design

Subway as Transect

Affectionately called the International Express, the 7 line runs from Manhattan's dense core, under the East River, and through a dispersed mixture of residences and parklands, terminating in downtown Flushing, Queens—the nation's most ethnically diverse county. Safari 7 imagines trains as urban classrooms, and provides maps and podcasts for travelers to engage the immediate environment of their city.

Rikers Island Channel

Bowery Bay

Ditmars/
Steinway

Hell Gate

Astoria

Bruckner Expressway

East
Elmhurst

Astoria Blvd

Junction Blvd

Ravenswood

Steinway St

Broadway

Jackson Heights

Northern Blvd

Woodside

61 St

69 St

74 St

82 St

90 St

Junction Blvd

103 St

33 St

40 St

46 St

52 St

Sunnyside

Queens Blvd

69th St

Broadway

Elmhurst

Queens Blvd

Long Island Expressway

Long Island Expressway

Newtown Creek

Maspeth

Maspeth Creek

Ridgewood

Plaza

Hallet's Cove

Brooklyn-Queens Expressway

SAFARI 7 LINE

HISTORIC
WETLANDS

LANDFILL

C'mon Ride the Train

Safari 7 is at once a collective and individual experience. The project invites subway-goers to act like park rangers in their city, learning about the complexity, biodiversity, conflicts, and potential of New York's urban ecosystems as they ride the 7 line. Podcasts on urban wildlife are timed with the elevated line's progress, and expose the hidden intersections between people, flora, and fauna at each stop and neighborhood along the route.

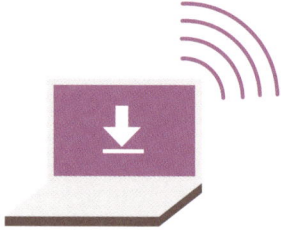

Download the Safari 7 self-guided tours from Safari7.org.

Listen to podcasts on your mp3 player during your 7 line train ride.

Check out the urban wildlife along the 7 line.

Listening to Urban Wildlife

Each story reveals a new relationship—whether it be canine demographics or subway car reef condos—and offers a lighthearted entry into the broader field of urban ecology.

TIMES SQ — 42 ST

IMMUNITY BOOSTERS
A close look at the micro ecology of NYC's smallest commuters.

GRAND CENTRAL — 42 ST

U THANT ISLAND
Off the grid and hidden in plain sight, U Thant Island is made from the leftovers from the 7 line's Steinway Tunnel and is home to NYC's cormorant population.

VERNON BLVD-JACKSON AV

OYSTERS
Back in the day Queens Bay was NYC's raw bar, home of the largest oyster population on the East Coast.

HUNTERS PT AV

FISH PHARM
The East River's high level of estrogen has the local fish swimming sideways.

| QUEENSBORO PLAZA | 40 ST — LOWERY ST | 52 ST | | 82 ST — JACKSON HTS | 90 ST — ELMHURST AV | JUNCTION BLVD |

SQUIRRELS
The expansion of Manhattan's East River parks mean a real estate boom for the indigenous eastside squirrels.

DOGS
From 5th Avenue to Times Square, the price of real estate is directly related to what size dog you keep.

ECOLOGY OF DEATH
Calvary Cemetery, one of the largest urban necropolises in the nation, has an ecology and chemistry all its own. A look at what goes in, what comes out, and what we should know about NYC's dead.

COOP COURTYARDS
Away from the street and behind walls of brick are well-tended garden oases.

REEF CONDOS
Homo sapiens aren't the only New Yorkers riding the subway. Aquatic New Yorkers strap-hang in decommissioned cars used to build reefs around Manhattan Island.

PIGEONS
New Yorkers have tried dozens of techniques, all unsuccessful, to control the population of the urban freeloaders known as rock doves.

Reaching Out

Safari 7 is an experiment in engaging the public in a dialogue about urban space. The project has taken multiple forms to reach a broad audience for the work, moving past typical design products of "master plan report" and "public workshop" to test more fluid and lively techniques for communication. Safari 7 lives as an app, a downloadable podcast, a series of exhibitions, a curriculum, a series of subway banners, and as an updateable website. Since the project's launch, Urban Landscape Lab has facilitated similar Safari studies in São Paulo and Beijing, extending the reach of the effort and building urban-ecology consciousness worldwide.

Uncovering the City

Large-scale section and perspective drawings on free guides illustrate the layered relationships between people and urban wildlife along subway stops.

For example, a zoom on U Thant Island reminds us that even the remotest and most isolated environments of New York have been shaped by urban actions. In 1890, rubble from the Steinway subway tunnel creation was piled on an existing reef outcropping, which created a tiny island in the East River. While this "off the map" space is not habitable to people, it hosts over twenty-four nesting pairs of the double-crested cormorant, who prefer the artificially constructed landform's dead trees for nesting.

Exhibition panel; *Steinway Tunnel: Cut-and-fill habitat*

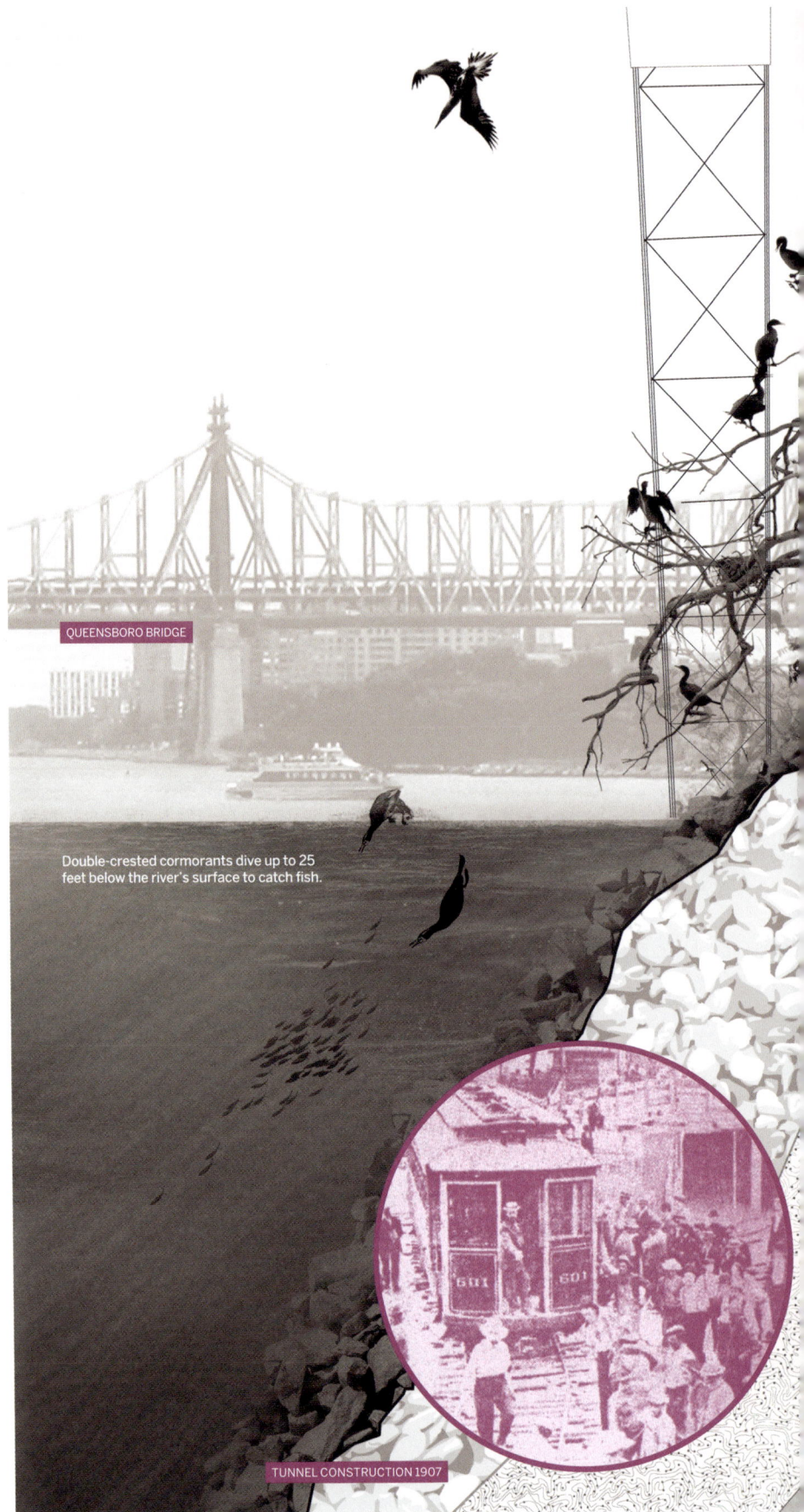

QUEENSBORO BRIDGE

Double-crested cormorants dive up to 25 feet below the river's surface to catch fish.

TUNNEL CONSTRUCTION 1907

The droppings of the double-crested cormorants slowly kill the trees they nest in, preventing other bird species from colonizing their nesting grounds.

The metal arch commemorating united national secretary general U Thant is a nesting site for double-crested cormorants, who build nests from branches, leaves, and trash collected along the river.

STEINWAY TUNNEL FILL

RIVER SEDIMENT, SAND

INWOOD LIMESTONE

Once threatened due to pollution and overfishing, striped bass have recovered in New York and are a popular catch for East River fishermen.

The Ecology of Death

A ride through Queens reminds Safari-goers that the borough is home to more dead inhabitants than living. The so-called "cemetery belt" aligns with a geologic formation of terminal moraine; this high ridge was repurposed as burial grounds for bodies disinterred from Manhattan during the real estate boom and cholera epidemic of the mid-1800s. Conventional burials don't encourage natural decomposition; instead, the anaerobic conditions in a typical casket encourage the production of methane gas and sludge. Safari 7 podcasts and drawings also explore the ecology of death, offering insights into emerging natural burial technologies that satisfy the deceased's relatives' desire for traditional burials while enhancing worm- and bacteria-driven decomposition cycles below ground.

Exhibition panel; *Woodside–61 St: Decomposers*

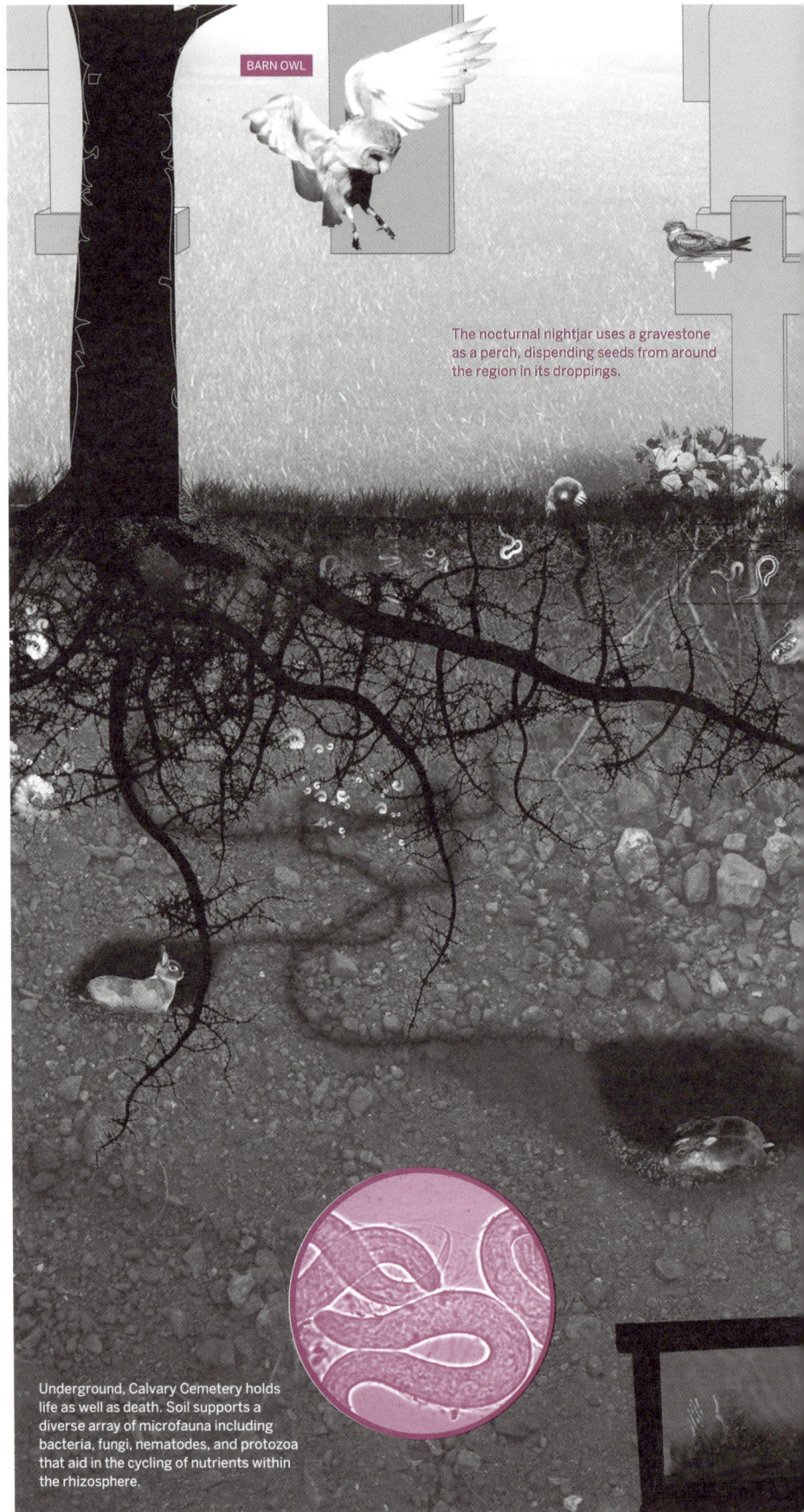

BARN OWL

The nocturnal nightjar uses a gravestone as a perch, dispending seeds from around the region in its droppings.

Underground, Calvary Cemetery holds life as well as death. Soil supports a diverse array of microfauna including bacteria, fungi, nematodes, and protozoa that aid in the cycling of nutrients within the rhizosphere.

Established in 1848 by the old Saint Patrick's Cathedral, Calvary Cemetery was created after the 1847 Rural Cemetery Act allowed non-profits to operate commercial cemeteries free of property tax. One of the oldest cemeteries in the United States, this once-rural cemetery now operates as a major open space within the dense neighborhoods of Queens, providing valuable habitat for local urban wildlife.

A squirrel feeds on a cluster of fungi that has grown in the shaded, moist microclimate at the base of a tombstone.

BURIED PET DOG

EARTHWORM

The body of an illegally buried pet dog slowly decomposes over time with the help of microorganisms, which break down the organic matter of the body into beneficial nurtients and gasses and release them into the soil.

BLISSVILLE
PART OF
LONG ISLAND CITY
Queens Co. L.I.

CALVARY CEMETERY

Weed Walk

The Weed Walk podcasts then turn our attention to some prominent vegetal members of the urban ecosystem—weeds. Ecologist Steven Handel walks the listener through an industrial stretch of the 7 line between Thirty-Third and Fortieth Streets, illustrating the diversity and resourcefulness of plants that manage to thrive in the mean streets of New York City.

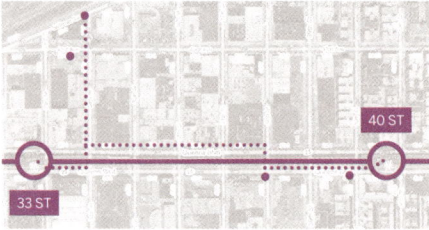

33 ST — VACANT LOT

PLANTAIN
Check your shoes! These sticky brits, also known as ribwort, have been known to stiffen collars and pants in Ye Olde NYC for two centuries.

MILKWEED
Don't put this poisonous weed's juice in your coffee, although caterpillars love it! That's how they develop their toxic chemistry that keeps the birds away.

BITTERSWEET
Those beautiful orange seedpods disguise a stone-cold tree killer!

BOUNCING BET
After a rough day, lather up with a fistful of sudsy bouncing bet, aka "soapwort."

33 ST — SUNNYSIDE YARDS

40 ST — QUEENS BLVD

RAGWEED
Not to be confused with goldenrod, these mustard-tasting weeds have NYC eyes watering and itching every fall.

OPPORTUNISTS
If you think the stakes are high and conditions crowded in the NYC real estate market, check out any pile of gravel in the street, where weeds are working hard to gain a root-hold and stake out a life on the mean city streets.

FOXTAIL GRASS
See a small, green squirrel tail sticking up in that alley? It is more likely to be NYC's fastest-growing weed.

MCDONALD'S GARDEN
Even in man-made gardens, gregarious mother nature joins the plant party. Stealthy weeds lay low to avoid detection, and lovable three-leafed clovers hope to get lucky.

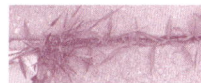

TREE BOXES & WIND POLLINATION
In NYC, even the insects have their own agenda, so self-reliant street weeds get down to business and pollinate themselves.

WHITE NIGHTSHADE
Although its edible relatives are the tomato and potato, this yellow-and-white beauty is a feast for the eyes but not the mouth.

Safari 7
P

The 7 Line is a physical, urban transect through New York City's most diverse ecosystems and communities. It runs from Manhattan's dense core, under the East River and through neighborhoods and park lands before terminating in Flushing, Queens, the nation's diverse

Park Raising
Intergenerational Space
Free Play Zone
Urban Hydrology
Research Incubator
Social Infrastructure Advocate

Park Raising

Regenerating underutilized public space in collaboration with community members as co-builders is a rare event in urban areas. By working with impacted neighborhoods to understand their direct needs, parks can successfully be built by neighborhood residents from the ground up.

—

103rd Street Community Garden
New York, New York

What is community-generated design? SCAPE worked in collaboration with the New York Restoration Project (NYRP) to engage a group of neighborhood residents in a design-build process that began with a public charrette and culminated in a "park-raising" day. The park design needed to accommodate young children, gardeners, teenagers, athletes, and seniors in less than a quarter of an urban block. Over several months, volunteers came together to share ideas, review drawings, and shape the design of the park into a multiuse public commons complete with vegetable plots, refurbished basketball courts, an open picnic area, a playground, a composting toilet, and two water-harvesting shade structures. Energy and enthusiasm abounded at the Park Raising, during which neighborhood volunteers helped plant and construct the revitalized community space. Perhaps what we need in our urban ecosystems are not merely more parks, but more "raisings" that regenerate underutilized spaces while creating and strengthening social infrastructure.

Intergenerational Space

Spaces are typically designed for just one subset of the population—old or young, not both. Spaces that serve multiple age groups can be successful recreational areas and forge new relationships between often-stratified members of society.

—

Blake Hobbs Park
New York, New York

The renovation of Blake Hobbs Park transformed an existing asphalt playground into a dynamic public commons that serves people of all ages. The site is adjacent to a senior center, new affordable housing units, office space for a nonprofit community-based youth development organization, and the permanent home of the Harlem RBI Dream Charter School. Students, faculty, senior citizens, all frequent users of the park participated in design sessions that scripted out space for rest, recreation, circulation, and ecosystem restoration. All new programming accommodates the preservation of an established grove of London plane trees. The understory is activated and organized with vegetation, play surfaces, low fences, and color, transforming the formerly inert and generic asphalt ground plane into a multilayered, intergenerational space and source of pride for the East Harlem community.

Free Play Zone

Imagination and interaction are key to childhood development, and free play zones foster just that—flexible spaces that accommodate multiple types of people and play.

—

PAVE Academy
Brooklyn, New York

The typical New York City schoolyard consists of a fenced-in amalgamation of asphalt, safety surface, and standard play equipment. SCAPE worked in close collaboration with PAVE Academy, a K-8 Charter School, to develop a swiftly constructible landscape that goes beyond the standard-issue urban schoolyard while working with a similar suite of low-budget and readily available materials. More than just a play space for students, the new schoolyard provides a multifunctional community gathering space for both the school and surrounding neighborhood. Colorful pavers and lush plantings transform the school's front and back courtyards into inviting spaces that support a diversity of uses. A front courtyard provides ample space for recess and school events, while a back courtyard plays host to outdoor classes and school meetings. These new landscapes are publically accessible at moments throughout the day, serving jointly as schoolyard and community gathering space. By making more shared spaces like the schoolyard at PAVE Academy, we can maximize our community assets, create new public-private connections, and expand educational and social networks within a neighborhood.

The hydrological cycle of precipitation, water flow, and evaporation has largely been driven underground, into culverts, and generally cut off from view in urban contexts. Urban hydrology reconnects residents to their immediate environment by sharing information through research, storytelling, and participation.

—

Town Branch Water Walk
Lexington, Kentucky

Why would someone care about a culvert? SCAPE received a grant from the Department of Environmental Quality to develop a public education campaign about urban water systems that would complement the Town Branch redevelopment project in Lexington, Kentucky. The result, Town Branch Water Walk, is a self-guided tour of downtown Lexington's formerly hidden waterbody, Town Branch Creek, with content developed together with University of Kentucky students. The design intervention is not a physical landscape, but a communication tool—using podcasts, maps, walks for the interpretation of urban systems. The Water Walk gives a broad understanding of the biophysical area around the Town Branch, reveals the invisible waters that run beneath the city, and demonstrates some of the impacts each resident of Lexington can have on the river and its water quality. By sharing how water systems and people are interrelated, the Town Branch Water Walk makes stormwater quality relevant, linking it with the history, culture, and ecology of the city.

SCAPE

How did you come up with the idea to stage an urban safari on the No. 7 subway line?

Kate Orff

Janette, Glen, and I are all friends and we were interested in collaborating on a guerilla art and research project about the urban ecology of the city that would be out there, engaging New Yorkers. I had assigned a case study called the "Wild A Train" in an early Columbia graduate seminar, since the A train links a relatively untouched, primitive forest in rocky Inwood to a coastal barrier island at the Rockaways. But obviously Safari 7 sounds much better and it cuts through these amazing neighborhoods! The 7 line acts as a sort of natural east-west transect through the geology and communities of Queens and Manhattan. We thought about this transect as something that would hit upon social systems and offer a lens for looking at human and animal life in New York City.

Glen Cummings

We conceived the project as a guided safari, not unlike the kind developed by National Parks and corporate adventure parks. Except instead of simply delivering content, Safari 7 encourages the public to contribute to the creation of the content.

Janette Kim

We liked the idea that even in the everyday space of Manhattan's subway cars, you can immediately engage in the city and become your own park ranger. That's the basic concept of the self-guided tour: by observing the city in a new light, you start to wonder why it's constructed in particular ways. You can scratch the surface behind the signs of life that are typically overlooked. You have to become an interpreter.

S

Once you had the idea, how did you develop the project?

JK

Much of the content for the first Safari 7 podcasts emerged from a seminar I taught at the Department of Architecture at Barnard and Columbia Colleges. It was a class on urban nature, which was great because we could read and explore topics like the political history of New York's infrastructure or the ethics of animal-human relationships. The students then went out into the city and did their own research along the 7 line. They gathered footage and created audio podcasts using very simple editing techniques. ULL and MTWTF and a big team of young designers interpreted the work into drawings, edited the audio podcasts, and created a design for the installation at Columbia's Studio-X New York that formed the basis of our launch with the MTA, which allowed us to reach a wide audience.

S

What inspired the multimedia approach, using podcasts and graphic design?

GC

Audio is a great medium for communicating with the public! Instead of asking people to read a long text to get involved, Safari 7 is much more immediate and direct. Anybody—anybody with a smartphone or MP3 player, anyway—can listen to this. It's informative, it connects to you, and it's also fun. But audio also has its limits.

When you're communicating with a broad public—like we were with Safari 7—not everyone might speak the same language or have the same level of oral comprehension. Think of a nonnative speaker listening to the podcast or the ways that a first-grader versus a college student would engage with the content; graphic design becomes crucial at this juncture. And when we brought the Safari framework to São Paulo and China, graphic design proved a really effective way not only to synthesize all of the diverse content that we collected, but also to bridge the language difference within these cross-cultural contexts, making content visual too.

JK

Audio turned out to be the perfect tool for getting students to engage with the city because there's something so immediate about it. I loved the process. Students visited locations along the 7 line every day; they found unexpected sites or information just by chatting with people on the street and grabbing found sounds. They also interviewed experts, such as researchers at the Parks Department. It was a great way for students to spark conversations about contemporary issues.

KO

This idea of having a shared community experience is part of what we were going for with the project—for the students and for the public. We wanted people on the 7 train to be listening to podcasts and looking at their maps and learning about the environment that they were traveling through—and then thinking about a podcast that they themselves might compose! From a graphic standpoint, we had been experimenting with giant drawn sections in the SCAPE office as a means to communicate complex phenomenon connecting above and below ground. The podcasts, sections, maps, and plug-in model work together to make a thick and interactive experience.

S

How does the Safari 7 framework encourage the public to engage with urban ecology?

KO

Reframing the 7 line as an urban safari forces you to experience your environment differently. Rather than just reading the newspaper as you're going through the Steinway Tunnel under the East River, you're thinking about the cut-and-fill and dredge operations that happened as they excavated the basin of the river and piled it up to make an island. You're not just on the receiving end of this scientific concept that is brought to you by experts; instead you're generating and sharing observations.

JK

The graphic map and audio narratives complement subway riders' views of the passing landscape. As they listen and look out into the city, riders form their own active and interpretive responses. They can question and celebrate what they're seeing, and continue to research and discuss these ideas with the people around them.

KO

It gets people to see, too, that urban animal life isn't just cockroaches and rats—there is this incredible mixture of animals that live and exist at every level in every sort of niche that you can imagine. The popular perception is: "Oh yeah, we've got pigeons here." But then you actually look at migratory maps and there are rare and endangered neotropical migrants that fly through and over New York's skyline every fall and every spring.

GC

As people we make up artificial binaries. It's the water and the land, the nature and the city, or whatever. And those things come from—who knows where they come from? They come from some sort of negotiation that's not exactly helpful or meaningful, and they cause us to think in a way that's nonproductive. I think the big message of this project is to see the world as an integrated whole, in which elements perceived as different are not actually in

different piles, they're all connecting. It's changed the way I think about things.

S

Did taking the project to other cities—with Safari 4 Beijing, Safari 1 São Paulo, and Safari SZHK in Shenzhen and Hong Kong—transform the way you thought about these ideas of urban nature further?

GC

Most people are interested in animals, so that provided an easy entry into talking about urban ecology in New York City. When we brought the project to Grand Central Terminal, everybody had some sort of urban animal story that they were excited to share, no matter how banal. But I think your experience, Janette, was that what people wanted to talk about differed substantially by city, is that right?

JK

We did encounter varied attitudes along the way. In New York, people would smile and laugh when I spoke with them about this project. They'd share funny experiences their kids had with pests that had invaded their apartments, and talked about squirrels who stole sandwiches straight from their hands. But in São Paulo, the response centered on complaints about infrastructural investment in the city. We arrived one or two weeks after the height of protests challenging government overinvestment in the 2014 World Cup. So the attitude was more, "What are we going to do with our city?!" At the forefront of everyone's minds was the need for civic investment to make significant changes in the city. Concerns about the lack of equity in relation to the environmental future of the city were omnipresent. So, we talked a great deal about the slums, waterways, development, and traffic congestion. If discussions about the environment and community involvement are considered relatively uncontroversial in New York, in China these topics were extremely delicate, and potentially threatening to government images of stability and progress. The authorities started to get very nervous about our research and methods of interacting with the public. The fear was that we might, for example, uncover that a river has been polluted with raw sewage, and stoke public outrage in response.

S

Do you think the Safari projects were able to open up cross-cultural dialogues in some way?

KO

What became clear as we took the projects to new places was that the Safari 7 "method" was a powerful way of generating group work, discussion, and knowledge in a way that is participatory and engaging. It gets people—students and faculty, neighbors, local

experts, or whomever—immediately talking with each other, looking at the world around them in a new way, and sharing their findings. With multiple cities, you could compare and contrast not only the animal/plant content but the cultural context—how much base data is available in what sort of political context, where people are connected to one another versus somewhat disconnected, and so on.

JK

In every city, we have worked with local residents. In the case of São Paulo, where we conducted a five-day workshop, we were very excited because the participants had such intriguing insights into the city. For example, one participant talked about the way security barriers play a huge role in the urban life of São Paulo. Because crime is so significant, many people board up their properties. This woman knew the neighborhood around Praça da Árvore quite well, and was able to explain how the residents' desire to sequester themselves behind these walls also pushed up against their desire for collective public space.

S

The Safari projects have a website, the materials are still available for download. What do you see as the future of the project?

GC

Even though the Safari project has run four times now, there's still so much possibility for it to continue growing. One way of engaging with the project is as a self-guided urban nature tour: you load podcasts, you go on the train, you listen to it in one of these four cities. But another way to engage with it is to get involved as a researcher or content-maker. I think we always imagined that guided authorship was as much a way to discover things as self-guided listening. I've always believed that Safari 7 could be an NPR radio program. The content and premise of it are really relevant now, especially since the entire world is urbanizing. What could be more interesting than how infrastructure, urbanization, and nature intersect? I think the whole thing has tons of life still left in it.

Social Infrastructure Advocate

Designing cities and landscapes to foster social cohesion is a primary challenge for the next century. Social infrastructure can increase interaction and generate new forms of engagement, prioritizing the human experience.

—

Inteview with Eric Klinenberg

Eric Klinenberg is professor of sociology and director of the Institute for Public Knowledge at New York University. He is the author of *Going Solo: The Extraordinary Rise and Surprising Appeal of Living Alone* (2012), *Fighting for Air: The Battle to Control America's Media* (2007), and *Heat Wave: A Social Autopsy of Disaster in Chicago* (2002), as well as the editor of *Cultural Production in a Digital Age* (2005) and of the journal *Public Culture*. Eric was director of research and a juror for the Rebuild By Design (RBD) competition.

SCAPE

So, for us the revelation of Rebuild By Design wasn't the concept of "living with water" or working in tandem with scientists—both of which we have been exploring for some years—but working with you, a sociologist. As infrastructure and ecology nuts, we tend to think about robust networks as physical systems. Can you talk about the concept of social infrastructure and how it relates to resiliency? Did this line of thought start with your *Heat Wave* research?

Eric Klinenberg

It did start with *Heat Wave*. The work I did in Chicago taught me how much social factors can determine who lives and who dies during a crisis, and also which places will fare better than others. I noticed that there were neighborhoods in Chicago that looked similar on paper—in terms of their poverty, segregation, and vulnerability—but that had dramatically different outcomes in the disaster. When I did ethnographic research around Chicago, I saw that what made the difference wasn't the power grid or the water supply or the food network. It was the street- and sidewalk-level conditions that set the tone for social life. Places where there were active public areas with dense commercial resources and people on the sidewalks tended to have very low death rates in the heat wave, and places that were ecologically depleted were notably deadly. I came up with the concept of social infrastructure to account for this kind of difference.

S

What are the measures of social cohesion? How do sociologists begin to assess this?

EK

There are different measures. You can look at traditional measures such as how many social ties people have to their neighbors, and how many people they can trust. In the past decade, sociologists have developed a measure for "collective efficacy," which tells us the capacity of people and local groups to achieve common goals. The measure integrates different kinds of connections, resources, and capacities, but getting it requires a lot of research that we don't have for most people and places.

S

You've written about the Rockaway Beach Surf Club as an example of a "reserve of strength" in the aftermath of Hurricane Sandy. Are there particular types of multi-purpose landscapes or structures that can play this role of enhancing or increasing social cohesion, especially in times of stress or crisis?

EK

Yes. Places whose function is not overdetermined by design can work well during emergencies, because people can adapt them to meet emerging needs. The Rockaway Beach Surf Club was located in a flexible space and it also had a sizable protected outdoor area, so volunteers were able to quickly convert the building and the yard into a community relief center. Having visited it and several other places nearby after Hurricane Sandy, I can say that it was a lot more welcoming and hospitable than the official evacuation centers. Another example from Sandy is the Red Hook Initiative, which not only had a large open space that could be converted to a relief site, but also had resilient vital systems in the building because there was no basement where cable lines and generators could flood. As a result, they mounted one of the most successful local relief efforts in New York City.

Both of these examples point to another important factor in social cohesion, particularly around disasters: tight integration with the neighborhood. The people who worked at the Surf Club and the Red Hook Initiative had made special efforts to develop trust with their neighbors. Red Hook Initiative even had a policy of mainly employing people who lived or grew up in the neighborhood. Neither would have been so effective without these deep ties.

S

In your experience, does the design process serve as a vehicle for dialogue, and generating new connections, or does it balkanize?

EK

It depends on the outcome! The design process can inspire people and bring them together, but there has to be follow-through or it can easily disappoint. Today there are a lot of neighborhoods where residents are exhausted and cynical because they've endured decades of malign neglect punctuated by cruel super-storms and crueler public policies. Go there with a design project and then disappear, or ram something from on high through the local leadership, and you'll alienate them even further. That said, an honest and well-executed collaboration can inspire everyone and do wonders for community integration. If only that happened more often!

S

During Rebuild by Design you stated in various ways that the engagement process itself is a project. Do you still think this? Has it helped to generate constituencies?

EK

It is absolutely a project, and we are far from perfecting it. After all, at least half of the communities that participated in the final stage of RBD didn't get the funds they needed to mount their projects, so we're batting .500 at best. How do you set realistic expectations when the design possibilities are limited. When the budget isn't big enough to do everything? When there will inevitably be losers? I don't have the answers.

S

At the same time, we tried to be honest with everyone about the risks and limitations of the project. And from what I understand, a lot of the relationships that started with RBD continue today, even in places that won't get RBD funds. After all, adapting to climate change is going to take a very long time, and we all need to be in it for the duration.

S

Your research seems to suggest that rather than investing billions of dollars in physical projects, our time and money might be well spent building civic society, talking to our neighbors. This is exciting, but we're also intrigued by developing a better understanding of how to pair a physical landscape and a "unit" of civic life—say a nonprofit group, club, or school program. We see immense potential in trying to discover how the scale of a local landscape and the scale of an organization within a neighborhood can interface—how they can literally build each other up through work and shared purpose. Do you see any promise here?

EK

I do see promise, but I want to be clear that you can't repair a fractured neighborhood or

society by pushing everyone to talk to neighbors and pleading for them to just get along. The concept of social infrastructure implies that social connections are rooted in material conditions that we often don't recognize. Community building isn't just a moral exercise; it also requires tangible investments in places and institutions—as your plans for New York City recognize. I really hope that's clear.

S

Yes, that's clear—what's exciting is that your research and writing opens up a zone of focus and generates a lot of really productive questions for designers. In a tangible way, how can material, physical spaces be designed to foster human connections and play a role in making us more resilient? And, more broadly, how can we design for climate change not with just a "nod" to social equity but with robust social systems at the center of the process and outcome? Time to get to work!

INFRASTRUCTURE INSIDE OUT
Emily Eliza Scott

"I dreamed that I could make public art grow from inside a public infrastructure system outward to the public and that the growing would affect both the
inside as well as the outside."[1]
—Mierle Laderman Ukeles

In his geologic page-turner from 1989, *The Control of Nature*, the American
writer John McPhee profiles three mid-twentieth-century, Herculean efforts to
thwart, stall, or otherwise tame earthly forces: massive navigation locks
installed along the Mississippi River to maintain its flow to Baton Rouge
and New Orleans; seawater sprayed furiously upon molten lava to forestall
its encroachment on the port of Vestmannaeyjar, Iceland, after a volcanic
eruption; and sublime-scaled debris basins erected at the base of the swiftly eroding San Gabriel Mountains to trap mud and dirt before it inundates
the metropolis of Los Angeles.[2] Each of these cases highlights the monu-
mentality of modern technology coupled with (and driven by) a deeply hierarchical approach toward urban versus environmental realities—one that
expressly *dis*-engages the two.[3] In an interview shortly after the 2011 Tohoku
earthquake and tsunami, which led, among other things, to spectacular infrastructural failure in the partial meltdown of the Fukushima Daiichi Nuclear
Power Plant, the Japanese architect Toyo Ito cited the utter anachronism of
such a human-over-nature paradigm, insisting we must abandon it at once:

> "Our way of life is still based in twentieth-century ideas, specifi-
> cally a modernist philosophy that assumes we can use science and
> technology to conquer nature. So we try to isolate ourselves from
> nature; our cities are completely segregated from the environ-
> ment. [. . .] That kind of modernist thinking has reached its limit."[4]

With current proposals to manipulate the climate in order to stem global
warming, however, it seems we are in fact facing an unprecedented intensi-
fication and culmination of geo-engineering. In this new phase, interventions
are designed for Earth systems at the planetary scale. In all of the various
schemes tossed about—from the sequestration of carbon via artificial plankton blooms catalyzed by ocean "fertilization," to the deflection of sunlight
away from Earth by means of aerosols injected into the stratosphere, the
placement of reflective sheets atop glacial ice, or "space mirrors" launched
into orbit—humans are figured to be in dire combat with a nature of their
own making.[5]

    SCAPE's Living Breakwaters, building from its ongoing Oyster-tecture
research, reverses such a control-nature modus operandi, instead drawing

attention to complex human and natural ecologies (see pp. 236–59). In "thickening" New York City's coastline with oyster reefs to mitigate storm surges resulting from rising sea levels and increasingly destructive weather patterns, infrastructure is reimagined as connector rather than barrier. More accurately, it functions as a substrate, or scaffold: not solid ground, but a platform upon which multiple human and nonhuman actors are set into motion and interactions are expected to evolve over time. As opposed to canonical modernist paradigms, the emphasis here is on networks, processes, flexibility, and porosity, or "soft" edges.

Living Breakwaters is exemplary of a new orientation in which hyper-specific solutions supplant a clean slate, one-size-fits-all approach; interdisciplinary collaboration is highly valued; and primary concern lies with users rather than monuments. Here, the work of feminist thinkers who have long been concerned with questioning and counteracting (inherently patriarchal and anthropocentric) cohesive, view-from-above perspectives by insisting on the partial, embodied, and situated nature of all knowledge—not to mention the presence and importance of more-than-human assemblages—is highly pertinent.[6] An endeavor like Living Breakwaters furthermore coincides with a surge of interest in landscape and ecology within the field of architecture, reflected not least in the emergence of "landscape urbanism" and "ecological urbanism" as influential discursive vectors. The urban theorist Charles Waldheim points to a "disciplinary realignment currently underway in which landscape replaces architecture as the basic building block of contemporary urbanism."[7] Landscape's move to center stage entails a fundamental rethinking of the city relative to environmental contexts (e.g., hydrological, biological, geological, climatological) as well as broader territorial scales. The field of architecture, in this version, pertains no longer to discrete objects but rather to intricate and dynamic systems.

To turn something "inside out" can mean to flip it, but also to investigate it thoroughly, to consider it from all possible angles, to know it anew. Within contemporary art, there is indeed a rich vein of work that has engaged the urban built environment, and especially infrastructure (e.g., freeways, sewage systems, levees, sidewalks, power grids, oil and gas pipelines), probing its function within the city as well as the ways that it connects the city to broader structures and operations. At the root of many such projects is a desire to bring that which is largely invisible, because too big, naturalized, or subterranean (the prefix "infra-" denotes below, under, beneath), into the light. In the process, they actively alter our urban-natural imaginaries.

In the 1970s, Mierle Laderman Ukeles inaugurated a multi-decade body of work on what we might call the "social ecology" of waste in New York City. Having claimed "the *whole city* as her site," she studies her subject "through a system that keeps it running."[8] Since 1977, she has been the official artist-in-residence of the New York Department of Sanitation, a position she created for herself (which was previously both nonexistent and arguably unthinkable). Many of her pieces have focused on the marginalization and stigmatization of sanitation work. Within the context of her *Touch Sanitation* series of performances from 1978–80, she spent nearly a year meeting face-to-face with each and every one of the 8,500 employees in the department to shake their hand and say, "Thank you for keeping New York City alive." *Follow In Your Footsteps* involved the artist traveling into the field with workers, where she carefully observed and mimicked their movements— thereby enacting a choreography of everyday tasks. These gestures, in addressing people as part of infrastructure rather than separate from it, recast infrastructure as being as much about specific actions as about built forms—thereby also implying the potential for new kinds of (inter-)action, engagement, and intervention. Elsewhere, Ukeles has participated in union efforts, orchestrated a "barge ballet" at the transfer station where garbage is off-loaded from trucks and shipped from Manhattan, and contributed to reclamation designs for the Fresh Kills Landfill, the longtime repository for much of the city's refuse. The art historian Miwon Kwon has noted that Ukeles's art, while specializing in the social and physical infrastructures of trash, opens onto "the economy of labor that structures our entire society— from homes and offices, to communities, institutions, and cities."[9]

Mierle Laderman Ukeles, *Touch Sanitation*

Meanwhile, the Center for Urban Pedagogy (CUP), founded in 1997, is a New York-based nonprofit organization busy creating research-intensive projects to "demystify the urban policy and planning issues that impact our communities, so that more individuals can better participate in shaping them."[10] Dozens of projects, generated by even more contributors, have addressed topics ranging from zoning laws to air pollution, affordable housing, and geographies of electrical power. CUP's efforts are directed at the interface between governance, administration, finance, and the urban lived environment—where the rubber hits the road, so to speak. Damon Rich, one of its founders, explains that the group's prolific and diverse production is cohered by its "use of design and art in the service of popular education around cities and how they work."[11] As suggested by its name, education is central to CUP's practice. Roughly half of its activities are carried out with public school students, the rest with community-based and advocacy groups focused on particular issues. In contrast to a top-down model of teaching, CUP's programming emphasizes mutual, on-the-ground learning, ultimately meant to foster empowered civic engagement.

Mierle Laderman Ukeles thanking sanitation workers for keeping New York City alive

In one final example, the British artist Nils Norman, in his 2000 book, *The Contemporary Picturesque*, documents the profusion of small-scale infrastructures throughout London in the 1990s, meant to curtail loitering, heighten surveillance, and prevent the public from assembling en masse.[12] His deadpan photographs capture spiked windowsills, caged entryways, anti-climb and anti-graffiti paint, bus shelter benches angled to make sure no one lingers too long, and more. When brought together, this constellation of curious, if by now familiar, fixtures spurs all sorts of questions about the surreptitious refashioning of contemporary urban space, including the rampant privatization and "securitization" of once-public sites that have in many cases transpired in broad daylight yet largely under the radar.

This type of work takes a direct interest in the civic sphere, grappling head-on with the politics of public space. Often associated with what the artist Suzanne Lacy in 1994 termed "new genre public art" and has more recently been called "social practice," it often involves a dialogical component, as well.[13] A key aim is to stimulate critical debate about thorny spatial issues and/or to expand frameworks for citizen involvement in ground-up planning.

Within architecture, too, there seems to be growing consensus that infrastructure represents a crucial nexus for socially and politically relevant design. Architect and urban theorist Dana Cuff argues that, rather than representing a purely pragmatic or technical "other" to architecture, infrastructure is the site "where design is most needed" and "the heart of the next generation's public sphere."[14] Urban infrastructure, as a form of commons, becomes the terrain for architects who "give a damn"—who want to reconfigure cities in meaningful ways, to enrich civic life, to wrest at least some power from urban planners and, increasingly, from private developers. Architect Stan Allen similarly identifies infrastructure as one locus where architecture might assert its "capacity. . . to actually transform reality."[15] He advocates a move beyond the prevailing concern with form and representation in architecture and toward a renewed emphasis on architecture's usefulness as a material practice. He is clear, however, to differentiate this material orientation from earlier, technologically deterministic varieties, declaring: "architecture's instrumentality can be reconceived—not as a mark of modernity's demand for efficient implementation but as the site of architecture's contact with the complexity of the real."[16]

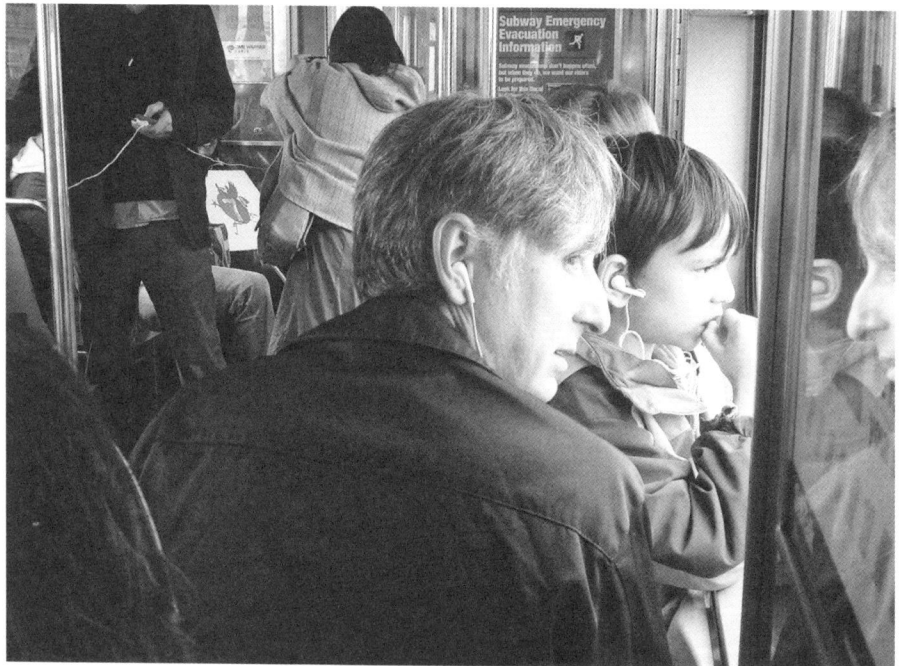

Safari 7 tour

Safari 7, led by Kate Orff and Janette Kim of the Urban Landscape Lab at Columbia University and Glen Cummings of MTWTF, delves precisely into "the complexity of the real" (see pp. 150–65). Designed as a self-guided podcast tour for riders of the Metropolitan Transit Authority's 7 subway line, it maps and interprets urban wildlife in New York City. This project resonates closely with the artworks discussed prior in its objective to render insights into the city as a vibrant, multidimensional, socio-ecosystem. It furthermore aligns with a strain of "critical tours" by contemporary artists intent on complicating our understandings of the hard-to-see forces that condition the world around us.[17] In the case of Safari 7, a heavily utilized infrastructure—the public transportation system—is transformed from a medium used to get from one place to another into a platform from which to see the city anew. The 7 line offers a specific transect of the urban environment, narrowing our focus to a handful of points between Times Square and Flushing Meadows, in Queens. Along the way, we are introduced to a series of thoroughly entangled human-nature tales that serve to defamiliarize both habitual ways of looking *and* assumptions about any clean division between nature and culture. One stop on the tour, for example, explores a vacant lot. "Whole lot—of nothing?" it asks. "Not at all," the narrator proceeds. "The microclimates of vacant lots are just as complex as the financial systems that leave them vacant." This vignette asks us to think simultaneously across vast scales and registers, recognizing links, for instance, between bacteria or insects in the soil and globalized capitalism— to see them as part of the same story.

Living Breakwaters, of course, encompasses a significant shift from interpreting ecosystems to designing them. This sort of large-scale, permanent, built project is categorically distinct from the more ephemeral, representation-based interventions typical of social practice by artists, even as it shares many of the same imperatives. It does a different kind of work in the world, we might say. Physical form here enables new human-nature interactions. If, in Ito's assessment, science and technology have been employed in the past to establish dominance over nature, in this case, they are put to work precisely in the service of reintegrating the social and environmental. It is no coincidence that the primary science influencing Living Breakwaters is ecology, which itself focuses on interrelations and, as such, stands apart from more specialized branches like hydrology or even biology. Rather than an attempted return to some sort of "baseline" nature (if we believe that ever existed), the work of SCAPE comes closer to what some forward-thinking scientists are now calling "ecological novelty," a concept that acknowledges the constant flux and entwined human and nonhuman elements-processes characterizing all environments today.[18]

Orff refers to the eastern oyster, a species that has played a key role in the ecology, economy, and culture of the New York Harbor historically, as an "environmental engineering partner." In addition to this collaborative approach to nature, Living Breakwaters diverges sharply from most (infra-) structural engineering in its prioritization of layered multifunctionality. Many parts are meant to do many things at once. Artificial reefs, as they agglomerate over time, protect the coastline from flooding and erosion by attenuating waves while at the same time expanding recreational opportunities for beach users, creating new habitat for aquatic life, and invoking the highly textured landforms from the pre-dredging days of the harbor. Equally important, infrastructure is intended to grow over time in tandem with growing community involvement and stewardship. A number of ambitious outreach programs are integral to Living Breakwaters, many of them geared toward middle- and high school students. Together, they aim to extend a network of people on the ground, who will help cultivate and sustain the project through enhanced ecological awareness, water awareness, risk awareness, and so on. Design itself is here meant to network, to be responsive, to engage humans and nonhumans on an even playing field, and to gain its power exactly through distributed agency.

Living Breakwaters clearly needs also to be considered relative to the anthropogenic climate change it explicitly addresses. Perhaps more than any other environmental phenomenon imaginable, climate change is dizzyingly convoluted, entailing many (often correlated and at times seemingly contradictory) things happening in many places at once, at varying rates and scales, and with myriad types and degrees of consequence. Orff has argued that a problem of the magnitude of climate change demands solutions on the same scale.[19] The Office of Mayor Bill de Blasio, upon releasing the New York City Panel on Climate Change's 2015 report—with its bleak predictions for increased heat waves, cold snaps, and rain, spikes in certain diseases, and coastal inundation from rising sea levels—noted that the findings "underscore the urgency of not only mitigating our contributions to climate change, but also adapting our city to its risks."[20] There has been a flurry of activity in the last several years toward developing innovative measures for such urban modification, with cultural and governmental institutions joining forces in certain cases to underwrite it.

Along with this swell of public-private investment in preparing cities for threats associated with climate change, the notion of "urban resilience" has taken hold with remarkable swiftness and potency, especially in the United States. Resilient: robust, able to spring back, irrepressible. It is indeed hard to argue with something that promises to hold catastrophe at bay, preserve human settlements and ways of life, grow the economy, and foster a seemingly more balanced relationship with the natural world all the while. As was the case with "sustainability," one of its discursive-rhetorical precursors, part of the power of "resilience" lies in its projected sense of inevitability as the only appropriate mode with which to face the present and future. This apparent neutrality or even benevolence, from another perspective, however, might be read as eclipsing and/or de-politicizing equally urgent (if less spectacular) matters at hand. Activists and scholars working toward "climate justice," for instance, maintain that attention to climate change must be coupled with attention to issues like the stark unevenness between those cities that bear the brunt of the climate crisis and those which are most responsible for its existence (and furthermore have the most resources with which to confront it).[21] Others point out that, as with countless urban revitalization efforts carried out since the 1980s in the name of "sustainable development," nature is harnessed by resilient urbanism in ways that are not only ecological in character, but also (if not foremost) meant to consolidate power and generate revenue.[22] A handful of critical geographers and political ecologists have offered especially incisive commentary on "resilience" as an extension of neoliberal governance, asserting that "the anxious race to reconnect New York City's natural surrounds, technical systems and human communities into a resilient system appears not only as a new mode of government or regime of accumulation, but as a desperate attempt to keep the present system on life-support."[23]

Distinct from plain old "sustainability," "resilience" has folded within it the idea of a disaster that is imminent, even underway—the future as present. In her 2007 book on the "rise of disaster capitalism," Naomi Klein demonstrates the extent to which global capitalism and its free market ideologies and policies have facilitated the exploitation (if not, in some cases, the blatant engineering) of new investment opportunities opened in the wake of various catastrophes.[24] With resilient urbanism, in a slight twist, imagined future crises likewise become fuel for commercial development. In this light, qualities such as flexibility, adaptability, and softness take on another, darker guise—more suggestive of the capacity to seep into any available space and to fill it.

If McPhee's mid-twentieth-century urban planners and civil engineers were up against risks of a primarily geological variety, today, cities are increasingly structured by the paradigm of risk itself, with perceived threats—whether potential storm surges, terrorists, or lawsuits—being the proclaimed basis for the massive reordering of urban built environments. The increasingly prevalent rhetoric of resilience in many cases facilitates a one-size-fits-all approach to urban design that sweeps aside crucial questions of difference—by whom, for whom, at cost to whom—plowing through and leveling all in its path. How might we carefully evaluate such trends, without being fully swept up in changes that are so fast as to make the head spin or in images so arresting as that of Manhattan underwater?

One role of critical art and design practices, I would argue, is precisely to help carve out time and space, while sharpening our tools, for scrutinizing transformations of contemporary urban space and their intended and unintended, visible and invisible, repercussions. What is at stake in a project like resilient urbanism, for instance, and for whom? How does it relate to earlier modernist-technological paradigms as well as to current and emergent ones? Which publics are most impacted by climate change, within a particular city and across global expanses? When might retreat make more sense than adaptation? The kinds of projects examined in this essay push us to turn over and inside out the city and its infrastructures, including the specific powers and ideas that shape them. The most compelling among them, to return to Ukeles's vision, moreover contribute directly to the cultivation of a lively public sphere, in which there is ample debate and even dissensus, perhaps especially about "the commons."

1. "Interview: Mierle Laderman Ukeles on Maintenance and Sanitation Art," in Tom Finkelpearl, ed., *Dialogues in Public Art* (Cambridge, Mass.: MIT Press, 2000), 322.

2. John McPhee, *The Control of Nature* (New York: Farrar, Straus, and Giroux, 1989).

3. Among the vast literature on modernity and infrastructure, see, for example: Paul N. Edwards, "Infrastructure and Modernity: Force, Time, and Social Organization in the History of Sociotechnical Systems," in Thomas J. Misa, Philip Brey, and Andrew Feenberg, eds., *Modernity and Technology* (Cambridge, Mass. MIT Press, 2003), 185–225.

4. Toyo Ito, interview with Julian Rose, "The Building After," *Artforum* (September 2013): 344.

5. Clive Hamilton, *Earthmasters: The Dawn of the Age of Climate Engineering* (New Haven: Yale University Press, 2013).

6. See Donna Haraway, "Situated Knowledges: the Science Question in Feminism and the Privilege of Partial Perspective," *Feminist Studies* 14, no. 3 (Autumn 1988): 575–99.

7. Charles Waldheim, ed., *Landscape Urbanism Reader* (New York: Princeton Architectural Press, 2006), 11.

8. "Interview: Mierle Laderman Ukeles," 295.

9. Miwon Kwon, "In Appreciation of Invisible Work: Mierle Laderman Ukeles and the Maintenance of the 'White Cube,'" *Documents* (Fall 1997): 17–18.

10. Center for Urban Pedagogy website: http://welcometocup.org (accessed by the author 14 November, 2014).

11. Damon Rich, interview with Cassim Shepard, *Urban Omnibus* (January 29, 2014): http://urbanomnibus.net/2014/01/walking-to-the-water-environmental-justice-and-newarks-riverfront-park/.

12. Nils Norman, *The Contemporary Picturesque* (London: Book Works, 2000), 32–54.

13. Suzanne Lacy, ed., *Mapping The Terrain: New Genre Public Art* (Seattle: Bay Press, 1994).

14. Dana Cuff, "Architecture as Public Work," in Katrina Stoll and Scott Lloyd, eds., *Infrastructure as Architecture* (Berlin: Jovis, 2010), 18.

15. Stan Allen, "Infrastructural Urbanism," in *Points + Lines: Diagrams and Projects for the City* (New York: Princeton Architectural Press, 1999), 50.

16. Ibid, 52.

17. See Sarah Kanouse, "Critical Day Trips," in Emily Eliza Scott and Kirsten Swenson, eds., *Critical Landscapes: Art Space Politics* (Berkeley: University of California Press, 2015), 43–56, and "A Post-Natural Field Kit: Tools for the Embodied Exploration of Social Ecologies," in Sébastien Caquard, Laurene Vaughan, and William Cartwright, eds., *Mapping Environmental Issues in the City: Arts and Cartography Cross Perspectives* (New York: Springer, 2011), 160–77.

18. Christoph Kueffer, "Ecological Novelty: Towards an Interdisciplinary Understanding of Ecological Change in the Anthropocene," in Heike Greschke and Julia Tischler, eds., *Grounding Global Climate Change: Contributions from the Social and Cultural Sciences* (New York: Springer, 2014), 19–37.

19. Kate Orff, "Rebuilding Eco-Infrastructures," talk given at the Urban Nature: Between Human and Nonhuman conference, Columbia GSAPP, May 16, 2014. Video documentation available at: https://vimeo.com/96855705 (accessed by the author March 17, 2015).

20. Official Website of the City of New York: http://www1.nyc.gov/office-of-the-mayor/news/122-15/mayor-de-blasio-releases-npcc-2015-report-providing-climate-projections-2100-the-first.

21. See Ashley Dawson's forthcoming book, *Extreme City: Climate Change and the Urban Future* (New York: Verso, 2016).

22. The artist Martha Rosler has written an insightful series of essays on the connection between greening and gentrification in New York City, at points directly addressing waterfront development: "Culture Class: Art, Creativity, Urbanism" (pts. I-II), *e-flux journal* (November 2010): http://www.e-flux.com/journal/culture-class-art-creativity-urbanism-part-i/.

23. Bruce Braun and Stephanie Wakefield, "Inhabiting the Postapocalytic City," introduction to a special forum edited by the two, "A New Apparatus: Technology, Government and the Resilient City," *Society and Space* 32, no. 1 (February 2014): http://societyandspace.com/material/article-extras/theme-section-a-new-apparatus-technology-government-and-the-resilient-city/bruce-braun-and-stephanie-wakefield-inhabiting-the-postapocalytic-city/.

24. Naomi Klein, *The Shock Doctrine: the Rise of Disaster Capitalism* (New York: Metropolitan Books/Henry Holt, 2007).

Scale

"Reason will dictate continuous renewal of the environment at every scale, not massive blight followed by massive reconstruction."[1]
—Shadrach Woods

Scaling a project—up or down—allows us to alter the influence of our work. This approach to design seeks replicable, networked, exponential impacts that act at multiple amplitudes simultaneously to catalyze widespread and lasting positive change. The disconnect between scales of action and scales of consequence defines the paradox of global climate change. Seemingly unrelated human acts—individual fires burning, personal cars emitting carbon dioxide, power plants combusting coal—have together contributed to a globally shared predicament.[2] Effecting positive change on global issues can feel well beyond the capacity of designers. How can we draw boundaries around complex, open systems in order to intervene? The potential of the intermediate scale or neighborhood-scale landscape as a defined zone from which we can scale up (to nitrogen cycles, water quality) and down (to streetscapes, sites) is a powerful tool to get beyond the paralysis of "global" and "local." Urban ecology projects at the landscape scale can begin to activate communities, inform policy, and create lasting and meaningful change.

$$[REVIVE+COHABIT+ENGAGE]^{10}=SCALING$$

The Living Breakwaters project featured in this chapter combines the insights described in the previous three chapters, and advances a suite of interrelated projects. In *Revive*, *Cohabit*, and *Engage*, urban ecology is described in various ways: as a proactive overlay of cultural and natural systems, as an extension of design thinking beyond our own species, and as a creative stance of engagement—but mostly as work to be done. Rather than pleasant backdrops to be consumed visually and manicured by an unseen labor force, SCAPE landscapes are closer in concept to preindustrial agriculture in that they bind the social and the natural with definable measures of joint participation. As productive landscapes embedded in communities, they seek to affect change, create new patterns of action, and develop spaces for growth.

Living Breakwaters represents years of hard work for our research-driven, activist practice and also combines and builds upon a range of other SCAPE initiatives. Early research and mapping of Jamaica Bay deepened our conviction that a mode of urban gardening could double as stewardship—and fueled an obsession with shellfish. From there, we engaged in simultaneous testing of ideas, from small, in-water mussel pilots and differently textured concrete structure samples to urban-scale, coastal-resiliency planning approaches to regional climate change analyses. Some were internally initiated, some were paid planning projects; over time, we were able to advance a range of studies that investigated ecological infrastructure and social resiliency, and to form a creative network of like-minded colleagues. Our team's shared knowledge of regulatory systems and legal planning at federal, state, and local levels grew. We accumulated hydrodynamic modeling knowledge and monitored oyster gardens. These parallel efforts created the conditions that allowed the full project to come into being. By the time Hurricane Irene hit in 2011 and Superstorm Sandy leveled houses with wave action and flooded entire neighborhoods in 2012, our team was well informed about local conditions and ready to respond.

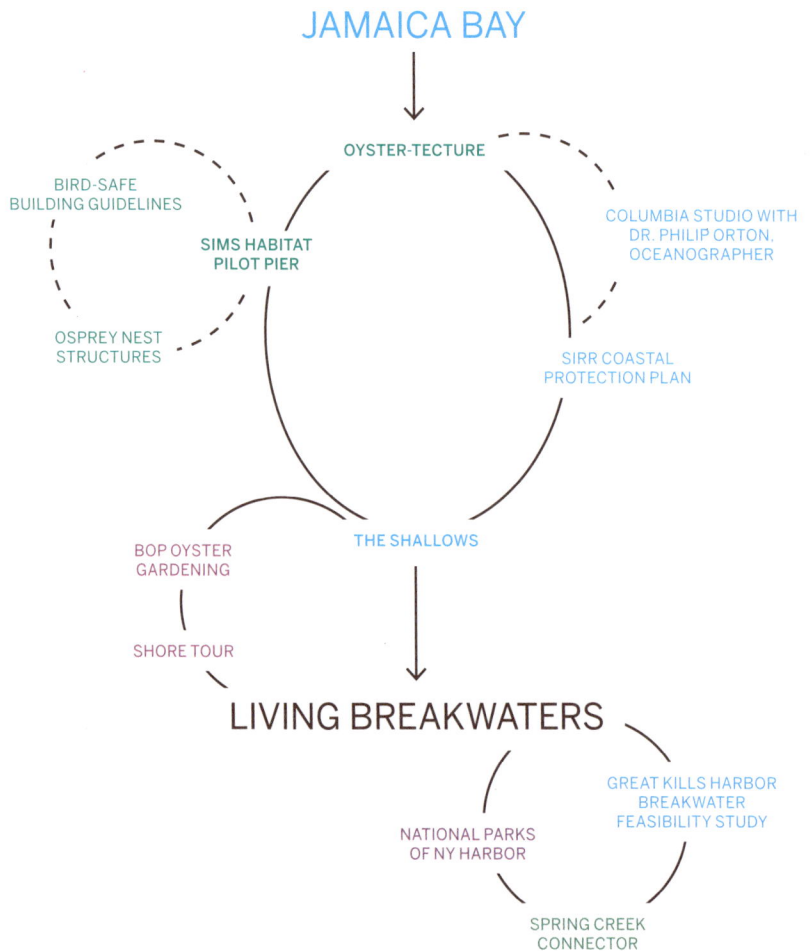

SCIENCE WORKING WITH DESIGN

A key task of designers and scientists is to come together around methods of modeling that imaginatively enact environmental scenarios and help evaluate options. SCAPE's approach to the Living Breakwaters project bridges the quantitative and the qualitative aspects of landscape and overcomes the typical compartmentalization of scientists, designers, and engineers, driving an iterative design process alongside a rigorous engineering evaluation. The scientific method is to ask a question, develop a hypothesis, test the hypothesis through experimentation, then analyze results—if we can extend this method to include iterative testing and modification to achieve desired outcomes, and bring together scientific models with 3-D sketching and scenario testing, the common ground between science and design-driven modeling methods can be exploited. Looking to merge large-scale gray solutions—that is, ecological infrastructure with traditional civil engineering solutions like culverts and levees—with ecological protection and enhancement, the team worked with regulators, fishermen, and local, state, and federal agencies to analyze resiliency goals. Through sketch sessions, geographic information system (GIS) and hydrodynamic modeling, aerial mapping, and sediment collection, our interdisciplinary team integrated insights from multiple perspectives. As conveners of this process, SCAPE bridges the realms of science and design by bringing together engineers, marine biologists, hydrodynamic modelers, and graphic designers to harness hybrid concepts that engage communities, ecologies, and infrastructure.

Our role is to take this knowledge, develop its spatial consequences, and make it read on a human scale through compelling, clear visualization. We also extrapolate scenarios to understand how an intervention will impact or benefit the entire ecosystem and bioregion that we are working within. The multi-scalar approach to scenario-based planning allows us to transcend an infrastructural design process that can be insular and aimed only at one aspect of intervention at any given moment in time, as well as to project multiple futures and potential scenarios. This type of systemic and collaborative thinking has the potential to flip the discourse of landscape architecture from professional expertise into one of engendering shared solutions.

SCALING HABITAT

A traditionally engineered breakwater constructed of uniformly sized rock has little habitat value. At the same time, oyster reefs are susceptible to changes in water quality and potentially vulnerable to damage in powerful storms. Living Breakwaters melds the risk-reduction capacity of a traditional breakwater with the ecological benefits of a thriving oyster reef. The structure's form has been modified to include reef street pockets of ECOncrete units designed to maximize diverse, three-dimensional habitat. Variable pore spaces at both a micro and macro level create niches for finfish and attract a host of other species such as crabs, lobster, and mussels. The breakwater itself will be seeded with oysters from the Billion Oyster Project schools on shore.[3] Oysters will agglomerate and build upon one another to create a reef of the biological glue calcium carbonate, which will protect its own surface while adding roughness to the bay to further reduce wave velocity. As they grow, the oysters will continue to accrete vertically—keeping up with rising sea levels and slowing new wave patterns. On shore, the wave-attenuating breakwaters will also have gradual and substantive effects. Over time, they will allow the eroded shoreline to replenish itself, making onshore recreational beaches for people and additional shallow-water habitat for a range of endangered wading birds and marine life. This is truly seeding a living landscape at the scale of the city.

SCALING ENGAGEMENT

Landscape architecture used to stop at a property line, but scaling embraces an extended realm of efficacy and human engagement. Scale is a strategy of effect, activism, and service. Rather than make static landscapes, we try to envision how the making of a dynamic landscape can engender new forms of community. One particularly illustrative example of this is our work partnering with the Harbor School; its students and teachers relate all curricula to New York Harbor, rendering it one gigantic classroom and science lab. With an accredited science curriculum, its Billion Oyster Project helps science teachers reach thousands of kids across the city in chemistry, biology, and physics while reintroducing oyster larvae to harbor waters. Students then upload and share their data through an online platfrom with other classrooms in New York City.[4]

Key to the notion of scale in the Living Breakwaters project is the concept of recruitment: recruiting teachers to teach the Billion Oyster Project science curriculum, in turn reaching thousands of students, and recruiting biological life onto the structure, which itself generates a substrate that is hospitable for many other species. The oysters themselves filter excess nitrogen out of the water, thereby jump-starting a positive chain of cleaner, slower water for all to enjoy. Eelgrass begins to grow around oyster reefs and provide a haven for scallops, crabs, threatened fish, and their natural predators. The program reinforces that there are no actual divisions between land and water, between urban, energy, and landscape systems, or between teaching and learning. Melding educational and design processes and creatively engaging communities in an intergenerational dialogue about the future should become our primary task moving forward.

SCALING SCALE

In the spring of 2015, SCAPE signed a contract with the New York State Governor's Office of Storm Recovery to continue to lead the design process for Living Breakwaters. Beyond serving as team leader, SCAPE works as a catalyst to spark ideas, integrate design concepts, and interweave socio-natural components with practical considerations such as construction budgets and regulatory and permitting challenges. The physical extent of the project, funded with $60 million in disaster recovery money from the

US Department of Housing and Urban Development, has been identified as an optimum spatial envelope for piloting ecological, social, and risk-reduction hypotheses.[5]

Living Breakwaters is a joint urban and ecological endeavor. It builds a physical landscape that fosters education, stewardship, and recreation for communities on shore and in turn strengthens and protects those communities over time. It channels the combined power of a simple life-form into a positive feedback loop that shifts and reboots a negative cycle of erosion, sea level rise, decreasing water quality, habitat loss, and increasing risk from storms. It illustrates the potential of combined disciplines to quite literally turn the tides: the systems that cause interdependent species to fail and communities to splinter can be countered by the patterns that make ecological systems and people grow and relate.

As this project began to take on its own momentum, it became clear that its effects would quickly go beyond those intended for its original, site-specific location—it triggers regulatory reform, finds new legal pathways for similar development, organizes community meet-ups, generates school curricula, and provides data about shoreline replenishment and fish and shellfish habitat regeneration to a larger audience. The project has become part of a very real movement.

Climate change demands synthetic, integrative thinking. Although the pilot underway now in Staten Island has a defined spatial extent and location, in concept Living Breakwaters works at multiple scales simultaneously. And rather than creating a top-down "master plan," it sketches a replicable cross section that links a unit of community, a zone of protective topography, and a program for ecological regeneration connecting people to each other as well as the landscape in a mutual stance of stewardship and interdependence. It prefigures both a different physical future world and summons the capacity to act.

The Copenhagen Accord of 2009 established a long-term goal of limiting the maximum global average temperature increase to no more than two degrees Celsius above preindustrial levels, subject to a review in 2015. Here we are, in 2015, with binding action plans and the enforcement of carbon pollution limits still seeming beyond the scope of existing governmental structures; a two- to four-degree increase in warming is anticipated. What will this world that we are making—intentionally or not—look like? Moving forward, a range of futures remains available. We need to ask not only what the real and interesting questions are now, but also what can design do?

Across the globe, climate shocks will interact with vulnerable and exposed populations in increasingly uncertain ways, with impacts distributed unfairly, and conflicts amplified. We need to design with science to develop scenario-driven methodologies that actively model and interpret future contexts: hotter, colder, wetter, drier, and generally less predictable. Designers must embrace uncertainty as productive design fodder and move away from fixed, easily marketable design products and toward crafting strategic approaches to infrastructures and urban fabrics. A focus on new energy landscapes and adaptive multipurpose infrastructure that is embedded within contexts and communities will drive the design professions toward new ways of working within the short window to act.

Addressing climate change transcends the limits of understanding for any one discipline or sector. The goal of scaling up smaller projects to something that approaches the scale of the problem has been outlined on these pages. At the same time, finding the nexus where a physical landscape intervention can be generative of social cohesion, and landscapes are synchronized with communities that care for them, presents an opportunity for change. Next-century infrastructure will be simultaneously technical and political, social and ecological, pragmatic and empowering. It is the epoch of urban ecology.

1. Shadrach Woods, "What U Can Do," *Architecture at Rice* 27 (Spring 1970): 35.
2. Even beyond steady agglomerating effects we can see accelerating, non-linear models of change. In the Artic the albedo effect contributes to a steepening curve of ice melt that exponentially builds upon itself. As explained by Elizabeth Kolbert's reporting, as ice (a very highly reflective, high albedo surface) melts and is replaced with open water (a very low albedo surface) the feedback look is accelerated: the more open water is exposed via melting, the more solar energy goes into heating the ocean. This leads to warmer oceans, rising seas and nested, looped impacts at every level of humanity. Scientist Donald Perovich explains: "It takes a small nudge to the climate system and amplifies it into a big change" (Elizabeth Kolbert, "The Climate of Man," *The New Yorker* [April 25, 2005]). As a designer, I want to know how can we construct a regenerative, positive feedback loop?
3. Landscapes and their constituent organisms can be cultivated to regrow via wind-based seed dispersal, oyster and mussel larvae, soil building techniques, or afforestation, among many other processes.
4. To support this initiative, our team, along with the graphic designers MTWTF, developed a freely downloadable Oyster Gardening Manual that ultimately will help seed the breakwater reefs.
5. Via the HUD Rebuild By Design Process, for more information, see rebuildbydesign.org and stormrecovery.ny.gov

SCALE

208

Community Pilot
Novel Ecosystems
Consensus Building
The Layered Approach
In Situ Study
Ecological Infrastructure
Bay Nourishment
Hydrodynamic Modeler
Urban Diver

Pilot projects are increasingly important in urban areas, to test the potential and techniques of green infrastructure. Community-driven design and citizen science help to drive these pilots and create a vocal constituency for urban nature and stewardship.

—

Fuzzy Rope Weaving Evening
New York, New York

How can active marine industrial areas support underwater life? SCAPE invited a group of community collaborators to actively participate in a small-scale test of this question. The Fuzzy Rope Weaving Evening welcomed friends, local business owners, and watershed activists in weaving simple and replicable habitat panels. Fuzzy rope, a polypropylene material explored in the Oyster-tecture proposal, is a tactile cable used in the aquaculture industry to cultivate mussel colonies—it adds much-needed underwater surface area to depleted shorelines and a microstructure for habitat recruitment. This material, applied as vertical net structures along an industrial barge-mooring pier, was tested as a temporary underwater habitat near an active recycling facility. Over thirty volunteers thought it worth a try, and their many hands fabricated fourteen fuzzy rope panels, seven intertidal and seven subtidal, which were later installed at a Sims Metal Management site in Brooklyn. SCAPE interns designed a shareable pamphlet that described the weaving process and invited others to design and monitor their own *in situ* experiments.

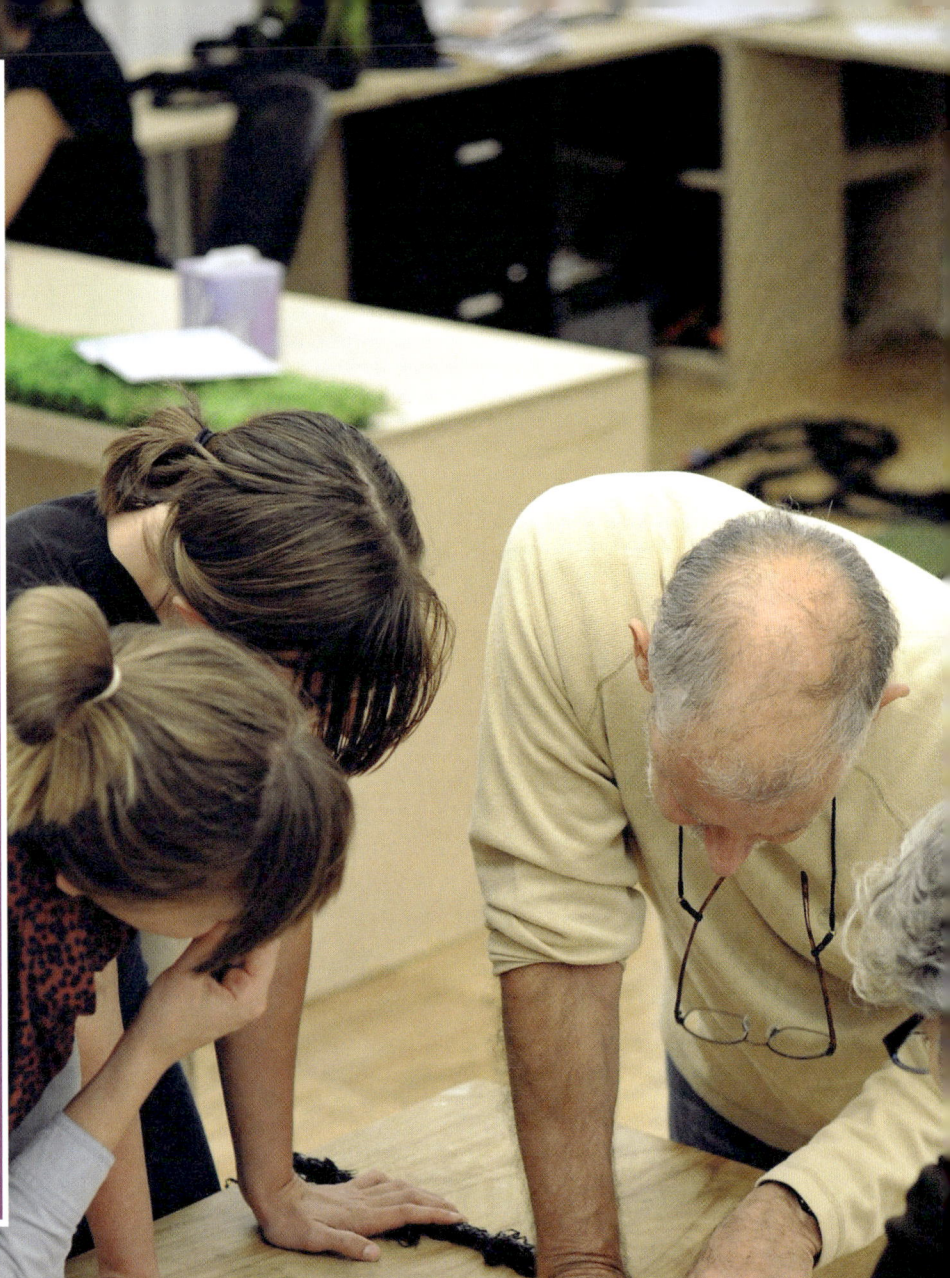

BRAIDED MARINE ROPE STRUNG
THROUGH TOP OF PANEL

BRAIDED MARINE ROPE LENGTH
VARIES TO ALLOW FUZZY ROPE
PANEL TO HANG AT SPECIFIED DEPTH

WOVEN FUZZY ROPE PANEL
FROM AN 18"-GRID, TIED WITH
CARGO KNOTS AS SPECIFIED
BY MANUFACTURER

5" BRAIDED MARINE ROPE

ANCHOR, (2) PER PANEL

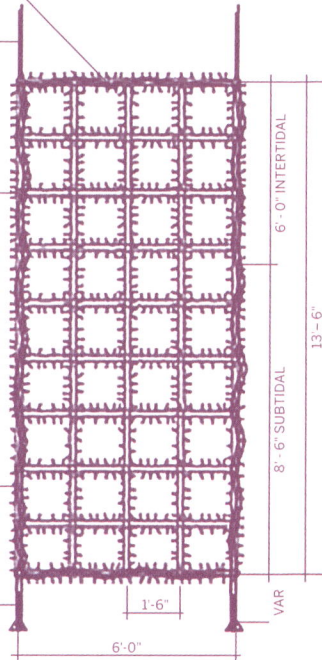

6' - 0' INTERTIDAL

13' - 6"

8' - 6' SUBTIDAL

VAR

1'-6"

6'-0"

These human-built and modified systems are products of the Anthropocene, and so lack analogs in prior natural systems. Global warming, invasive species, and mass extinctions give rise to new niche habitats molded and structured by human agency.

—

Sims Habitat Pilot Pier
Brooklyn, New York

Fourteen community-made fuzzy rope panels and a series of ECOncrete tiles were installed along the Brooklyn waterfront in March 2013. Monitored in collaboration with Michael Judge of Brooklyn College, the *in situ* experiment embraces the potential for creating urban habitats with new materials and investigates what species can thrive in an active maritime industrial zone. The fully functioning barge-mooring pier now supports a diverse and changing composite of aquatic life; in June of 2013 the fuzzy rope panels supported between six and twenty blue mussels per linear foot and a host of associated species including green crabs, colonial and solitary tunicates, barnacles, amphipods, algae, and sea squirts. While the installation has a maximum life span of five to seven years and is considered temporary, it reveals how even active industrial shorelines can function as critical parts of New York City's coastal habitats, and how simple materials can be repurposed as habitat probes.

PILOT PIER SECTION AND ELEVATION

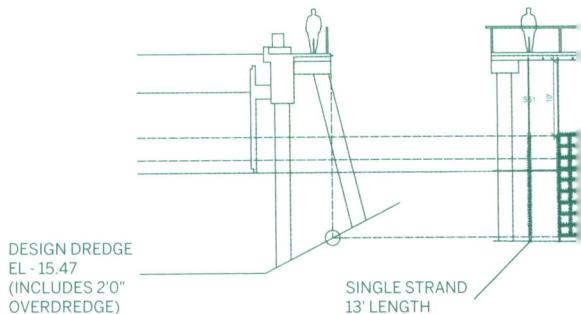

DESIGN DREDGE
EL - 15.47
(INCLUDES 2'0"
OVERDREDGE)

SINGLE STRAND
13' LENGTH

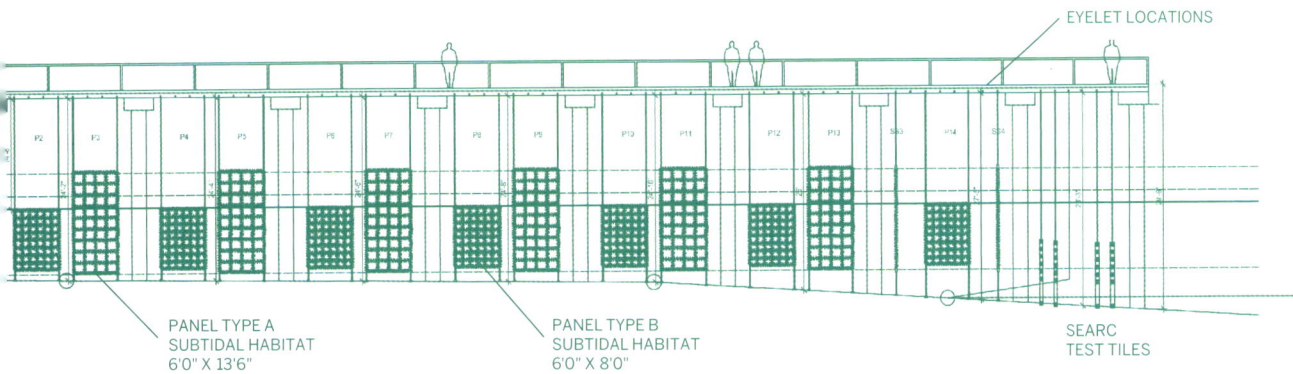

EYELET LOCATIONS

PANEL TYPE A
SUBTIDAL HABITAT
6'0" X 13'6"

PANEL TYPE B
SUBTIDAL HABITAT
6'0" X 8'0"

SEARC
TEST TILES

Consensus Building

Every designer knows that gaining consensus on a project is never an easy task. Thinking through collaborative, bottom-up approaches and solutions to complex urban problems is the charge of twenty-first-century landscape architects.

—

New York Rising Community Planning
Brooklyn and Queens, New York

As part of a New York State initiative to respond to storm damage from Hurricane Sandy, SCAPE consulted with part of a larger team that worked with hard-hit communities on developing their own planning framework for the use of federal recovery funds. Rather than imposing a technically driven solution, the team solicited community suggestions and asked residents to identify opportunities. These were developed into a series of possible projects, and the consultants provided technical expertise, feasibility review, and cost estimates. They also helped community leaders prioritize the work in relation to their expressed needs and the realities of site constraints. SCAPE worked with the Jamaica Bay communities of Broad Channel, Canarsie, Howard Beach, and Mill Basin/Bergen Beach to integrate ecological services and landscape solutions into small-scale water system upgrades including revetment walls, tide gates, berms, stormwater swales, as well as to plan urban forest regeneration. This detailed type of planning and bottom-up design is driven by transparency, listening, and idea exchange, and sets up a feedback loop for long-term stewardship and investment.

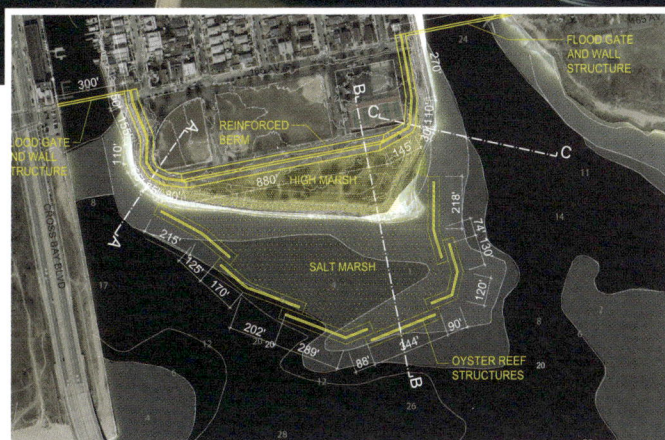

FLOOD GATE
AND WALL
STRUCTURE

FLOOD GATE
AND WALL
STRUCTURE

REINFORCED
BERM

HIGH MARSH

SALT MARSH

OYSTER REEF
STRUCTURES

The Layered Approach

Heat waves, drought, heavy precipitation, hurricanes—all of these unpredictable weather patterns need to be considered for our uncertain future. Designers need to confront traditional static and monofunctional approaches to infrastructure, and to understand that there is not a panacea solution to climate change.

—

SIRR Coastal Protection Plan
New York, New York

SCAPE helped frame and test harbor-wide strategies for coastal protection measures that could reduce risk for the five boroughs of New York City as part of the Mayor's Special Initiative for Rebuilding and Resiliency. Working in a "war room" context as part of a team of engineers, cost estimators, and planners, hard engineering solutions were overlaid with performative natural systems and tested through hydrodynamic modeling. As designers, SCAPE emphasized the importance of including several different strategies for enhanced coastal protection and ecosystem health—a layered approach. This resulted in strategic advice and design recommendations that contributed to New York City's award-winning report titled "A Stronger, More Resilient New York" —released only six months after Superstorm Sandy. This city-scale collaboration is not an implementation mandate; rather it provides a framework for consensus-building and organizing around the risks of future climate change impacts, as well as establishes New York City as a leader in resilient coastal design and planning.

COMPREHENSIVE COASTAL PROTECTION PLAN
FULL BUILD RECOMMENDATIONS

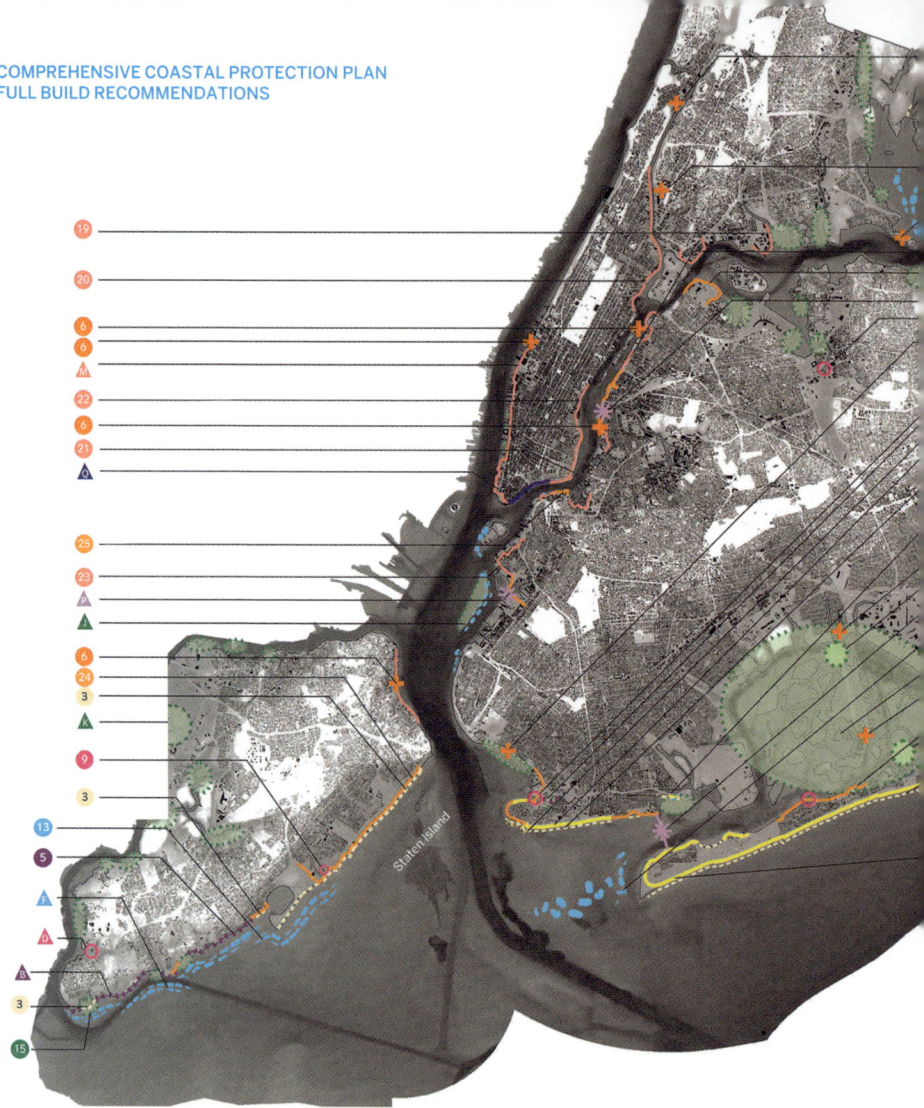

● PHASE 1 INITIATIVES
▲ ADDITIONAL FULL-BUILD RECOMMENDATION

INCREASE COASTAL EDGE ELEVATIONS
● BEACH NOURISHMENT
● ARMOR STONE (REVETMENTS)
● BULKHEADS
● TIDE GATES / DRAINAGE DEVICES

MINIMIZE UPLAND WAVE ZONES
● DUNES
● OFFSHORE BREAKWATERS
● WETLANDS, LIVING SHORELINES, AND REEFS
● GROINS

PROTECT AGAINST STORM SURGE
● INTEGRATED FLOOD PROTECTION SYSTEM
● FLOODWALLS / LEVEES
● LOCAL STORM SURGE BARRIER
● MULTI-PURPOSE LEVEE

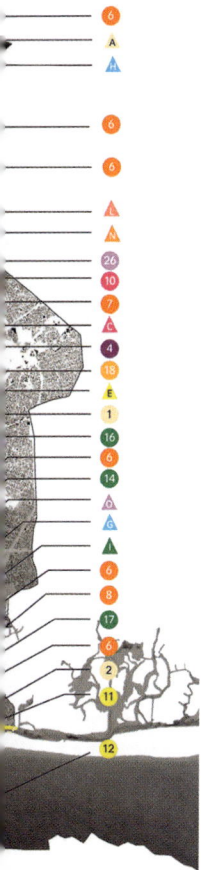

WETLANDS / SHOALS

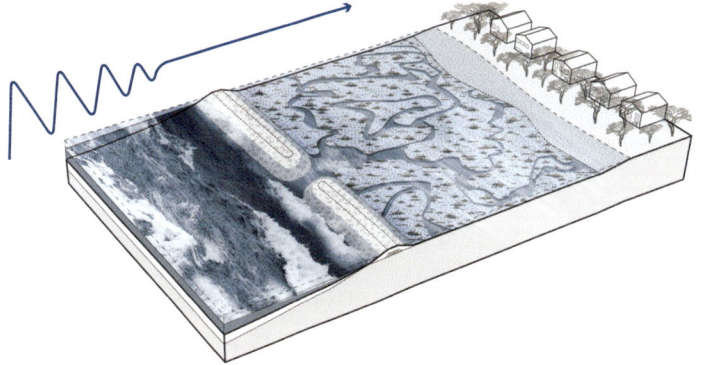

OFFSHORE BREAKWATERS

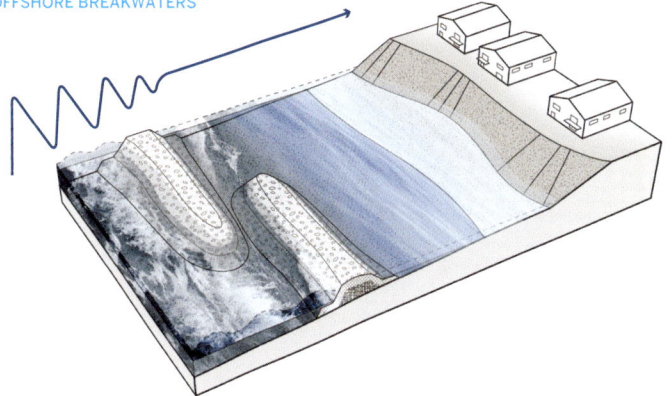

LOCAL STORM SURGE BARRIER

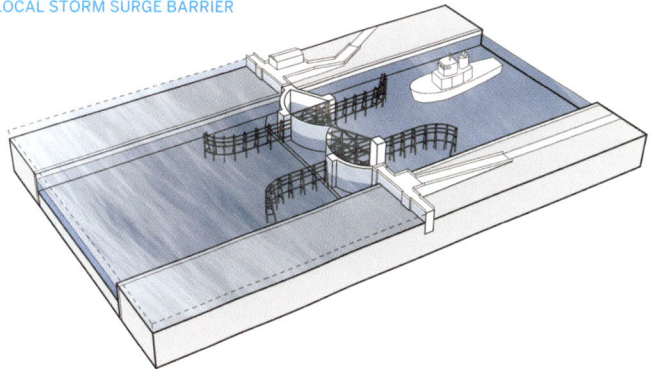

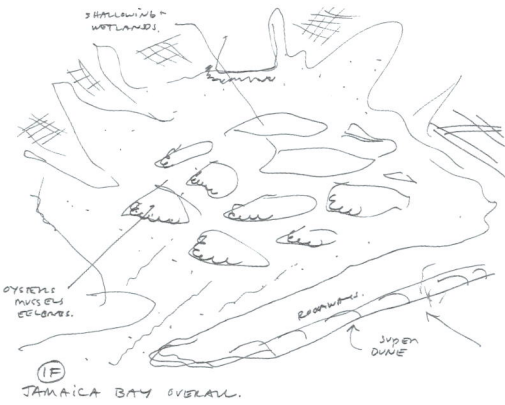

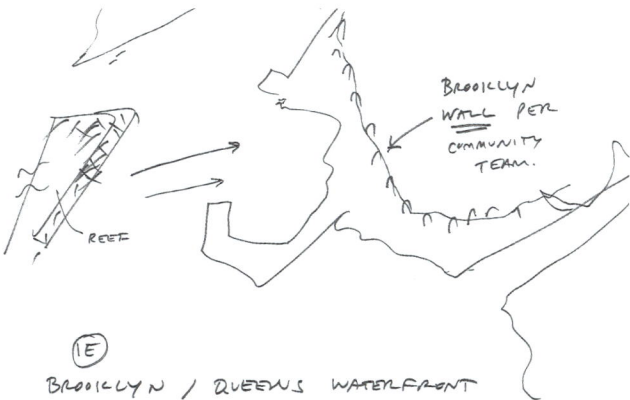

SHALLOWING + WETLANDS.

OYSTERS MUSSELS EELGRASS.

ROADWAY.

SUPER DUNE.

(1F)
JAMAICA BAY OVERALL.

BROOKLYN WALL PER COMMUNITY TEAM.

REEF

(1E)
BROOKLYN / QUEENS WATERFRONT

Many ecosystems in our cities have not been studied in enough detail to suggest clear plans of action. It is critical to gain on-the-ground information about urban ecosystems in order to understand the systemic impacts that potential design interventions could have on cities before enacting them.

—

Great Kills Breakwater Feasibility Study
Staten Island, New York

Feasibility studies at Great Kills Harbor and Crescent Beach on Staten Island provided an opportunity to apply Rebuild by Design research at a granular scale. Working with engineering and planning partners, SCAPE advanced a series of alternative breakwater scenarios for vulnerable communities subject to erosion and land loss. The project placed a strong emphasis on studying habitat impacts—notably the displacement of hard clams (*Mercenaria mercenaria*) within the break-water footprint —and on *in situ* ecological classification and sediment sampling. The team gathered hard data that had not existed until then— most information on the area had been gathered anecdotally from fishermen.

Results suggested that breakwaters were an appropriate response for the Crescent Beach portion of the site exposed to direct wave action, and that while a breakwater footprint would impact existing hard clams, their construction could encourage sediment-rich zones to form along their shoreline edges, creating additional habitat for any hard clams displaced during construction. The study also emphasized the need for iterative modeling, testing, and refinement, and stressed the need for informed design decisions and collaborative conversations with residents and city agencies alike to achieve successful outcomes.

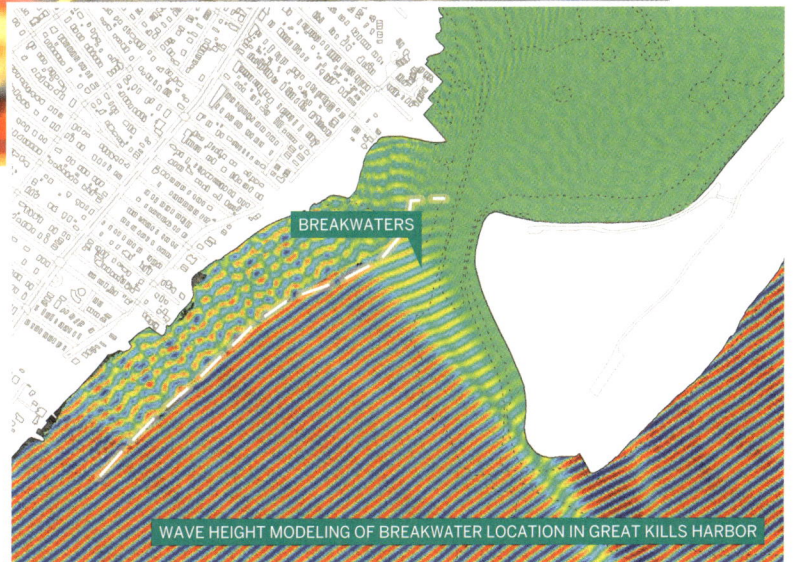

BREAKWATERS

WAVE HEIGHT MODELING OF BREAKWATER LOCATION IN GREAT KILLS HARBOR

Ecological Infrastructure

Simply put, ecological infrastructure refers to naturally functioning ecosystems that deliver valuable services to people. Within urban environments, this type of system can be amplified to help create resilient cities.

—

The Shallows: Regional Strategy
New York and New Jersey

The federal Rebuild by Design competition created the opportunity for the SCAPE team to combine knowledge with interdisciplinary partners—innovative engineers, marine biologists, and educators—about the best ways to assess risk in Sandy-impacted areas. Our regional research, entitled "The Shallows," identified nearshore shallow-water zones as critical to the city's economy and infrastructure, yet emphasized how and why their threatened ecosystems should be protected and regenerated for future risk reduction and habitat value. Regional landscape research was combined with hydrodynamic testing of shallow-water design scenarios, resulting in five clear project proposals, one of which is featured on the following page. All of the proposed strategies reinforce the validity of taking a layered approach to risk reduction; it became clear during the course of the study that interventions must extend from the shore to the seafloor while still inviting access to and use of the shoreline.

HUDSON RIVER

LONG ISLAND SOUND

GREAT SOUTH BAY

NEW YORK HARBOR

JAMAICA BAY

RARITAN BAY

SOUTH OYSTER BAY

SANDY HOOK BAY

BARNEGAT BAY

GREAT BAY

A CULTURE OF RESILIENCY

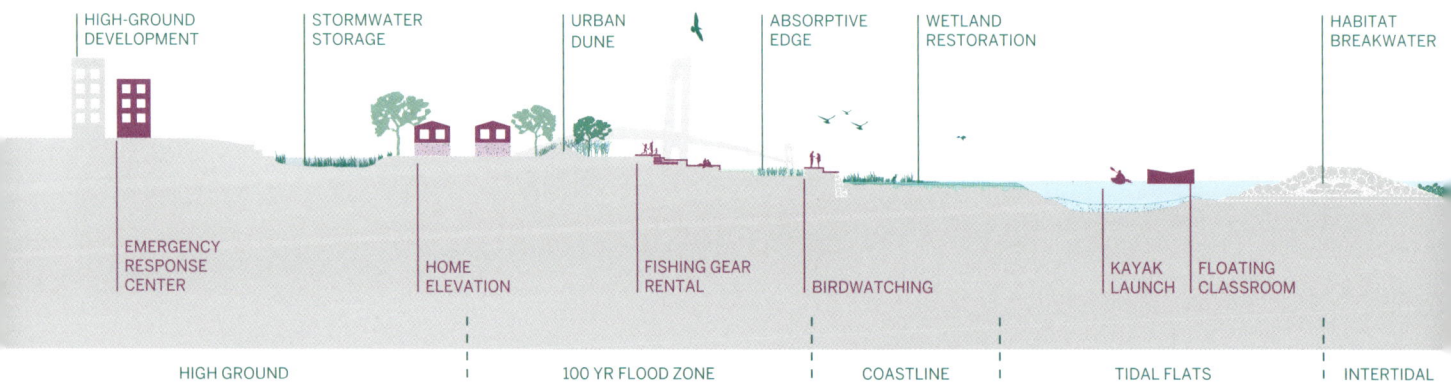

HIGH-GROUND DEVELOPMENT

STORMWATER STORAGE

URBAN DUNE

ABSORPTIVE EDGE

WETLAND RESTORATION

HABITAT BREAKWATER

EMERGENCY RESPONSE CENTER

HOME ELEVATION

FISHING GEAR RENTAL

BIRDWATCHING

KAYAK LAUNCH

FLOATING CLASSROOM

HIGH GROUND

100 YR FLOOD ZONE

COASTLINE

TIDAL FLATS

INTERTIDAL

DREDGE WETLANDS

TIDAL FLATS

FRICTION FORESTS

CONSTRUCTED REEFS

ABSORPTIVE EDGES

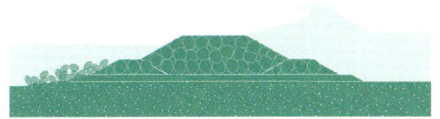

HABITAT BREAKWATERS

DUNES AND BERMS

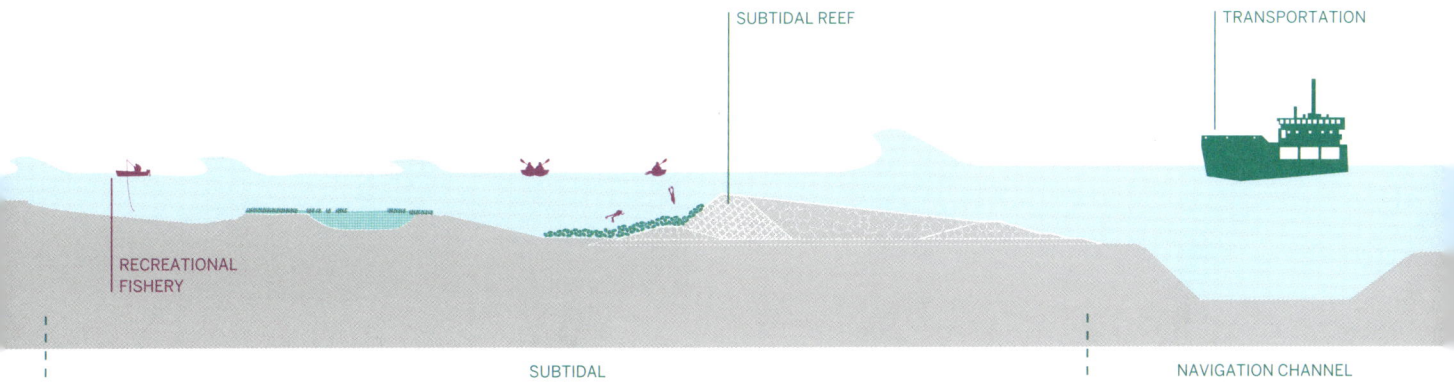

SUBTIDAL REEF

TRANSPORTATION

RECREATIONAL
FISHERY

SUBTIDAL

NAVIGATION CHANNEL

SCALE

Bay Nourishment

Beach and bay ecosystems are intricately linked in coastal environments, where water and sediment dynamics interact in an ever-changing interplay. By experimenting with scales of shallowing and modification of bathymetry, large-scale changes can be enacted to minimize the effects of sea level rise.

—

The Shallows: Bay Nourishment
Brooklyn and Queens, New York

Jamaica Bay is one of the nation's most urbanized tidal estuaries; it hosts a vulnerable and dense population of over 500,000 people and serves as critical breeding ground for hundreds of species of fish and birds. Its formerly shallow marine bathymetry, water quality, and flow patterns have been drastically altered by dredging, urbanization at its edges, and excessive nitrogen pollution from four wastewater treatment plants. Wetlands are succumbing to development and disappearing as sea levels rise. Deep, dredged channels into and around the perimeter of Jamaica Bay now quickly deliver storm surge floodwaters straight to populated areas, causing flooding and devastation.

While coastal infrastructure is often conceived of as walls or levees, the SCAPE team chose to investigate coastal adaptation measures in Jamaica Bay that are soft, subtidal, and muddy. Restoring dredged channels to their shallower water depths could help reduce flood risks for waterfront neighborhoods while contributing to marshland and mudflat regeneration. SCAPE worked with Dr. Philip Orton of the Stevens Institute of Technology to test and model bay nourishment approaches that encourage sedimentation within the bay while minimizing impacts to bay navigation and recreation. Early studies showed positive results— that protective benefits for neighborhoods could be accrued through a strategic restoration of shallow bay bathymetry.

HOWARD BEACH, QUEENS POP 26,150

18% REDUCTION IN WATER LEVEL

21% REDUCTION IN WATER LEVEL

CANARSIE, BROOKLYN POP 84,000

CHANNEL SHALLOWING

WETLAND RESTORATION

DREDGE CHANNEL PRESERVATION

BROAD CHANNEL POP 3000

BERGEN BEACH

12% REDUCTION IN WATER LEVEL

7% REDUCTION IN WATER LEVEL

BELLE HARBOR

BREEZY POINT

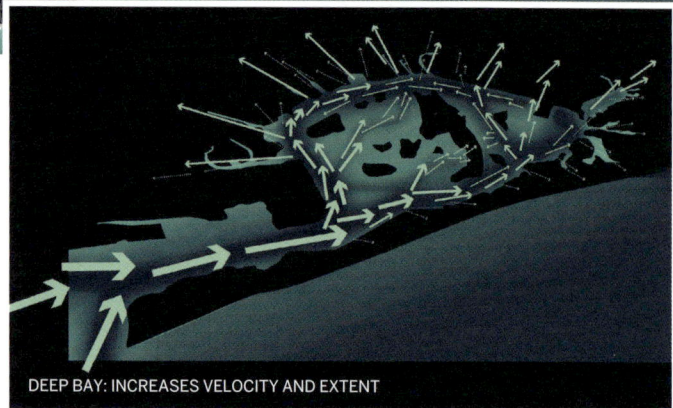

DEEP BAY: INCREASES VELOCITY AND EXTENT

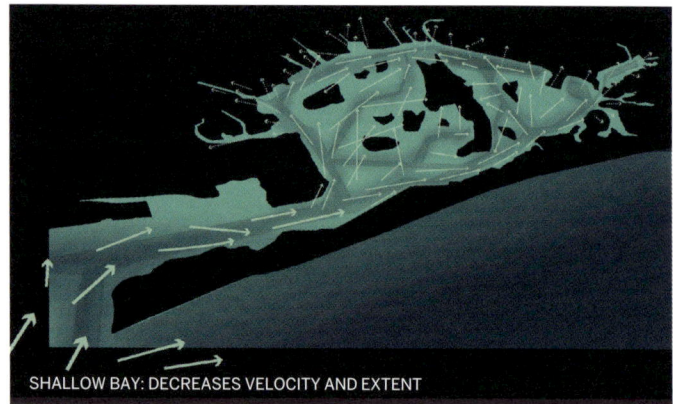

SHALLOW BAY: DECREASES VELOCITY AND EXTENT

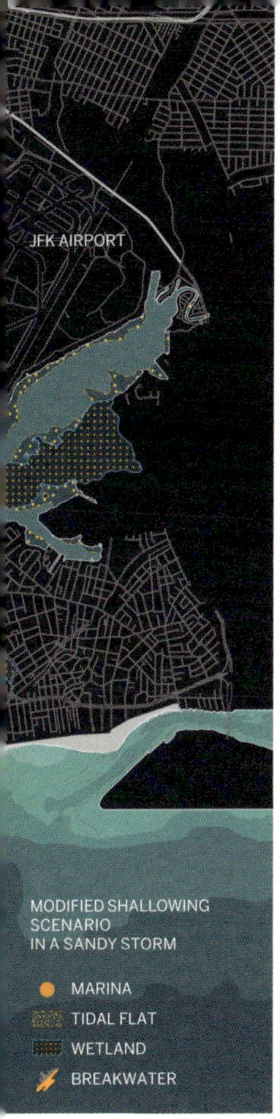
JFK AIRPORT
MODIFIED SHALLOWING SCENARIO IN A SANDY STORM
MARINA
TIDAL FLAT
WETLAND
BREAKWATER

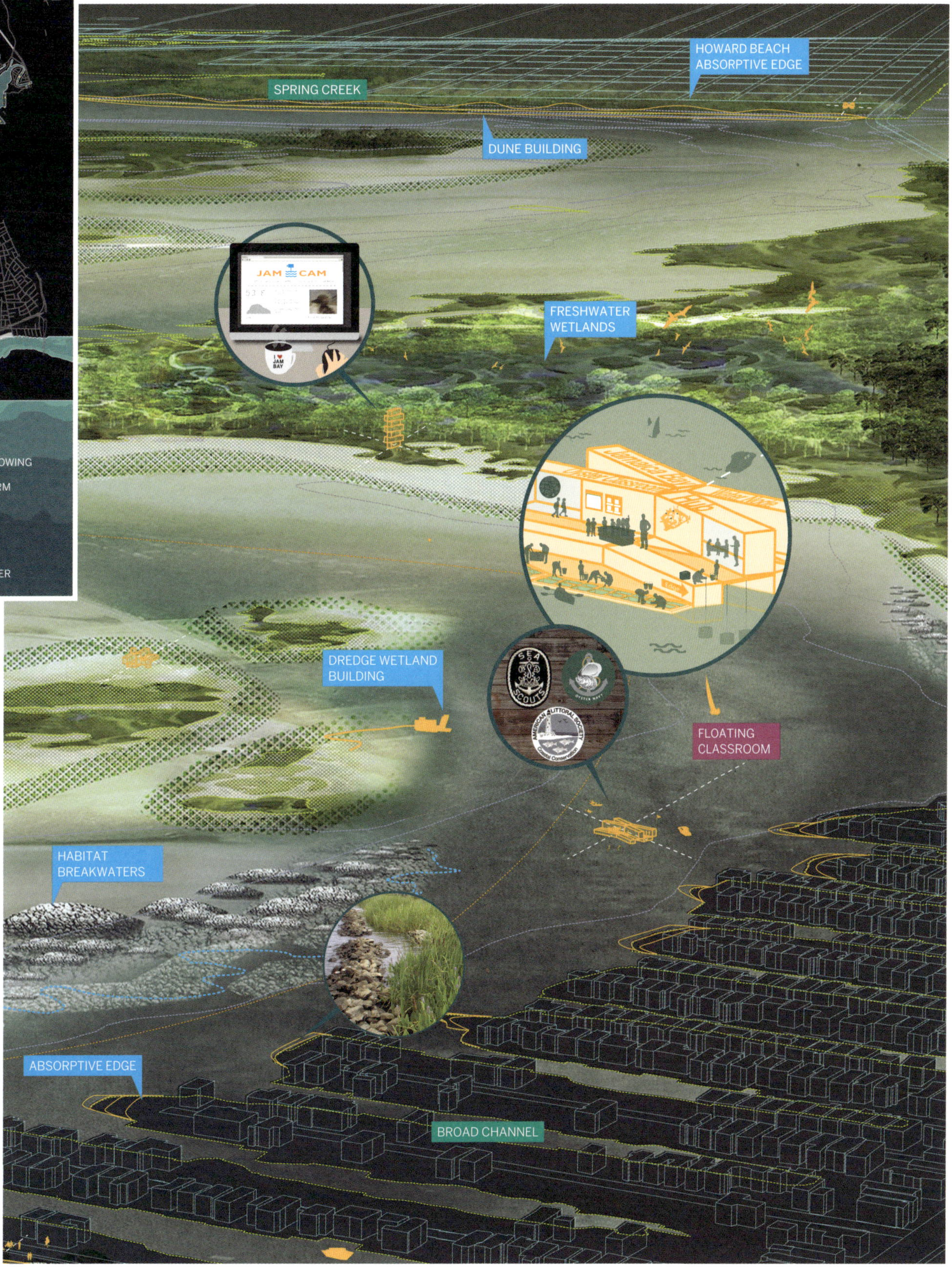
HOWARD BEACH ABSORPTIVE EDGE
SPRING CREEK
DUNE BUILDING
JAM CAM
FRESHWATER WETLANDS
DREDGE WETLAND BUILDING
FLOATING CLASSROOM
HABITAT BREAKWATERS
ABSORPTIVE EDGE
BROAD CHANNEL

SCAPE

Has Hurricane Sandy changed the type of modeling you're doing?

Philip Orton

Definitely. It's changed the modeling from being hypothetical risk assessment work to being about adaptation: What can we do? Prior to Hurricane Sandy, the work was all about trying to illustrate that flooding could happen here and talking about 1821, when the last big hurricane storm surge hit. Once we had Hurricane Sandy, that whole job was done. The big new thing was: How do we adapt and prevent flooding from ruining neighborhoods?

S

How can modeling teach about adaptation? Why are the kinds of coastal flood, storm surge, and inundation modeling you do at the Stevens Institute important?

PO

There's a real dearth of quantitative information on flooding, and what does exist is often simplistic. Take the FEMA results, for example, which when they came out were considered the most detailed, useful new thing. Yet they represent just one set of methods. That's not the only way of estimating flood zones and flood risk. So we can add to that by having our own assessment of flooding risk and running models. And we can also do forecasting of flooding when a storm is coming. Another thing that the federal government doesn't do is tailor information to local governments. They're very good at giving flood mapping or storm surge forecasting for the whole country, but they have to make it uniform. So we've been working

with the Department of City Planning, for example, to put information into a more locally useful language.

S

What made you reach out to SCAPE to begin collaborating with designers?

PO

Right as I was going from studying physical oceanography to thinking about storm surges and flooding, I visited MoMA and saw the *Rising Currents* exhibit. It was very inspiring, in part because there were so many cool ideas out there, but also because it seemed that there wasn't a lot of knowledge of the physics of flooding. So I felt motivated to reach out.

S

Starting with our early conversations over Oyster-tecture, we worked together to develop a design- and science-driven iterative process: designing, testing, modeling, redesigning, and so on. What has that process been like from your end?

PO

You know, at the start our capabilities were very coarse and large-scale. That first year when we worked together—with the student projects—everyone wanted to do small-scale things. It didn't match up quite right. But gradually our models have gotten to a finer scale, and we're now almost at a human-scale resolution where we can model buildings acting as barriers to water and water flowing down a city street. The collaboration process has always worked really well, but our capabilities have gotten a lot more appropriate for working with designers. We're building them up so that we can simulate the ideas designers come up with.

S

Much of the work we've collaborated on is about large-scale techniques for nature-based infrastructure, like wetland development or bathymetric modifications. Can you talk about how modeling informs decision making around nature-based systems?

PO

A big role we've been able to play in the decisions and debates about coastal adaptation is quantifying—really quantifying—some of these systems that people don't know the details of. For example, language is thrown around very loosely suggesting that a wetland fringe in Hoboken or Manhattan that's fifty feet wide or even a few hundred feet wide will help protect the area from flooding. But the best scientific knowledge says you need miles of wetland to reduce flooding by a significant amount of peak. So that's one thing we've done: to try to step in and point out what's unrealistic. But we're also trying to focus everyone's attention on the places where wetlands could reduce flooding, like Jamaic a Bay where there is a ten-kilometer space to work with.

S

During Hurricane Sandy, New York City was revealed to be a more fragile environment than most people expected. As someone who's been modeling and projecting the region's vulnerabilities since long before then, how do you think Sandy changed the conversation around climate resilience?

PO

Hurricane Sandy definitely made people feel that we suddenly were very vulnerable. And we were. But now there is this fear that it's going to happen again very soon, which it could—it's a random chance, you never know. But there's something like a 1–5 percent chance that we'll have a storm in the next six years similar to Hurricane Sandy or worse. Based on what we know, the probability is very low. So I definitely have a concern that people are going to want to put up walls right away to protect themselves from the flood they think could happen any year now, instead of taking more time and having a broader multilayered strategy, like we came up with in Rebuild by Design, that protects us in ways that aren't so simplistic as building levees and walls.

I'm concerned about reproducing what New Orleans did. New Orleans was always vulnerable to flooding, and New Orleans always put up walls. Once they did, the politics of the situation were such that if they got flooded again, they would raise the walls because people said, "Well, you need to protect me!" And the population was always growing, especially after the 1960s. In the 1960s they had a hurricane that overtopped their protections again, and they built the modern levee system. After that they had a big influx of people into neighborhoods that were not sustainable long-term at all—they were not places where people should have moved, as we saw in 2005 with Hurricane Katrina. That system failed, in some cases, and those areas of New Orleans's became very deadly places to be.

Maybe this wouldn't happen exactly that way in New York City, but there is a pattern of human reluctance to evacuate and leave your home, leave your property. That's always there, and if you tell people they're protected that gets exacerbated. There's also the pattern of development in which putting up barriers lets people feel safe and that causes them to move in. But it's a terrible idea to add more people to a neighborhood that's sinking below sea level like New Orleans. A lot of New Orleans is sinking at about three feet per century, which is exactly the situation sea level rise is supposed to create over the next century

everywhere around the world. It's like we're all in New Orleans' place now. And to keep building higher walls every time isn't a very good idea.

S

What's dangerous about levees and walls as flood-protection strategies?

PO

A levee protects you up to a certain flood level, but it has a maximum height. With a levee, you're protected, you're protected, you're fine... but once you get over that flood height, then things completely fall apart: you have rapid flowing of water into a neighborhood because the water level outside is much higher than in the neighborhood, it fills up the neighborhood in a matter of minutes, and people can't get away. That's what happened in New Orleans. A levee's a great example of fragility. With fragile systems, vulnerability increases because people feel safe and so they don't evacuate. That's considered to be a fragile system: one that collapses and makes things more dangerous.

S

The layered approach we developed for Rebuild by Design came largely from our discussions with you about the fragility of the condition of the South Shore of Staten Island. What is the value of a layered approach?

PO

Nassim Talem has put out a concept of the "anti-fragile." The notion is to build resistance to hazards or to variability that bends but doesn't break. That's a really useful way to think about it: how can we have anti-fragility with these protection systems? One way is to have multiple layers, none of which will break at any point. The layers can start at the

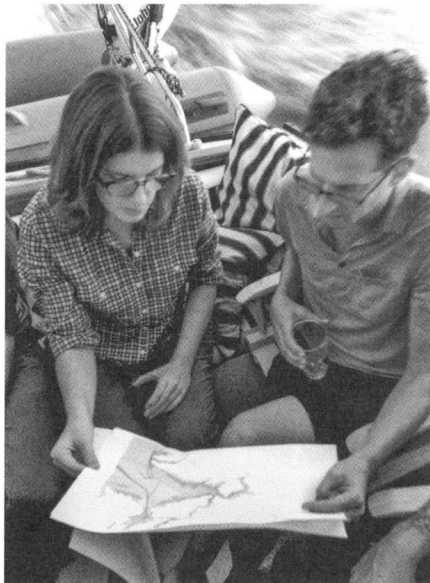

waterfront, reducing waves or flood height, but then they can extend to zoning regulations or community outreach. For example, if people interact more with the waterfront, they understand the fact that the high tide comes every twelve hours. That's something most people in the city didn't know during Sandy, but people in places like Breezy Point understood the ocean better. Nobody died at Breezy Point, and I think that's a factor. So you can have all these different layers of adaptation and protection—none of which says, "You're totally protected," but also none of which has a fragility that will cause it, at some point, to fall apart.

S

What is your hope for the work we're collaborating on now, modeling these different layers in Jamaica Bay?

PO

The number-one approach the city wants to study right now, with the support from a lot of communities, is storm surge barrier systems, which are more like a levee approach. But Jamaica Bay is one of the few places in the New York City area where we could add to that system or even replace those ideas with large natural systems. As I mentioned before, Jamaica Bay is about ten kilometers wide. In prior experiments, as part of the NYC SIRR study and Rebuild by Design, we looked at how wetlands or shallower shipping channels would reduce flooding. We found definite leverage on reducing flooding with these natural approaches.

It's going to be very difficult, I think, to stop the tendency to raise berms and just make them look beautiful—still have a levee that just doesn't look like a levee. So I'm hoping that by focusing on a few places like Staten Island and Jamaica Bay we could demonstrate a different alternative. That's what we're studying with SCAPE. SCAPE is designing different Jamaica Bay topographies and ecosystems such as wetland areas, and then we're modifying our model and running it with the dynamics of the water flows so that we can see how those changes to the landscape reduce flooding.

The past many decades have been all about concrete and steel and rock, but now there is an open door. And if we want to deal with sea level rise in a smarter way, we probably need to follow a different path. If we can plant some seeds and show people what can grow and how things could be different than just vertical walls, maybe these ideas will catch on.

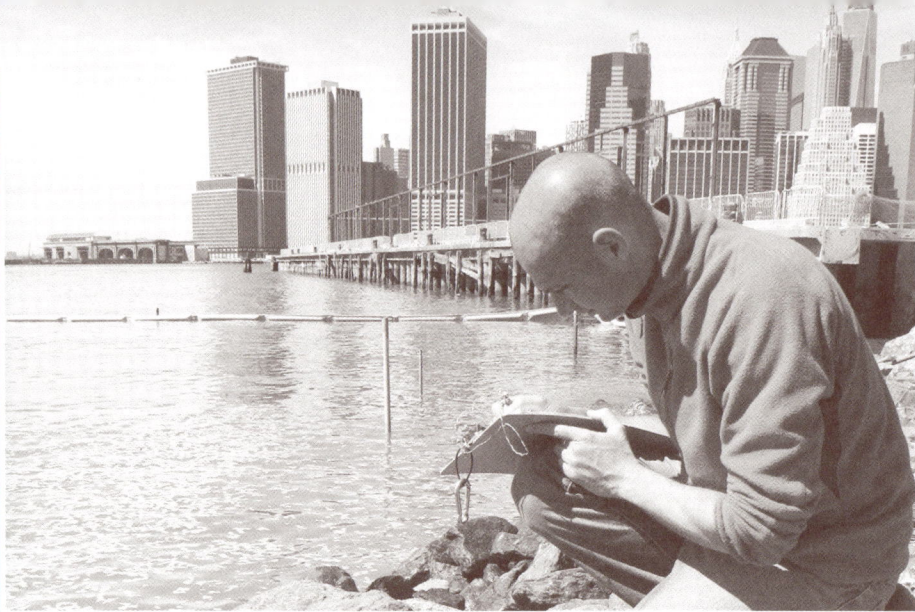

SCAPE

Our practice is inspired by people who can bridge different worlds, and you're bridging industrial fabrication processes with marine biology and scuba diving. How did you and Shimrit get to where you are?

Ido Sella

Shimrit and I are marine biologists. We've been dealing with different aspects of marine infrastructure for twelve years, from artificial reefs to industrial and urban waterfronts. With time we've learned something very straightforward—design affects biology. This is well known: if we increase complexity, we create more habitat and that affects biodiversity on the site. But if you don't do it the right way, you can cause undesirable effects. A lot of infrastructure is made of concrete—something like 60 or 70 percent of worldwide marine infrastructure—and concrete behaves differently from other materials on the water. For example, steel gets covered very quickly with healthy ecology and biology, but concrete is completely different.

S

In that it does not beget life?

IS

It begets life, but the substrate provides qualities that usually don't fit the local species, starting with the very high pH—it's very alkaline. But there are other issues too. If you mix different materials into the concrete, they sometimes leach to the surface and affect the surface of the substrate so that only a low number of species can survive. Then, because there's no competition and no other species is fighting for that same area, those few species spread really fast. So usually what we see on concrete infrastructure is very low biodiversity: the same species covering a lot of space.

S

How did you make that leap from being a marine biologist to being a designer of ECOncrete? Was it a case of seeing the need and developing a different response? Was it through a testing process?

IS

With concrete, it was by mistake. The concept of ECOncrete grew out of our consulting company, SeArc, where Shimrit and I perform ecological surveys and provide ecological services for coastal and marine projects. We conducted a large survey almost four years ago on coastal power plants in the Mediterranean. They have long stretches of seawalls, and we saw that some parts of the seawall were behaving completely differently than others. When we asked, they told us, "Well, it's the same contractor that did the entire seawall. Where you see changes in biology is where we stopped work from one day to the next." Which means: we noted a line on the wall where we saw a shift in the biology, and the only difference was that this area was cast on one day, and that area was cast on a different day. We started thinking that maybe it's these very subtle changes within the concrete that affect biology, so our team experimented. We asked concrete technologists to provide us with different mixes of concrete that fit the requirements for marine construction. They gave us fifteen recipes, and we mixed them and tested them in the lab and in the waters of the Mediterranean and the Red Sea. After a very short time, we noted that six or seven of them behaved much better than the others in terms of growing and recruiting biology. Through a testing process we focused on five different matrices that work well with biology. Some are more cost-effective than others, but all of them can be used in marine construction.

S

What was the next step from there?

IS

Then we wanted to know if we would see changes between different areas—tropical seas, moderate seas, north, south—so we extended the experiment and spread a series of test sites along the East Coast of the U.S. One of them was with you at Sims! So we had one in Florida, one in Georgia, a few around New York, and then going north to the fresh water of the Great Lakes. And we noted that the matrices behave differently in different environments. For example here in New York we have two mixes that work very well for recruiting oysters and increasing biodiversity. They're slightly different than what has worked well elsewhere.

S

A different color? What are the other factors?

IS

We haven't put our finger on it yet. There are a lot of unknowns in what we do. Everything is tested and retested, but sometimes we cannot say why a particular mix is working. If it's working once, twice—even if it's working all the time—we know that this mix promotes biology, but we don't really know why. We try to isolate the different factors. Sometimes we think it's the pH, but for example here in New York we have a mix that is a bit higher in pH and still working very well. So it's a working process. But at the end, after two years of experiments and getting the same results over and over again, we know they work. Now it's just a matter of finding out why—which is a very common situation in science.

S

We learned during Living Breakwaters that the larger New York/New Jersey Harbor lacks much structural habitat for fish. ECOncrete and the reef street concept are designed to be able to serve as this structural habitat, replacing what has been lost over time. Could you explain how the structure affects biodiversity?

IS

When we say it's important to increase complexity, it's not just complexity that affects biodiversity, it's the effect of the complexity that creates the habitat species need. Those reef streets are areas where the velocity of the water is changing, where you have changing micro-currents going in and out because of the design of the structure, and that brings food and oxygen to the reef—creating the right factors for biology. So if we provide the substrate, provide an area that gives species all they require, we can increase biodiversity. It's quite simple in the end. The issue is knowing what the factors are, because if you don't do it

the right way then one species can flourish while the other cannot. We try to achieve a balance in order to get high biodiversity: a lot of species on a very small area. For example in a riprap area, if you use just one size of stone, then you'll get a certain amount of species. If you mix different sizes of stones, then the quantity of species goes up: there are more ecological niches, there are more places for different habitats. If you change the texture of the stone, then you get even more.

S

Understanding the limits of the macro and of the micro has been really instructive for this office as a whole. And now, with the Living Breakwaters project, we'll be testing these concepts in an exciting way, at the scale of what could be conceived as an actual reef. Do you think the Living Breakwaters project is going to teach you some new things?

IS

I'm sure it's going to teach us something new about the biology but also about the incorporation of biological thinking into the design and construction processes. Usually in breakwaters —because they come from the engineers and the engineers are doing their math—

S

Calculating with just the typical 5-ton rock piled up at a certain slope—

IS

Right. If you change the size of the stone or mix in different sizes of stone, then you have already made a great change. But with Living Breakwaters now we're taking the next step and changing the substrate in the macro and the micro, creating some ecological niches within the stones and within the large concrete units. We did an ecological breakwater in Israel— the first large-scale project we did. We took the texture that was tested on six-by-six-inch tiles and we copied it into a structure that is almost fifty tons in the water. And it worked beautifully. Here, from the work we did at Sims and the work we did in other areas in the harbor, we have a lot of knowledge and now it's just taking all the small bits and pieces and putting them together into a project that can show them on a large scale.

S

With the Breakwaters project, we were able to plug into this informal network of people— you, Pete Malinowski, and Philip Orton— formed through research and a shared passion for something. In being so specialized in our expertise nowadays, one of the things we've lost is the ability to see outside of our own fields. But everybody on this team has a very broad lens, and just the action of actually collaborating around one particular study

has been very helpful for us. Has that been an interesting process for you?

IS

We worked quite a lot in the academy with engineers and modelers, but I think what is different in this group is that everyone is focused on the same goal while accepting the others' ideas and vision. Usually when you run a model, the engineers rarely care about the surface and microdesign. They say, "We don't look at the micro, we look at the macro—for this model it's going to be smooth cubes!" I think Philip Orton was the first modeler I ever worked with who noted the micro also. And Pete Malinowski—Pete is a designer, only instead of concrete and steel he works with oyster shells.

S

We really believe that design is about perceiving and understanding, modifying, testing, and advancing ideas, and bringing them out into the world. With this project we're getting to test everybody's design insights at a new scale— and then the next question becomes how to implement them at a large scale.

IS

That is one of the main issues we are working on now: how to create materials that are easy to use for the construction industry. We're putting a lot of effort into this: How do you provide them with steel that is better? How do you provide them with concrete that is as easy to use as ordinary concrete so it's a no-brainer for them—it's just a different mix of compounds. Usually the gap between green infrastructure and ordinary infrastructure is, first of all, cost, and second, methods. The construction industry is very, very conservative, and it doesn't change quickly. But if you change things in a way that doesn't require different working methods—they basically do the same work, with materials that they feel comfortable with, but which have added benefits—then that's the way to get blue-green infrastructure out there.

PUBLIC SEDIMENT
Brian Davis

"People do not just run together and join in a larger mass as do drops of quicksilver..."[1]
—John Dewey

Now more than ever before, landscape is the quintessential public medium. Our time of rapidly shifting climate, migrating populations, and crumbling infrastructure has thrown into relief the uneven and temperamental nature of landscapes, once assumed to be natural, stable, and relatively unchanging. Publics themselves are similar, although rarely considered in this way these days. A public is not a vague, indifferent, undifferentiated mass, nor is it a stand-in for society. Publics are very specific creatures formed in particular and mutable ways around a set of commonly held ideas, issues, or perceived problems.

A public is a community, but not one defined by geography or demographics. Rather, it is constructed through commonly held aspirations, heated debates about ideas, aesthetic experiences, and shared work. The pragmatist philosopher John Dewey defined the public as a form of association that comes into being whenever the effects of a transaction go beyond those parties directly associated.[2] Publics are always being created and destroyed, coming into existence, bringing about changes, and grappling with the issues at hand, then morphing into something new or dissolving entirely. An actual public is always provisional and incomplete, heterogeneous and uneven, yet robust and dynamic, possessing its own agency. And there is no better medium for forming, working with, and strengthening these unique affiliations than landscape.

This insight is at the core of SCAPE's practice. Their ongoing effort to rethink the relationship between people and infrastructure is built on a concern for public landscapes. By emphasizing the potential of landscape to mediate relations between communities and infrastructures, SCAPE's method suggests that it is possible to catalyze new forms of both. In this approach, landscape projects are not merely a solution to a problem but rather, to paraphrase the philosopher William James, *a program for more work*.[3] They are an incitement to reimagine the particular ways in which existing realities might be improved.

MAKING RESTORATION ECOLOGY GEOLOGICAL
In recent decades restoration ecology has become a vital discipline in understanding and reconstructing threatened or degraded landscapes. The sources of the threats are myriad: rising sea levels, legacy contamination from industrial processes, new pests and predators, expansion of major

urban areas, and shrinking municipal funds for maintenance, to name a few. The practice of restoration ecology is founded on the conceit of a stable ecological context and the idea that human intervention has degraded ecosystem health. While this approach has serious limits in a time of rapid climatic changes and intensifying urbanization, it has been an important tool for combating some of these issues and has significantly influenced policy and design in coastal cities.

There is one important process of coastal cities that remains largely unaddressed in restoration ecology efforts, however, and that is dredging. The uplift and transport of accumulated underwater sediments, dredging is a complex environmental and infrastructural practice that is critical in nearly all coastal cities, now even more relevant as the Panama Canal expansion nears completion.[4] Dredging is essential to the maintenance and deepening of ports and shipping channels for navigation; it maintains the function of critical flood control infrastructures and can help in the reconstruction of barrier islands and beach nourishment, as well as in the environmental remediation of industrial sites, including waterways. It is a fundamental practice for cleaning up the messes we've made over the last hundred years while preparing for ever-larger ships and storms in our own century. And it is one of the largest and most regular undertakings of contemporary coastal societies.

It is also a self-perpetuating practice. Dredging usually begets more dredging, since the deepening of channels tends to increase erosive processes that cause even more unwanted accumulation of sediment. This excess sediment has for a long time been thought of as waste—something to be disposed of as cheaply as possible. Just how to deal with the vast amounts of material being pulled from the bottoms of our bays and coastal waterways is a pressing issue right now in geographies from the Great Lakes to Los Angeles to New Orleans.

Yet because it generally takes place below the surface of the water, dredging is rarely considered and barely understood outside of the narrow group of policy wonks and engineers charged with the task. As landscape architecture has adopted and aligned with restoration ecology to take on new projects in coastal conditions, there has been a tendency to favor biology—switchgrass and spawning salmon, sumac trees and nighthawks—over geology. The shaping and molding of geological matter, such as soils, is one of the main preoccupations of landscape architecture when on firm ground. But as soon as it disappears below the surface of the water—the stuff that forms topography and bathymetry, that offers rooting medium and structural substrates, that shifts with storms and winds and tides, that gives shape to shallow bays and deep shipping channels—this stuff is taken as a given, something that can't be effectively manipulated.

INSTRUMENTAL SHALLOWS

The SCAPE team takes aim at this gap with their Rebuild by Design proposals for Barnegat Bay and Jamaica Bay. In these projects, shallow underwater areas are identified as key infrastructural, ecological, and cultural zones. As part of a team that includes local educators and community groups, as well as ecologists and hydrodynamicists, SCAPE locates these areas where they historically and currently exist and analyzes them for performance effects related to culture, ecology, and infrastructure. These shallow areas, made through the simple accretion of excess geological material over time, create conditions that are incredibly productive at a range of scales, from the microorganism to modern infrastructure.

Because of tides, the shallows experience a high rate of nutrient exchange over the course of each day. In addition, more sunlight reaches the seafloor in these shallow areas, and relatively small changes in elevation create a range of coastal typologies including protected pools, brackish marshes, intertidal beaches, and underwater habitat. The result is a variegated, nutrient-and sunlight-rich environment that is ideal for the growth of aquatic microorganisms and vegetation, and subsequently larger organisms such as shellfish, bivalves, and the birds, fish, and humans these attract. The ongoing construction of a varied and rich environment in a way that offers unique experiences to people living in nearby neighborhoods, requiring ongoing inputs of human ingenuity and energy, results in an adaptable and culturally significant landscape infrastructure.

These shallow areas and the organic structures such as plants and reefs that they accrete over time also provide unique protection against sporadic but devastating weather events such as hurricanes. Hydrodynamic modeling by the SCAPE team offers evidence that shallow areas have the potential to dissipate storm surges, lowering wave heights and velocities—meaning that these biologically rich landscapes can serve a supportive and protective function for human inhabitants as well. Unlike an impenetrable wall intended to keep water out in the event of a storm, the shallows, as a strategy, create room for water, acknowledging that flooding will occur, yet in a safe manner. Shallow landscapes tend not to exacerbate adjacencies and instead act as an infrastructure that is affected over longer periods of time. They constitute a robust protection system, not subject to catastrophic failure like the single-line-of-defense strategies currently used. During a storm, they would experience something like an exaggerated version of the tide coming in, thus giving residents time to respond and evacuate.

SHALLOWING INSTRUMENTS

Shallows are watery landscapes perched between city and sea that are both biologically rich and socially significant. Many people are drawn to these places for the food they provide, the recreational opportunities they allow, and the protection they offer. They are not only a historically sound defense strategy against rising seas and stronger storms, they also offer broad habitable zones, areas rich in habitat and aesthetic experiences. This combination of recreational, educational, economical, and infrastructural performance means many of these shallows have been culturally important for a long time. People, plants, animals, and sediments themselves grow literally attached to them.

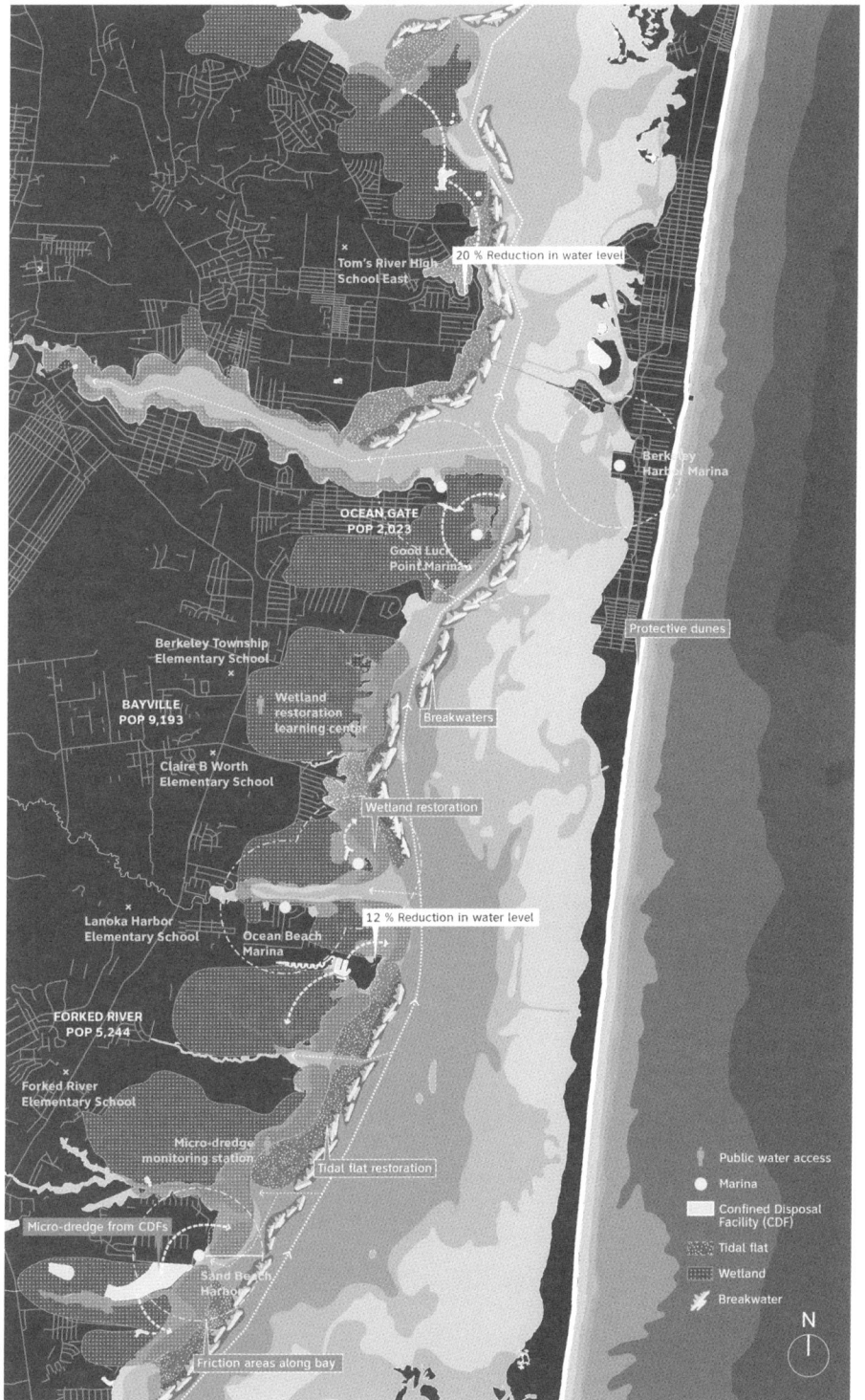

SCAPE's Dredge Wetlands Proposal for Barnegat Bay, New Jersey

The SCAPE team understands the importance and multiple functions of these shallow areas. They identify dredge material from the New York/New Jersey Harbor Deepening Project not as a waste product but as a source material, and they realize a very important potential symbiosis between processes of shallowing and dredging. Shallows need constant inputs of sediment at least as great as the sediment they lose to tides and during storm events over the months and years. Dredging is also a constant process, as it tends to create the need for more dredging. The SCAPE team seizes on this complementarity to propose that the material displacements of dredging might be *localized* and *situated*, creating tight relationships between local dredging sites and shallows through time.

While radical from within the standard logic of dredge, this proposal is familiar to a landscape architectural perspective, where the balancing of cut-and-fill within a given landscape has long been a strategy for negotiating the economical, ecological, and aesthetic demands of a project. The critical step SCAPE takes here is to apply this strategy underwater to similar effect—and to play it out in adaptive ways over long periods of time. Dredging and shallowing don't just occur during a singular moment at the beginning of the project, but rather must repeat in a cyclical way, each time with slight variations and modifications to adapt to changing circumstances and desired outcomes. A heavy rainy season or large storm surge may create a need for more dredging one year while at the same time yielding higher demand for new habitat for bivalves and shorebirds. The maintenance of navigation channels necessary for modern shipping and recreational boating requires ongoing dredging, but by putting to beneficial reuse what was formerly a waste product, dredging also becomes an activity of critical ecological value, and dredged material an important input to be managed in a responsive way.

By thickening the edge between land and sea, SCAPE proposes a wide zone of socially significant and ecologically resilient shallow coastal landscapes that mediate the contradictory dynamics and impulses inherent to coastal cities. This zone is not homogeneous—it is not a long slope stretching from beach to navigation channel, for instance, or a salt marsh all at the same elevation. Instead it consists of many undulations, a crenelated section where intertidal breakwaters and constructed reefs create calm tidal pools, followed by salt marshes and beaches that transition to floodable open spaces supporting maritime forests and shrubland at the edges of protected neighborhoods. This strategy not only reduces the likelihood of flooding and eliminates the possibility of catastrophic disaster, it fundamentally creates more space. The landscape becomes a place where people with particular and varied interests related to the harbor are brought together. Bird enthusiasts, schoolkids, cyclists, and dredge operators form a heterogeneous public with competing and complementary values, skills, interests, and workdays.

For SCAPE, the concept of shallowing becomes *both a method and a strategy*. Locating the shallows is the means of identifying sites, while creating or amplifying the shallows is the design objective. In this way, shallowing becomes pragmatic, or *instrumental*. It is neither simply an end goal nor a means to achieve it. Instead, the project places ends and means on a continuum: the objective also serves as a generative method in a continuing collaboration with the landscape itself. The result is a pragmatic landscape proposal that is not a solution, but a finely tuned plan for more work. It is something to be put into *practice*. This pragmatics of landscape implies an ongoing commitment on the part of all those involved. Designers, politicians, and clients cannot simply build, cut the ribbon, and move on. Each proposal is a protagonist in a scientific process driven by Bayesian inference[5]—spatial practices and their anticipated implications are updated as soon as new things are learned. Pilot projects, which are monitored and modeled, then inform the structure and placement of future iterations.

A WAY TO MAKE PUBLICS AND LANDSCAPES

There is a common attitude in these projects: the design proposal is seen as a collaborative, sophisticated plan for working towards what should be. Viewed in this way, it binds technical experts, high school students, local residents, and birding aficionados together with eelgrass, oyster reefs, sedimentary cycles, and storm surges. Such an approach is uniquely appropriate for public landscapes, which are dynamic and temperamental, cyclical and conflicted, and marked by overlapping boundaries and competing intentions. And it reorients priorities away from knowing the answer toward doing the work. Indeed, the work becomes itself a means of discovering what we want the future to look like. That actual experience of students and technicians and educators and designers collaborating with clams and shorebirds and recycled concrete reefs and tidal currents is what matters. Working towards what should be implies working out the question, not merely the implementation of an answer.

In this context, proposals become more like highly informed, finely tuned hypotheses—responding to new information, constantly subject to testing and evaluation, modification and adaptation through representations and modeled scenarios, as well as pilot projects and prototypes. They are design experiments in their own rights, and in reckoning with the presence and agency of complicating and contingent factors at work in the coastal landscapes of Staten Island, Jamaica Bay, and similar places, they conjure forth an ongoing engagement on the part of all those involved. In other words, they generate publics.

The ability to create specific publics—groups of people oriented around a set of issues and brought together through a specific problem—through landscape infrastructure is one promising way forward as our societies grapple with the need to adapt to changing demographics and shifting environmental and economic baselines. Landscape appears uniquely capable of knitting together publics from a motley assortment of peoples, ecosystems, technologies, and geological forces. The approach is particularly appropriate in the Americas—societies of postcolonial territories defined by pluralism, heterogeneity, and unevenness, marked by conflict and difference, and populated by large urban agglomerations of people with radically different cultural histories and values.

This pragmatics of public landscape embraces the political and environmental nature of infrastructure projects, and their necessity. It approaches their form, function, and location not as an inevitability—the rationalized outcome of positivistic science—but rather as something to take on actively and work out at many different levels of society simultaneously and forever. In this way, it is a method fit for our modern American landscape.

1. John Dewey, *The Public and Its Problems* (University Park: Pennsylvania State University Press, 2012), 45.
2. Ibid.
3. William James, "What Pragmatism Means," in *Pragmatism, A New Name for Some Old Ways of Thinking: Popular Lectures by William James* (New York: Longmans, Green, and Co., 1928), 53.
4. The Dredge Research Collaborative, of which Gena Wirth, design principal at SCAPE, and the author are a part, consists of a group of seven designers and writers investigating sediment handling processes and their effects on contemporary and future society as one of the primary operations of the Anthropocene.

They undertake research, design projects, and organize public events including tours of dredge sites, exhibitions describing and speculating on dredge futures, design workshops, and symposia bringing together members of government, industry, academia, and design together with the public.
5. Bayesian Inference is named for Thomas Bayes and his theorem. It is a method of statistical inference in which initial propositions are updated as new information is acquired. It is an important logical operation in science and engineering. See "Bayes' Theorem," entry in the Stanford Encyclopedia of Philosophy, http://plato.stanford.edu/entries/bayes-theorem/.

Living Breakwaters

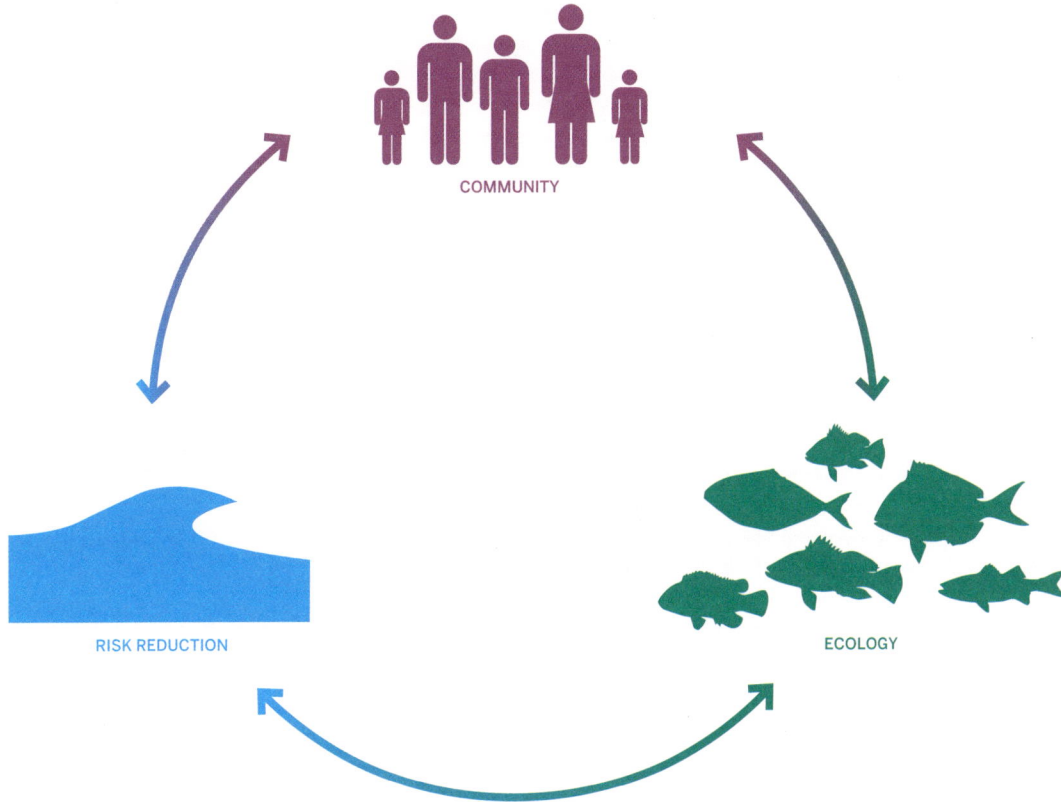

COMMUNITY

RISK REDUCTION

ECOLOGY

REDEFINING COASTAL RESILIENCY

New York City faces a high degree of uncertainty when planning for future storms. Staten Island in particular is vulnerable to climate change threats due to its location directly at the mouth of the New York Bight. Extreme storm events, like hurricanes, and smaller everyday storms erode the shoreline. Even as these systems falter, the Raritan Bay and beach experience remain essential to the identity of Staten Islanders and their livelihoods. The Living Breakwaters project reduces risk, revives ecologies, and connects educators to the shoreline, inspiring a new generation of harbor stewards and a more resilient region over time.

The concept design was developed by the interdisciplinary SCAPE team for the US Department of Housing and Urban Development's Rebuild by Design Initiative, and was one of six winning proposals in the global competition. The proposal was awarded to New

York State and the Phase I Tottenville Reach will be implemented by the Governor's Office of Storm Recovery with $60 million of CDBG-DR funding allocated specifically for this project.

Facing page: Staten Island coastal erosion

The Layered Approach

Living Breakwaters is a proposal to move beyond single-use flood infrastructure, like levee walls, and focus on a layered approach to risk reduction, mitigating the most life-threatening and hazardous elements of a storm while encouraging water access and shoreline regeneration on a daily basis. The project is a replicable system where the infrastructural "unit of change" is multi-purpose—a necklace of wave-attenuating breakwaters that reduce water speeds and slow erosion, designed for maritime habitat regeneration, and connected to onshore neighborhoods through an educational Water Hub and island-wide school engagement. The bird's-eye image at right shows the Living Breakwaters system adapted to the entire South Shore of Staten Island, envisioning a calmer, safer, and more productive relationship with water.

SOUTH RICHMOND
HIGH SCHOOL

PS 6

PS 1

IS 34

SHORELINE
STEWARDSHIP

TOTTENVILLE

COASTAL
MARITIME FOREST
RESTORATION

SHALLOWS
RESTORATION

LIVING
BREAKWATERS

TOTTENVILLE
HIGHSCHOOL

IS 7

PS 3

LEMON CREEK
WATER HUB

NAVIGATION
CHANNEL

TOTTENVILLE
WATER HUB

CULTURE

ECOLOGY

REPLICABLE CROSS SECTION

RISK REDUCTION

Piloting Change

While the entirety of the South Shore of Staten Island is threatened by coastal land loss and erosion, it contains distinct and varied neighborhoods, land uses, and geophysical conditions. Each reach, or stretch, of shoreline requires a unique and adaptive approach. Living Breakwaters proposes a replicable system, where each reach is designed to prioritize different needs of the adjacent community, including waterfront recreation, beach growth, critical ecosystem protection, boat access, and fishing and shellfishing economies.

Phase 1, the Tottenville Reach, enhances recreational use of the shore, builds beaches along the narrow stretch of Conference House Park, and reduces risk in this hard-hit community.

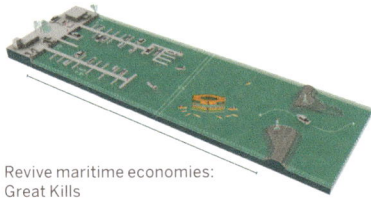

Revive maritime economies:
Great Kills

Enable new edges:
Annadale and Crescent Beach

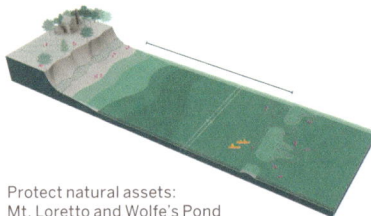

Protect natural assets:
Mt. Loretto and Wolfe's Pond

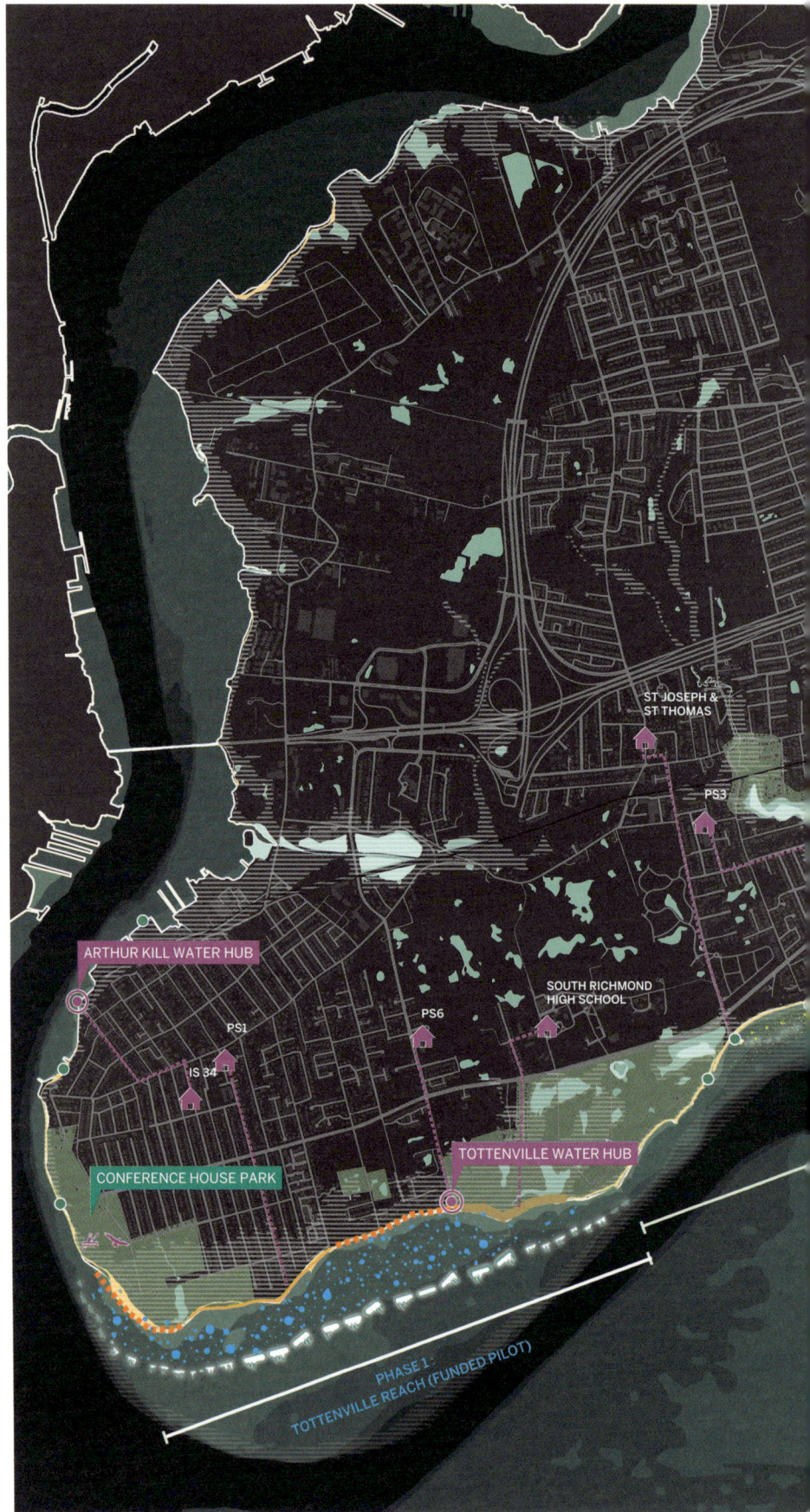

ST JOSEPH &
ST THOMAS

PS3

ARTHUR KILL WATER HUB

PS1

PS6

SOUTH RICHMOND
HIGH SCHOOL

IS 34

CONFERENCE HOUSE PARK

TOTTENVILLE WATER HUB

PHASE 1:
TOTTENVILLE REACH (FUNDED PILOT)

PS53

IS 24

GREAT KILLS WATER HUB

FRANCIS SCHOOL

ST CLARE SCHOOL

CRESCENT BEACH WATER HUB

PS 55

OUR LADY STAR
OF THE SEA

TOTTENVILLE
HIGH SCHOOL

ST JOSEPH BY THE
SEA HIGH SCHOOL

I S7

EMON CREEK WATER HUB

PHASE 2 :
ANNADALE AND CRESCENT BEACH REACH

PHASE 3 :
LEMON CREEK AND WOLFE'S POND REACH

WATER HUBS

SCHOOLS

BREAKWATER TYPE 1

WATERFRONT ACTIVITIES

BEACH GROWTH ZONE

SPAT SANCTUARY

EXISTING SHORELINE UPGRADES

PROPOSED SHORELINE UPGRADES

EDUCATIONAL CONNECTIONS

ACTIVE CLAMMING AREAS

What Do Breakwaters Do?

Conventional coastal infrastructures that "protect" inhabitants by erecting a barrier between people and water, like levees, ultimately sever our visual and physical relationship to the shore and potentially exacerbate the potential for catastrophic failure in the future. Breakwaters reduce risk while increasing awareness of these threats—they do not keep the water out; rather, they slow water, reduce wave action, encourage sedimentation and beach-building, and serve as a visual reminder to the intensity of the ocean. Philip Orton tested the strategy with the ADCIRC/SWAN storm surge and wave modeling system, showing that exposed breakwaters would have reduced wave heights approximately 3–6 feet during Superstorm Sandy.

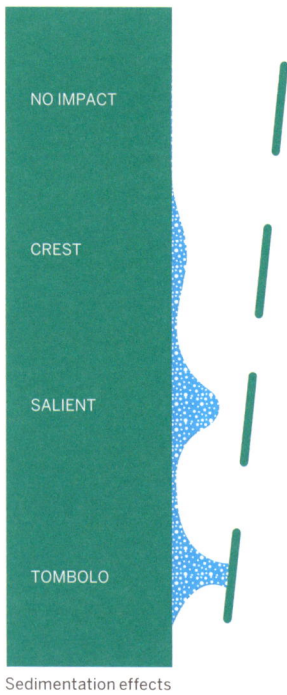

SUBTIDAL BREAKWATER

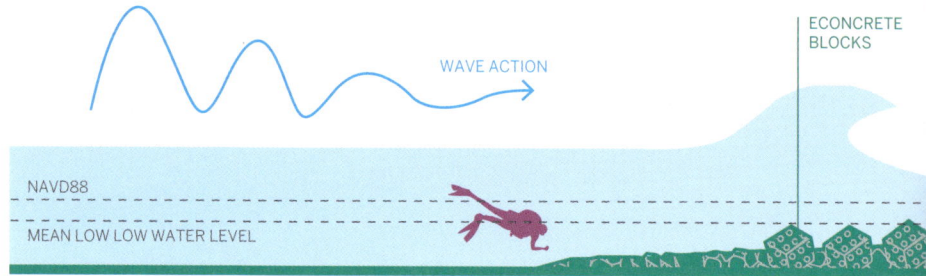

WAVE ACTION

ECONCRETE BLOCKS

NAVD88

MEAN LOW LOW WATER LEVEL

EXPOSED BREAKWATER

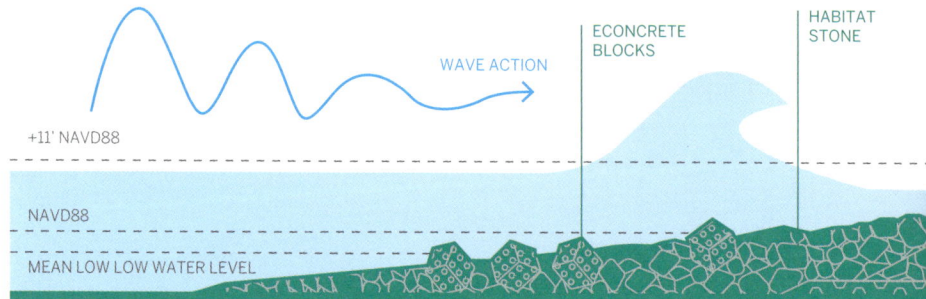

WAVE ACTION

ECONCRETE BLOCKS

HABITAT STONE

+11' NAVD88

NAVD88

MEAN LOW LOW WATER LEVEL

NO IMPACT

CREST

SALIENT

TOMBOLO

Sedimentation effects

SWAN WAVE MODELING OF EXPOSED BREAKWATERS

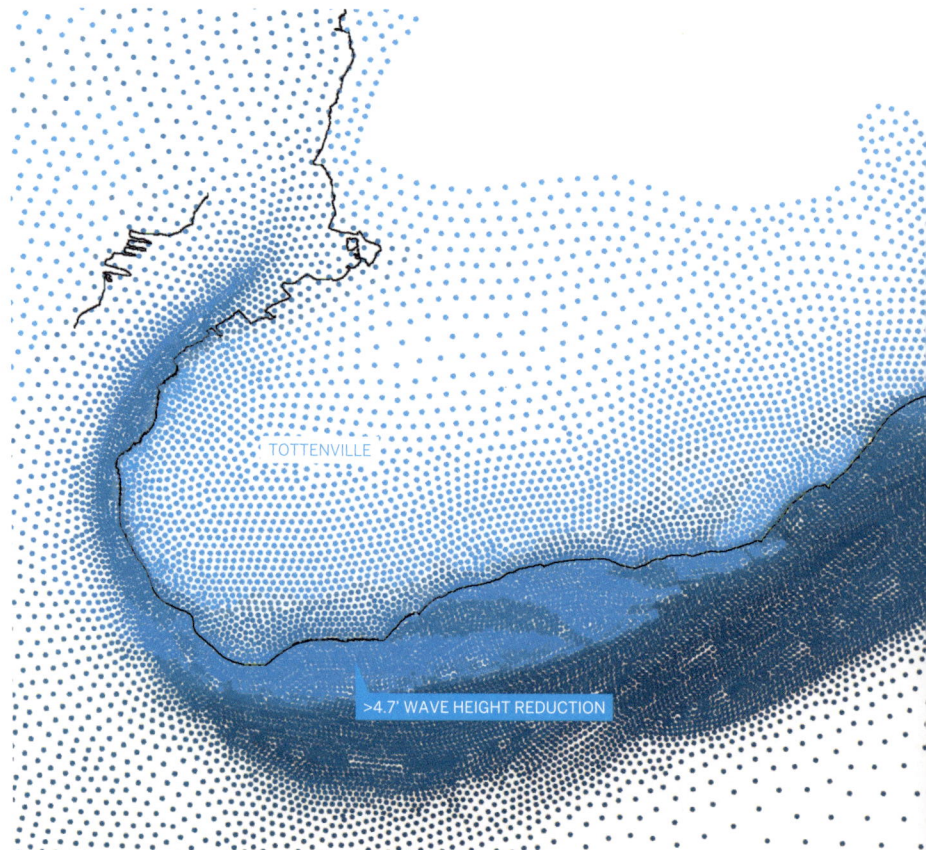

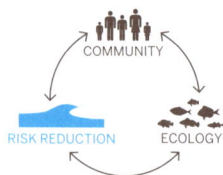

TOTTENVILLE

>4.7' WAVE HEIGHT REDUCTION

COMMUNITY

RISK REDUCTION

ECOLOGY

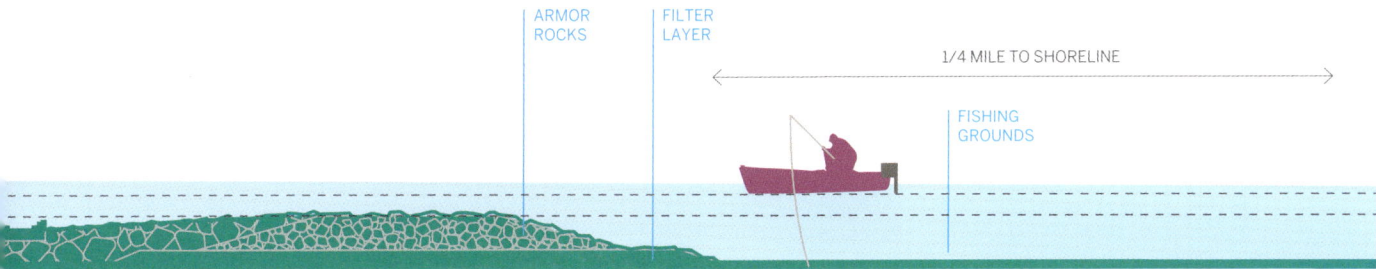

ARMOR ROCKS

FILTER LAYER

1/4 MILE TO SHORELINE

FISHING GROUNDS

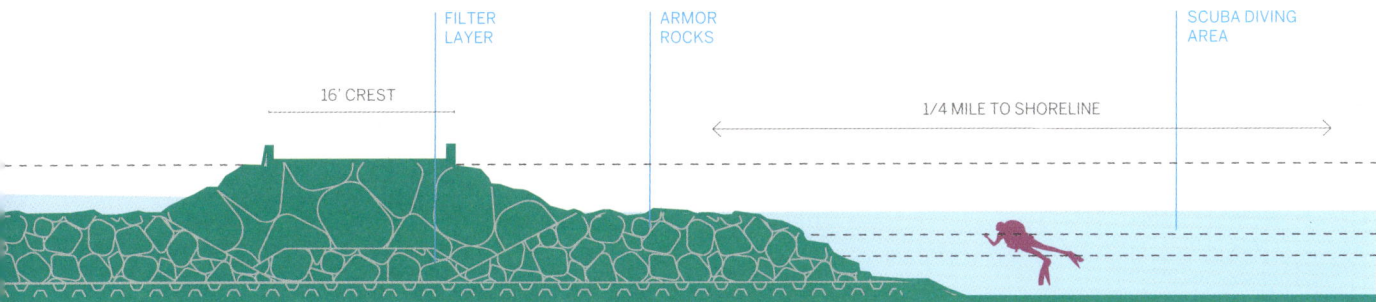

FILTER LAYER

ARMOR ROCKS

SCUBA DIVING AREA

16' CREST

1/4 MILE TO SHORELINE

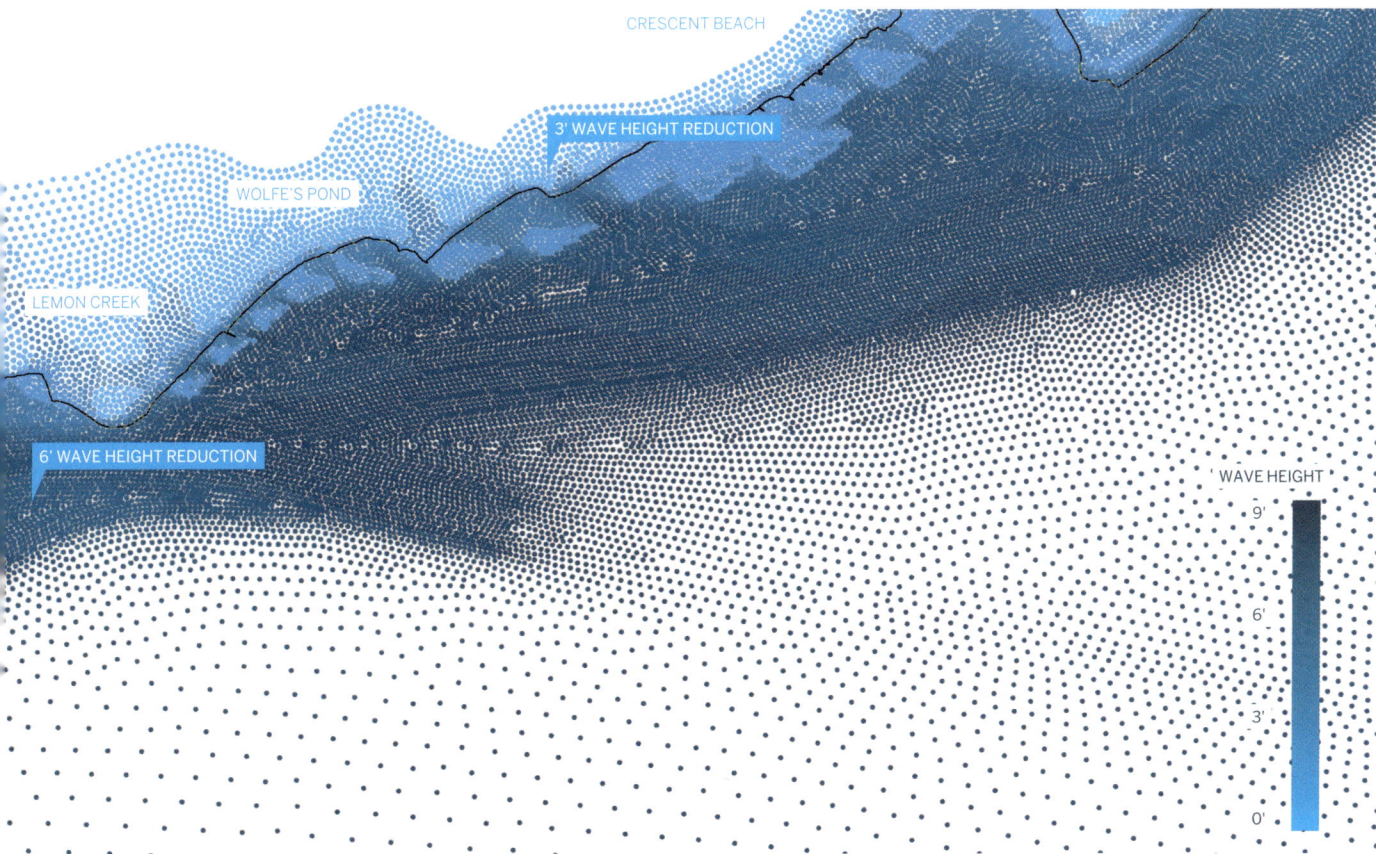

CRESCENT BEACH

3' WAVE HEIGHT REDUCTION

WOLFE'S POND

LEMON CREEK

6' WAVE HEIGHT REDUCTION

WAVE HEIGHT

9'

6'

3'

0'

Feed in the Street

Raritan Bay is prime habitat for juvenile fish which grow to adult size in the bay before venturing out into the Atlantic Ocean. Many of these fish species require rocky habitat and tiny pore spaces for shelter during this vulnerable phase of life. The breakwaters are designed to maximize complexity and habitat for a diversity of species, including finfish, lobsters, and shellfish. Pockets of maximum complexity, called "reef streets," mimic the historic reef habitats of Raritan Bay. Juvenile fish will be able to hide from predators in the extensions of ECOncrete and stone and will feed in the narrow and protected reef streets.

STRIPED BASS LIFE CYCLE

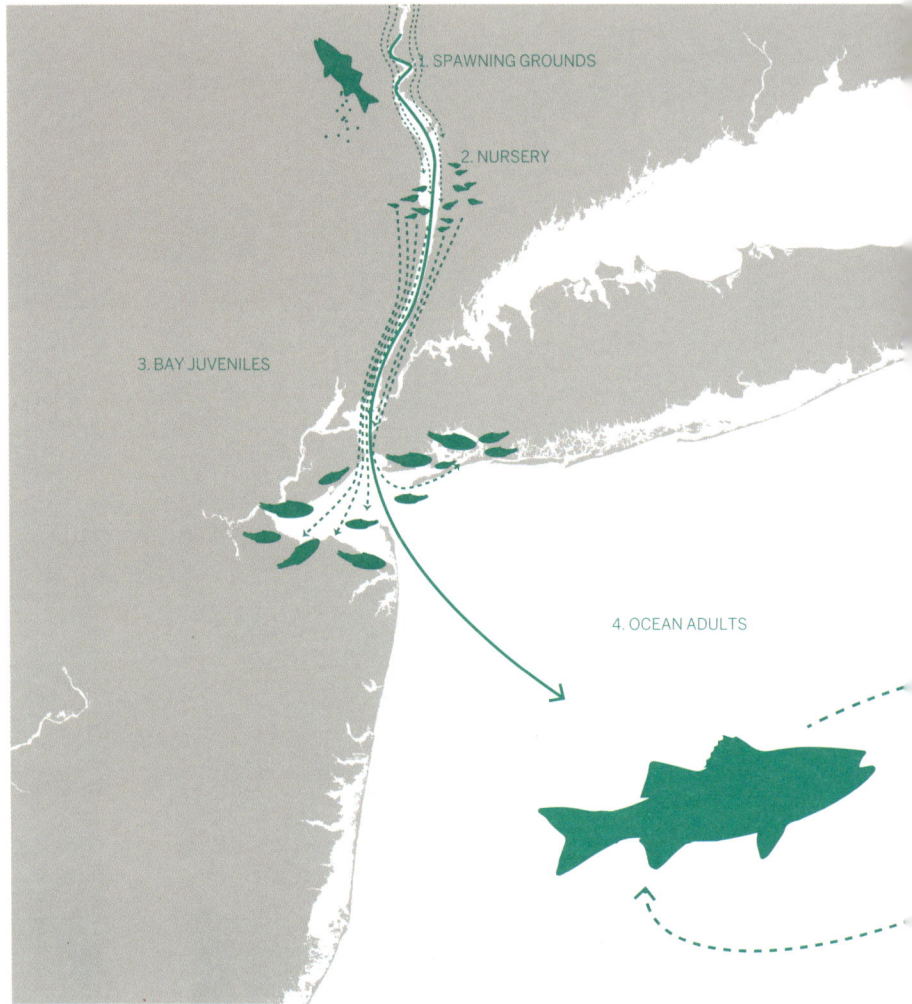

1. SPAWNING GROUNDS

2. NURSERY

3. BAY JUVENILES

4. OCEAN ADULTS

JUVENILE FISH HABITAT

LOBSTER

BLUEFISH

BUTTERFISH

SCUP

BLACK SEA BASS

TAUTOG

JUVENILE SIZE

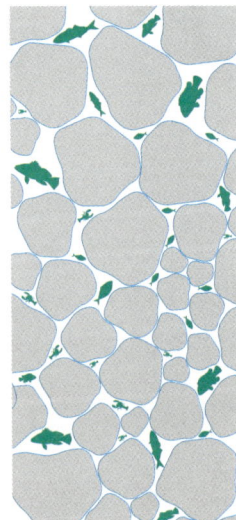

3–10 CM ROCK

20–40 CM ROCK

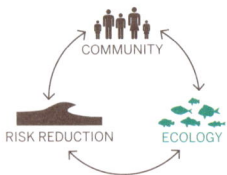

COMMUNITY

RISK REDUCTION   ECOLOGY

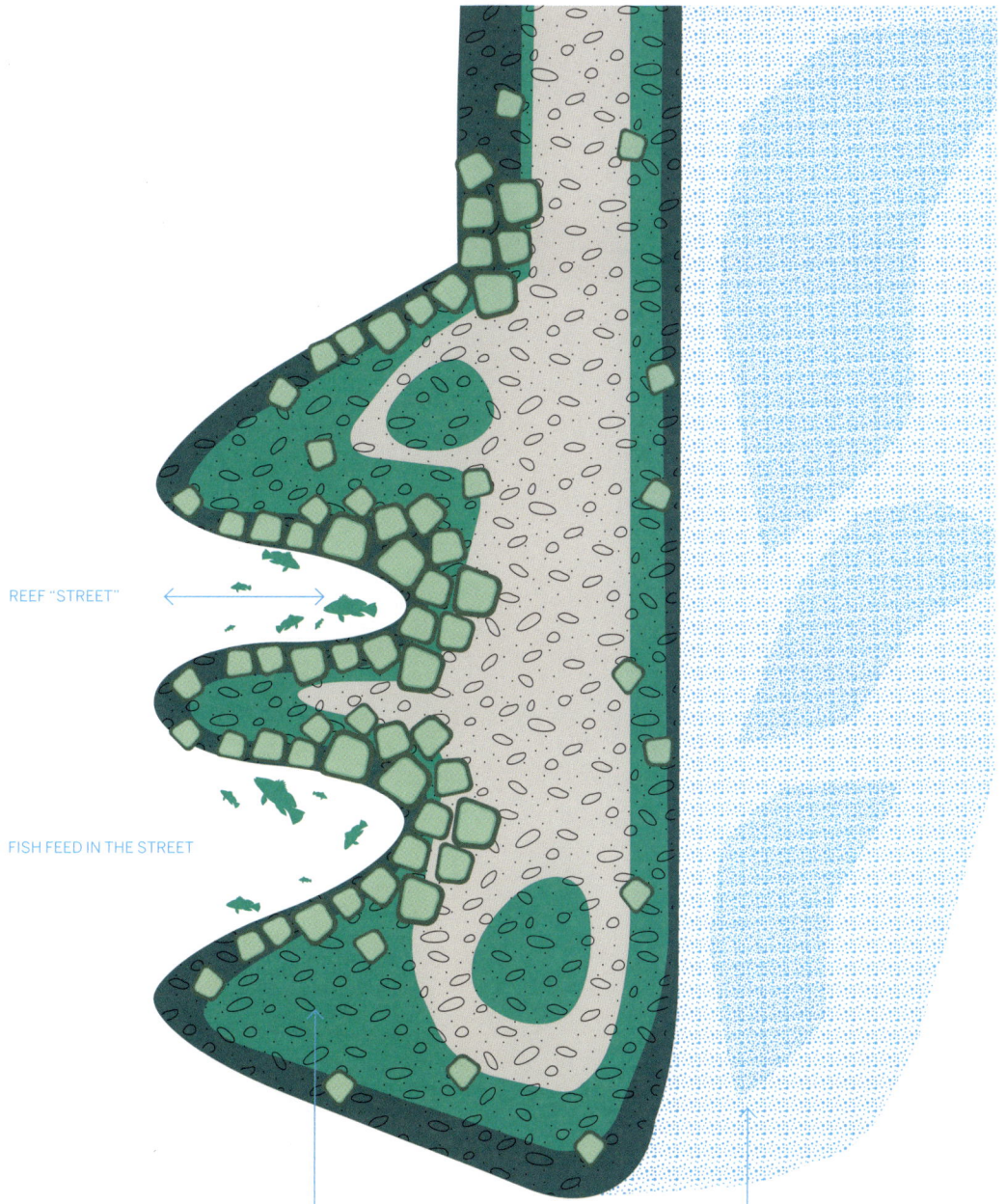

REEF "STREET" ⟷

FISH FEED IN THE STREET

ECONCRETE UNITS
CONCENTRATE AT "STREETS"
AND IN INTERTIDAL AND
SUBTIDAL ZONE

SEDIMENTATION ZONE
PROVIDES HABITAT FOR HARD
CLAMS, EELGRASS, SALT
MARSH DEPENDENT UPON
RATE OF SEDIMENTATION

SEDIMENT

STONE

ECONCRETE UNITS

OYSTER REEF

Breakwaters are designed to avoid critical habitat and integrate micro-complexity for a diversity of species. Living Breakwaters provides habitat throughout the water column, from subtidal structure to upland islands. Underwater, small-scale reef streets are incorporated into the breakwater and provide foraging and shelter for juvenile fish. Above water, the breakwaters can host harbor seals and nesting birds, again providing habitat away from predators. Other species, such as muddy bottom-loving eelgrass and hard clams, thrive in lightly sedimented zones in the lee of the breakwater.

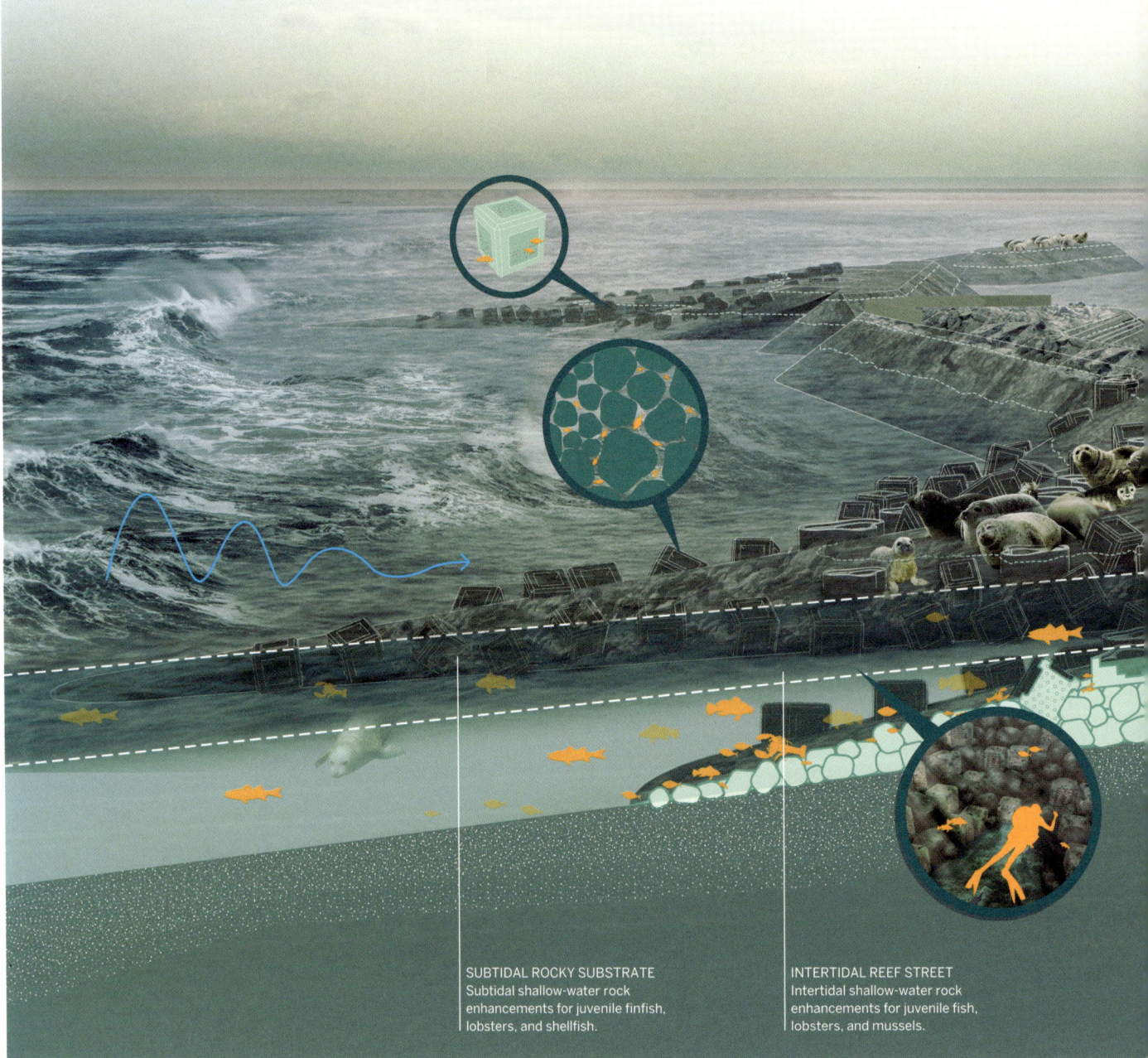

SUBTIDAL ROCKY SUBSTRATE
Subtidal shallow-water rock enhancements for juvenile finfish, lobsters, and shellfish.

INTERTIDAL REEF STREET
Intertidal shallow-water rock enhancements for juvenile fish, lobsters, and mussels.

1. TYPICAL
BREAKWATER

2. MODIFY FORM TO AVOID
CRITICAL HABITAT

3. MODIFY FORM FOR
LOCALIZED, MICRO-SCALE
COMPLEXITY

4. LOCATE HARD STRUCTURE
COMPLEXITY ON WAVE-WARD SIDE
TO PRESERVE PORE SPACE

WAVES

UPLAND ISLAND
Exposed island habitat free from
predators. Used by harbor seals
and colony nesting birds.

MUDFLATS
Zones of moderate sedimentation
create habitat for hard clams,
benthic fish, and eelgrass.

Oysters Past and Present

Reefs and leased oyster beds once extended across the shallow-water flats of Raritan Bay, reducing storm impacts and filtering water. Historic images show fishermen tonging for oysters in leased beds along the coast of Mt. Loretto and Lemon Creek, once a critical economy of the South Shore. Over time, shellfish populations declined due to sedimentation, water contamination, and channel dredging, though efforts are underway to restore this keystone species to the harbor. Oysters are ecosystem engineers, but they are also an educational tool—enthusiasm for oyster restoration has never been higher.

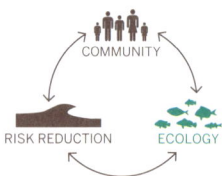

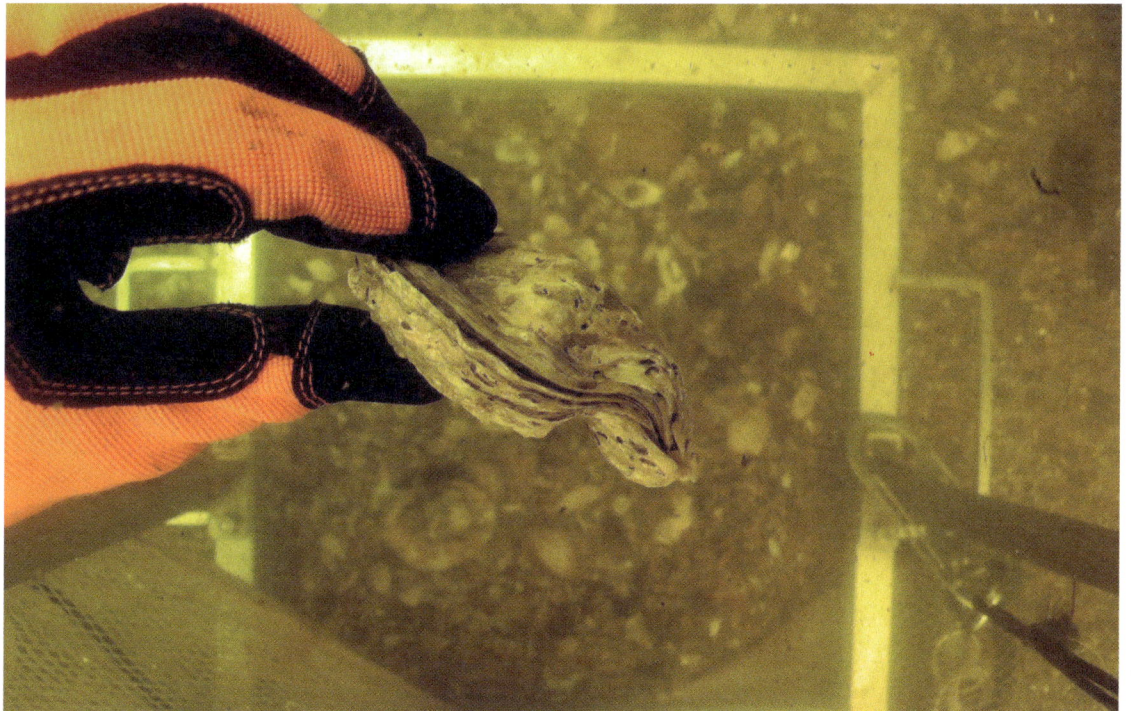

A Sanctuary for Spat

A rejuvenated oyster population would help strengthen the reef system, adapt to climate change and sea level rise over time, and filter nutrients out of the water. The breakwaters are a shoreline-scale experiment to test multiple types of restoration techniques, proven and experimental. In New York City, oysters are considered an attractive nuisance, as the harbor water is contaminated by sewage discharges and oysters are not safe for consumption. To prevent the illegal harvest of oysters, surveillance strategies are designed in tandem with restoration techniques.

ECOncrete units set with oyster spat will catalyze oyster reef development through time. ECOncrete is a new material developed by our partners at SeArc Consulting that enhances underwater biological recruitment through surface texture, concrete composition, and macro-scale design. As oysters grow, they biogenically build calcium carbonate deposits, strengthening and extending the lifespan of the man-made infrastructure.

Oyster restoration suitability in Raritan Bay

ECOncrete armoring unit with macro and micro texture

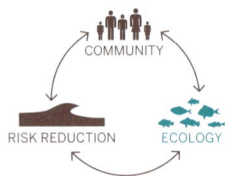

COMMUNITY

RISK REDUCTION   ECOLOGY

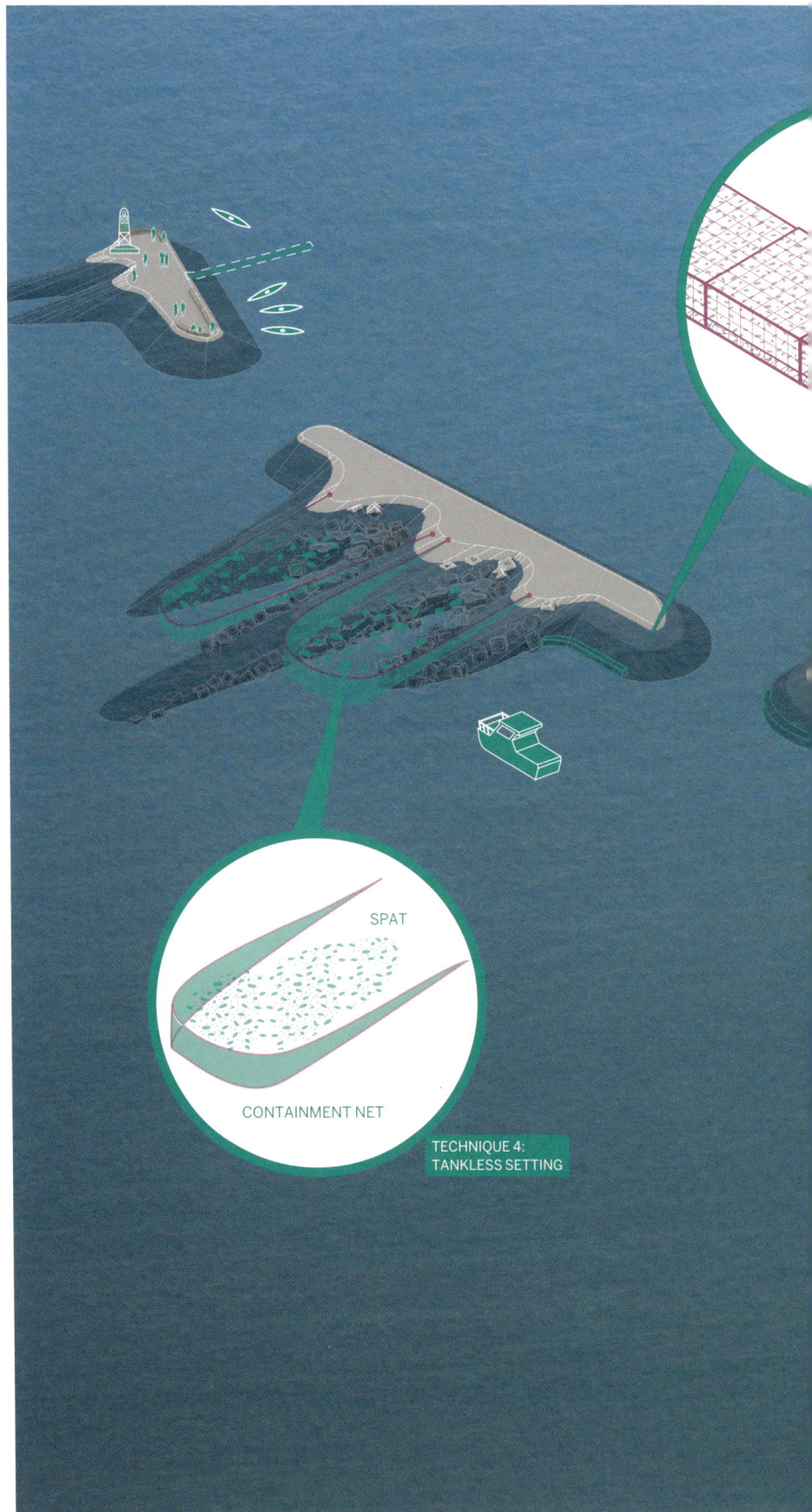

SPAT

CONTAINMENT NET

TECHNIQUE 4:
TANKLESS SETTING

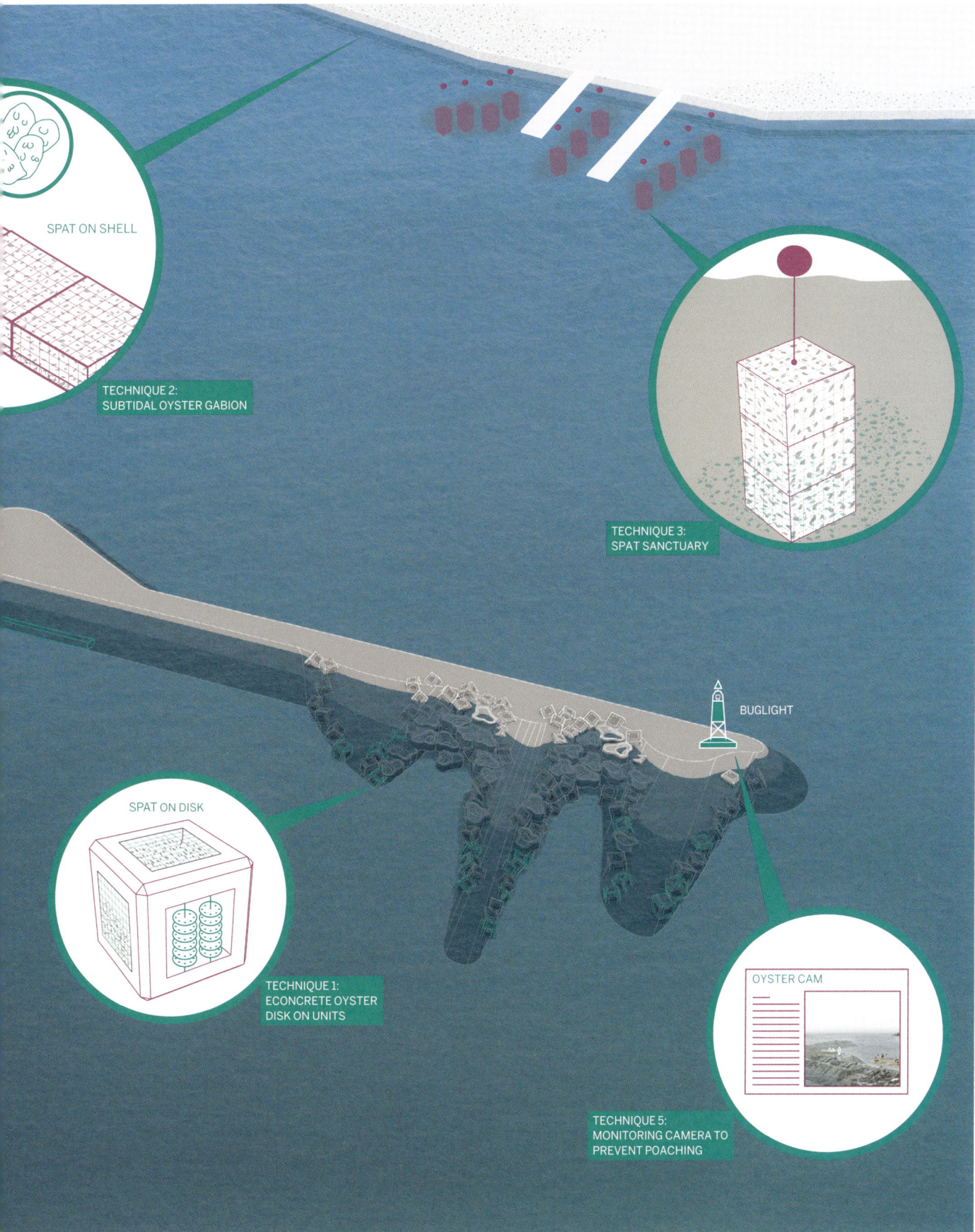

SPAT ON SHELL

TECHNIQUE 2:
SUBTIDAL OYSTER GABION

TECHNIQUE 3:
SPAT SANCTUARY

BUGLIGHT

SPAT ON DISK

TECHNIQUE 1:
ECONCRETE OYSTER
DISK ON UNITS

OYSTER CAM

TECHNIQUE 5:
MONITORING CAMERA TO
PREVENT POACHING

The Harbor as Classroom

The Billion Oyster Project is a long-term initiative linked to this proposal to restore one billion live oysters to New York Harbor and train thousands of young people to restore the ecology and economy of New York Harbor. As a first, actionable step, the team created an Oyster Gardening Manual to help schools use the shoreline as a classroom. With the help of the Billion Oyster Project and the New York Harbor School, multiple schools in Staten Island are using the manual to monitor oyster survival, health, and growth rate throughout the project area. The manual is a free and widely distributed pamphlet that extends the project's influence far beyond its physical extents.

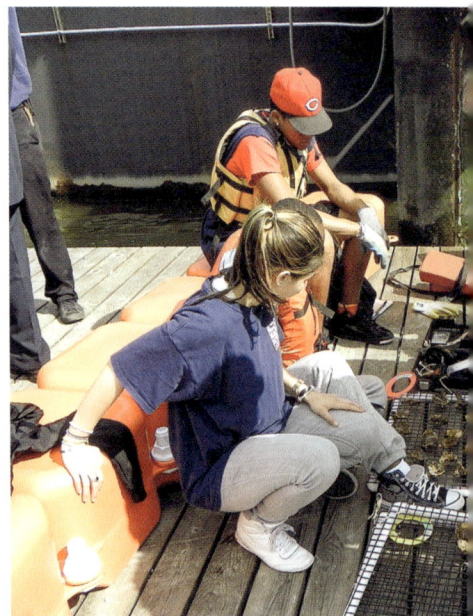

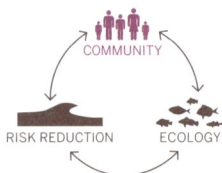

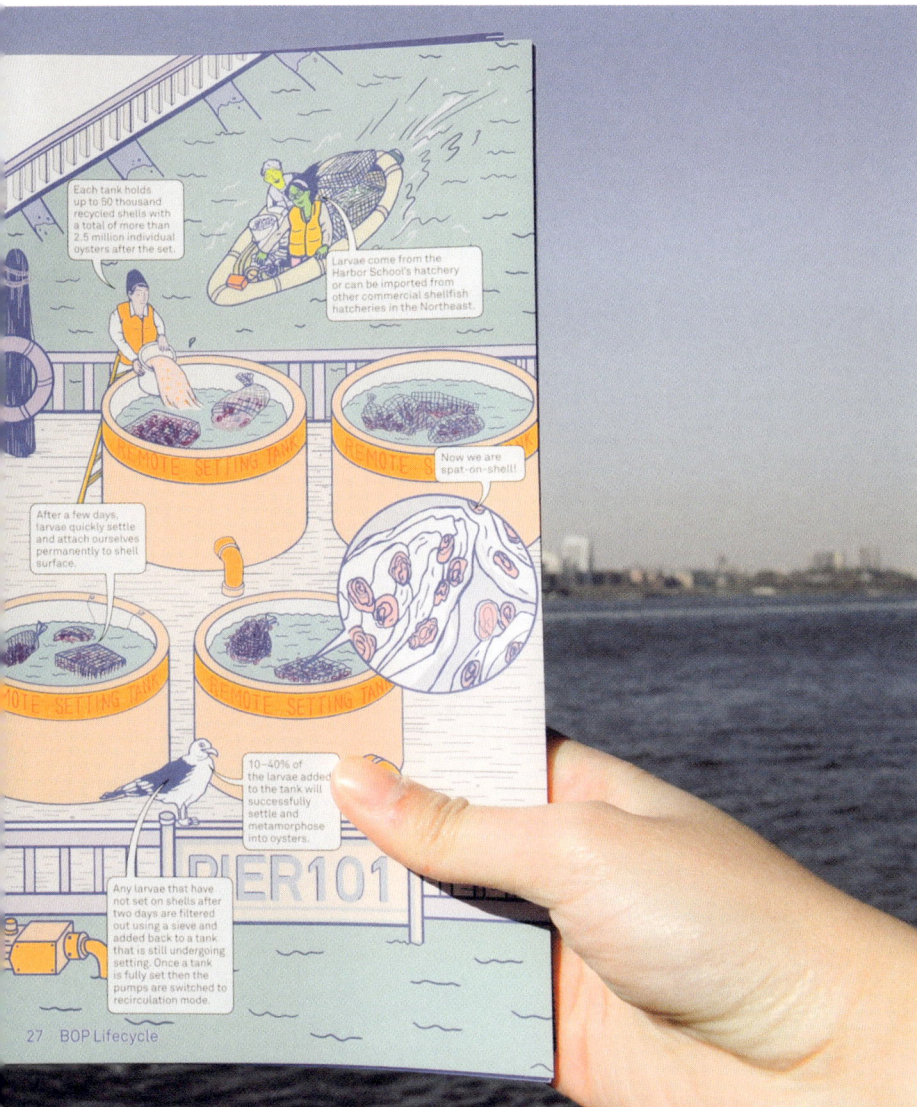

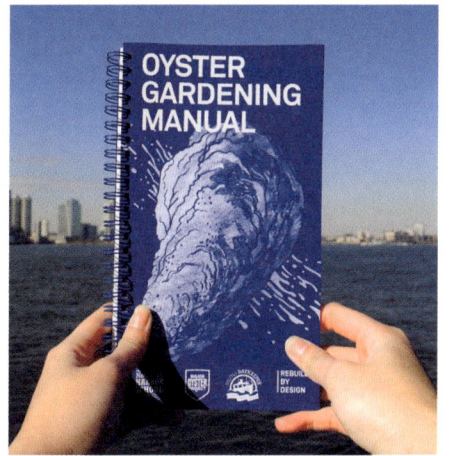

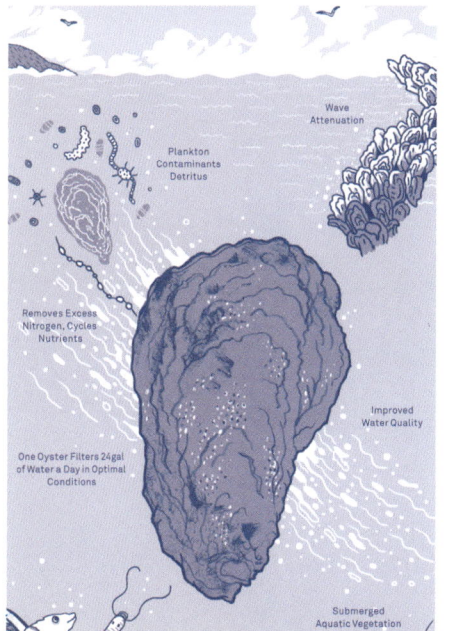

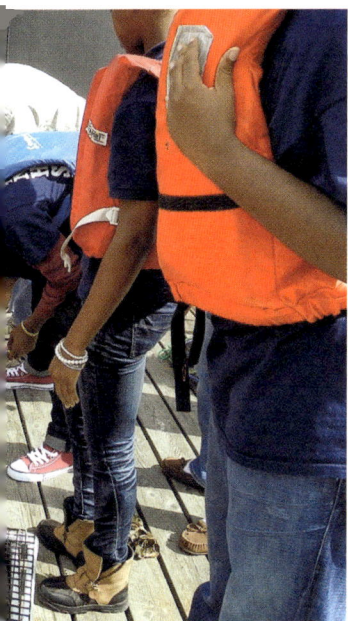

Building Social Resiliency

Living Breakwaters proposed a network of visible and programmed physical outdoor education spaces, called Water Hubs, which will create shoreline sites for outdoor classes, hands-on science-based education, and maritime skill-building. Water Hubs are also for local residents, and will be developed through community-design charrettes, through which needs are identified and incorporated into the structures. Each site condition and community need necessitates a different type of hub—embedded, floating, cantilevered, or elevated—and will be placed in relation to fitting community and natural resources.

Programming the Hub

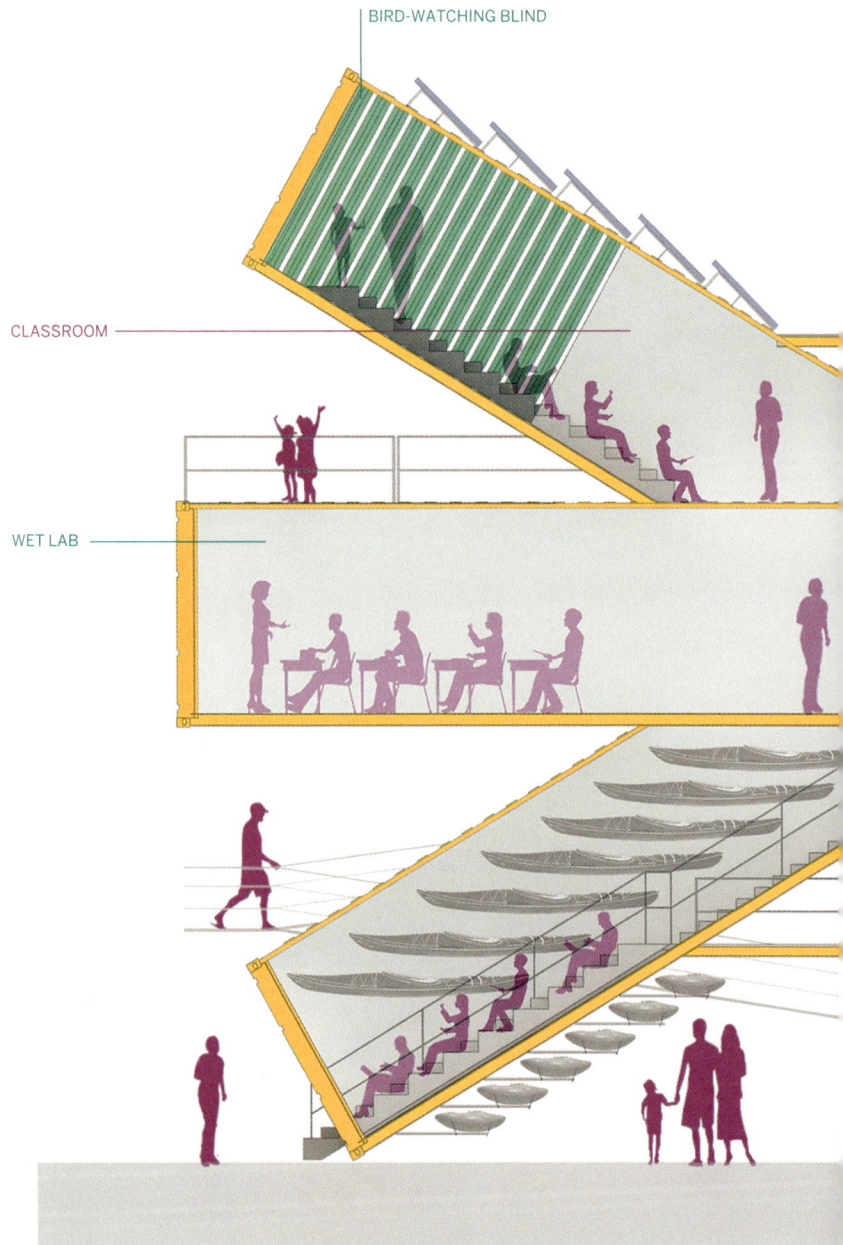

BIRD-WATCHING BLIND

CLASSROOM

WET LAB

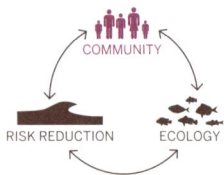

COMMUNITY

RISK REDUCTION

ECOLOGY

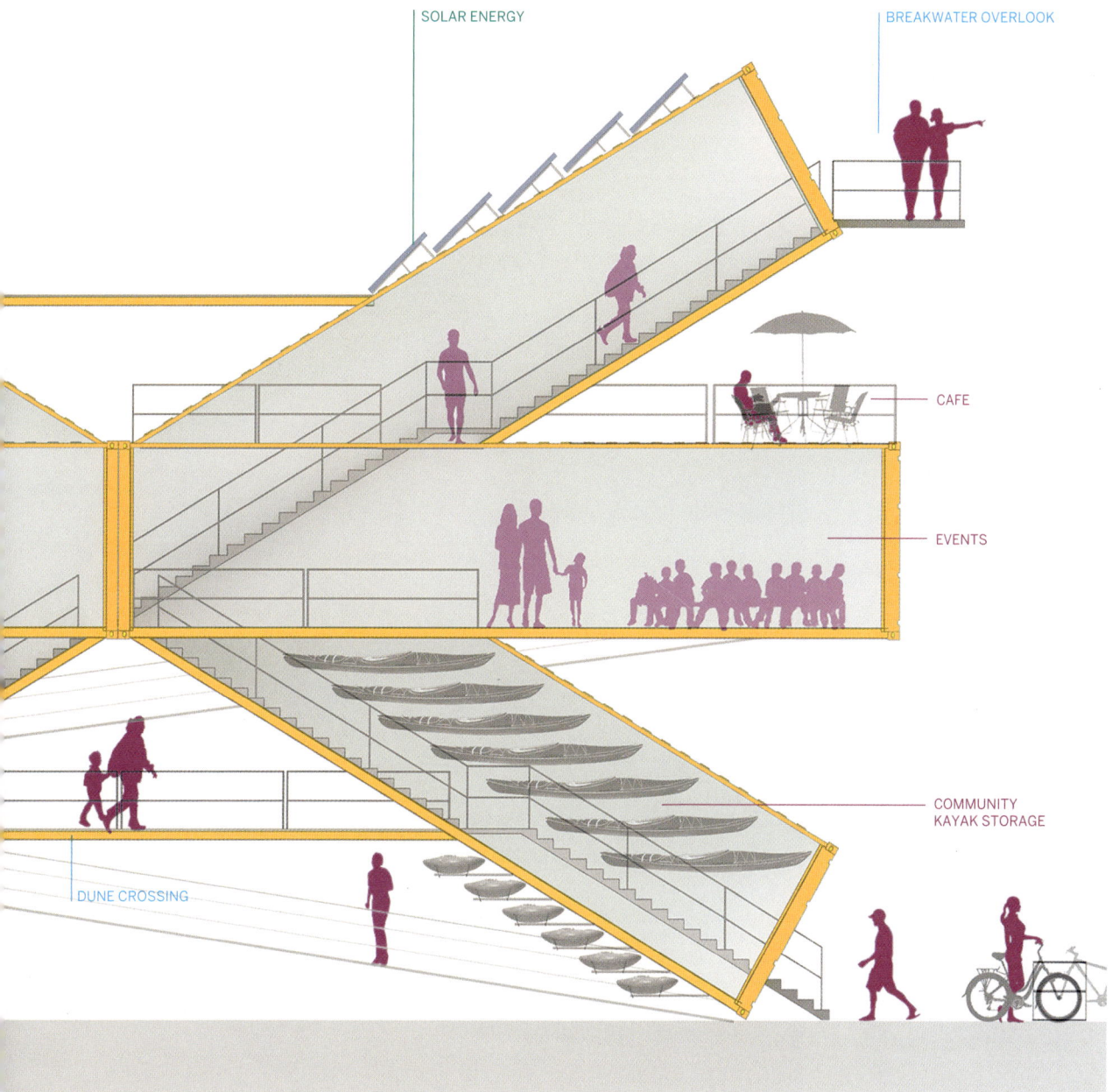

SOLAR ENERGY

BREAKWATER OVERLOOK

CAFE

EVENTS

COMMUNITY
KAYAK STORAGE

DUNE CROSSING

Future of the South Shore

Living Breakwaters is pictured at right in its proposed pilot location in Tottenville, Staten Island. Offshore breakwaters have the power to rebuild beaches and catalyze reef ecosystems, creating slower and calmer water for recreation behind. On shore, community-designed Water Hubs will provide a physical and perceptual link to the shore, creating a venue for water education and shore stewardship. Social, ecological, and physical resiliency are considered as equally critical elements of contemporary coastal infrastructure.

Continued Engagement

Living Breakwaters is equal parts design strategy and community conversation. Throughout the development of the project, the SCAPE team worked with neighbors, clammers, educators, community advocates, and shoreline users to revise and develop the hybrid system. A unique range of pedagogical tools were developed—including graphics, shore tours, charrette sessions, and models—to move past potential reactive "not-in-my-backyard" conversations and toward establishing a collective future vision. Particular attention went towards developing design and outreach tools for youth, as Staten Island's children will be responsible for breakwater and shoreline stewardship of the future.

Acknowledgments

I am grateful to the talented and dedicated people who have contributed to the SCAPE office in so many ways over the years and made "work" playful and meaningful. Special thanks to Elena Brescia, FASLA, committed partner in the office since 2007, and an amazing leadership group including Pippa Brashear, John Donnelly, Alexis Landes, Lanie McKinnon, and Gena Wirth, among other rising stars at SCAPE. Our office is interdisciplinary, with a mix of landscape architects, planners, and urban designers. The dynamism of this book is reflective of the multiple voices of many collaborators from within and outside the office walls. We strive to find the right mix of paying projects, intellectual tangents, built work, and speculative design problems on practically a daily basis.

We are proud to be a part of a wide community of architects, landscape architects, and academic colleagues, and our work has been sharpened by productive dialogue with many practitioners and cultural groups in New York, such as the Architectural League, the NY ASLA, Rebuild By Design (especially former HUD Secretary Shaun Donovan, Henk Ovink, and Scott Davis), the Regional Plan Association, The Hudson River Foundation, NY/NJ Baykeepers, the Fine Arts Federation, and Van Alen Institute. A Francie Bishop Good and David Horvitz Fellowship from United States Artists is gratefully acknowledged–it enabled financial recovery from *Petrochemical America* and renewed focus on this book. Critical support in the form of awards from the Buckminster Fuller Institute and The American Academy of Arts and Letters is appreciated.

I am grateful for the friendship of many colleagues at Columbia University including Kenneth Frampton, whose 1995 article sparked the title for this book, Dean Amale Andraos, and the Architecture and Urban Design faculty for constructive conversations over the many years. Linda Pollak, Scheri Fultineer, and Jeanann Pannasch provided helpful feedback and comments on early drafts of this endeavor.

Special and sustained thanks to the "book team": Glen Cummings, Aliza Dzik, Sarah Dunham, and Michela Povoleri at MTWTF Graphic Design, and Gena Wirth, Lauren Elachi, Alexis Canter Landes, Nans Voron, Renata Robles, Sara Jacobs, and Anya Kaplan-Seem at SCAPE who helped push the book's themes, structure, and visual identity forward. We were fortunate to work with editors Alan Rapp and Stacee Lawrence and are grateful that the Monacelli Press believed in us enough to let this manifestograph come into being.

Kate Orff
New York City, 2015

Contributors

KATE ORFF is a registered landscape architect and the founder of SCAPE/LANDSCAPE ARCHITECTURE. She is also an associate professor at Columbia University and the director of the Urban Design Program at the Graduate School of Architecture, Planning and Preservation. She lives in Forest Hills, New York, with her husband and two children.

BART CHEZAR was a research and development engineer and manager of electric transportation at the New York Power Authority for most of his professional career. Since retiring in 2002, he has initiated ecological restoration projects around New York City and collaborated with community and environmental organizations, schools, private companies, and volunteers. He was awarded an Environmental Quality Award by the United States Environmental Protection Agency in 2014 in recognition of his environmental stewardship efforts.

BRIAN DAVIS is an assistant professor of landscape architecture at Cornell University and has practiced in Raleigh, Buenos Aires, and New York City. His research and teaching looks at the relationship between landscapes and instruments, specifically focusing on urban rivers and watersheds, and emphasizes historical and theoretical relationships between landscapes throughout the Americas.

JIM GRAY is currently in his second term as mayor of Lexington, Kentucky, a vibrant university city surrounded by rolling bluegrass pasture and world-famous horse farms. As the former CEO of Gray Inc., an international engineering and construction firm, he has brought an executive's approach to the city government and is committed to building Lexington into a great American city through sustainable urban development. Mayor Gray received a BA from Vanderbilt University and, in 1996, was appointed a Loeb fellow at Harvard University's Graduate School of Design. He is also a graduate of the Mayors' Institute on City Design, which prepares mayors to serve as the chief urban designers of their cities.

HANS HESSELEIN served as executive director of the Gowanus Canal Conservancy, where he worked for three and a half years on projects involving environmental and ecological restoration of Brooklyn's coolest Superfund site. While at the Conservancy, Hans was responsible for developing and managing green infrastructure projects, watershed planning initiatives and volunteer stewardship programs. Hans received a BA in landscape architecture from North Carolina State University in 2004.

JANE HUTTON is a landscape architect and assistant professor in the department of Landscape Architecture at the Harvard Graduate School of Design. She is co-director of the Energy, Environments, and Design research lab and faculty director of the Loeb Library Materials Collection. Her work focuses on the extended relationships of material practice in landscape architecture, looking at links between the landscapes of production and consumption of common construction materials. Hutton is a founding editor of the journal *Scapegoat: Architecture, Landscape, Political Economy* and has co-edited several issues: 01 Service, 02 Materialism, and 06 Mexico D.F./NAFTA.

ERIC KLINENBERG is professor of sociology and director of the Institute for Public Knowledge at New York University. He is the author of *Going Solo: The Extraordinary Rise and Surprising Appeal of Living Alone* (Penguin Press, 2012), *Fighting for Air: The Battle to Control America's Media* (Metropolitan Books, 2007), and *Heat Wave: A Social Autopsy of Disaster in Chicago* (University of Chicago Press, 2002), as well as the editor, with Claudio Benzecry, of the Cultural Production in a Digital Age special issue of *The Annals of the American Academy of Political and Social Science* (January 2005) and of the journal *Public Culture*. Eric was director of research and a juror for the Rebuild By Design competition.

PETE MALINOWSKI grew up farming oysters with his parents and siblings on the Fishers Island Oyster Farm. His passion for the environment and education led him to The New York Harbor School where he founded the school's Aquaculture and Oyster Restoration Programs and spent five years as a teacher. Pete is now the director of the Billion Oyster Project and continues to work with Harbor School staff and students growing oysters and restoring them to reef sites around New York Harbor.

DR. PHILIP ORTON is a research assistant professor at the Stevens Institute of Technology in Hoboken, NJ, and specializes in coastal physical oceanography and storm surges. He holds a PhD in physical oceanography from Columbia University and has published over twenty articles in peer-reviewed journals, as well as three op-eds on climate change, coastal ecosystem health and coastal flooding in the *New York Times*. He is a technical team member of the NYC Panel on Climate Change (NPCC), and recently worked on NYC's Special Initiative on Rebuilding and Resilience after Superstorm Sandy.

EMILY ELIZA SCOTT is an interdisciplinary scholar focused on art and design practices that engage pressing ecological and/or geopolitical issues, often with the intent to actively transform real-world conditions. Currently a postdoctoral fellow in the architecture department at ETH Zürich, she co-edited with Kirsten Swenson *Critical Landscapes: Art, Space, Politics* (UC Press, 2015), and has contributed to *Art Journal, American Art, Third Text, Cultural Geographies*, and *Social Text*, as well as multiple edited volumes. She is a founding member of World of Matter (2011–),and the LA Urban Rangers (2004–). Before entering academia, she was a National Park Service ranger in Utah and Alaska.

DR. IDO SELLA, along with Dr. Shimrit Perkol-Finkel, is the co-founder and CEO of SeArc-Ecological Marine Consulting, and co-founder of ECOncrete Tech LTD. He is responsible for a number of biological inventions, and has over ten years of experience in the field of marine ecology, biomechanics, and life-history traits of marine invertebrates. He has a worldwide scientific experience, and led onshore and offshore projects in both temperate and tropical environments, such as the South China Sea, the Mediterranean Sea, and the Indian and Atlantic Oceans.

DR. THAÏSA WAY is an urban landscape historian teaching history, theory, and design at the University of Washington, Seattle. Her book *Unbounded Practices: Women, Landscape Architecture, and Early Twentieth Century Design* (University of Virginia Press, 2009) was awarded the J.B. Jackson Book Award. Other more recent books include the co-edited work with Ken Yocom, Ben Spencer, and Jeff Hou, *Now Urbanism: The Future City is Here* (Routledge, 2014) and *The Landscape Architecture of Richard Haag: From Modern Space to Urban Ecological Design* (University of Washington Press, 2015). She is currently finishing the monograph, *Landscape Architect A.E. Bye: Sculpting the Earth* (Modern Landscape Design Series, LALH & Norton). Dr. Way is a senior fellow at the Dumbarton Oaks Garden, Landscape Studies and is executive director of Urban@UW, an initiative of the University of Washington's Office of Research and CoMotion.

Current Staff

Kate Orff
Elena Brescia
Chris Barnes
Pippa Brashear
Ian Brennick
John Donnelly
Lauren Elachi
David Hanrahan
Martin Harwood
Kate Hayes
Brad Howe
Alexis Canter Landes
Michy McCreary
Lanie McKinnon
Marianna Mihalik
Gena Morgis
Juan Guzman Palacios
Renata Robles
Anna Speidel
Silvia Vercher
Nans Voron
Rich Li-Chi Wang
Anne Weber
Gena Wirth
Chunyao Xu

Former Staff

Benjamin Abelman, Carrie Agar, Björn Bracke, Melissa Brown, Martha Jane Burgess, Gabriel Burkett, Janice Tan Hui Ching, Danielle Choi, Jaewoo Chung, Jordan Crabtree, Mihai Craciun, Kelly Cusack, Samarth Das, Therese Diede, Taylor Drake, Gray Elam, Anna Eutsler, Sean Fagan, Alice Feng, Steven Garcia, Clara Goitia, Erin Greenwood, Ian Hampson, Peter Hanby, Fidelma Hawney, Rachel Hillery, Yen-ju Hsieh, Shih-Feng Huang, Sara J. Jacobs, Daniela Serna Jimenez, Emily Johnson, Nefeli Kalantzi, Anya Kaplan-Seem, Anne Kemper, Helen Kongsgaard, Bradley Kraushaar, Charlotte Leib, Ashley Ludwig, Hema Mangal, Julie Marin, Jeffrey Millett, Karli Molter, Idan Naor, Benjamin Nicolosi-Endo, Linh Kim Pham, Francisca Piwonka, Johannes Pointl, Natasha Polozenko, Devanshi Purohit, Ian Quate, Lucas Rauch, Leigh Salem, Marjan Sansen, Alison Shapiro, Katie Shima, Hye Rim Shin, Julia Siedle, Emily Silber, Angela C. Soong, Micah Stanek, Elizabeth Stoel, Katrina Stoll, Ryosuke Takahashi, Tse-hui Teh, Manolo F. Ufer, Jorge Waisburd, Yifei Wang, Zachary Youngerman, Cody Zalk, Sheena Zhang

Project List

103RD STREET COMMUNITY GARDEN
Location: New York, New York
Date: 2010
Client: New York Restoration Project
Project Team: Disney, KaBOOM!, East Harlem community members

BE'ER SHEVA QUARRY
Location: Negev Region, Israel
Date: 2014–ongoing
Client: Beracha Foundation, City of Be'er Sheva
Project Team: TOPOTEK1, LOLA Landscape Architects, Jonathan Cohen-Litant, Yael Moria-Klain
Note: This is a unique collaboration for which three landscape-architecture firms worked together to conceive the project.

BIRD-SAFE BUILDING GUIDELINES
Date: 2006
Client: New York City Audubon Society
Collaborators: E.J. McAdams, Hillary Brown, Glenn Phillips, Marcia T. Fowle, Bruce Fowle FAIA

BLAKE HOBBS PARK
Location: New York, New York
Date: 2012–ongoing
Client: HRBI DREAM Partners LLC
Project Team: New York Restoration Project, NYC Department of Parks & Recreation, NYC Housing Authority, Strandberg Associates

BLUE WALL CENTER
Location: Cleveland, South Carolina
Date: 2008–ongoing
Client: Dream Big Greenville
Project Team: Studio Gang Architects, Earth Design Landscape Architecture

BUFFALO NIAGARA MEDICAL CAMPUS STREETSCAPE
Location: Buffalo, New York
Date: 2011–ongoing
Client: Buffalo Niagra Medical Center
Project Team: Foit Albert, nArchitects, Tillett Lighting

COVE CO-HABITAT
Location: Sag Harbor, New York
Date: 2013
Client: Anonymous
Project Team: Vandeberg Architects

FIELD GUIDE TO THE FLOWERS THAT ARE STILL HERE
Date: 2009
Client: Hong Kong Shenzhen Bi-City Biennale Exhibition

FIRST AVENUE PLAZA
Location: New York, New York
Date: 2013–2016 (expected completion)
Client: JDS Development Group
Project Team: SHoP Architects, AKRF, Pine and Swallow

FUZZY ROPE WEAVING EVENING
Location: New York, New York
Date: 2011
Collaborators: Tom Outerbridge, Bart Chezar, volunteers

GLEN OAKS BRANCH LIBRARY
Location: Queens, New York
Date: 2006–2013
Client: NYC Department of Design and Construction
Project Team: Marble Fairbanks, BuroHappold, Plus Group, Richard Shaver Lighting, Langan Engineering

GREAT KILLS BREAKWATER FEASIBILITY STUDY
Location: Staten Island, New York
Date: 2014
Client: New England Interstate Water Pollution Control Commission, NYS Department of Environmental Conservation
Project Team: Ocean and Coastal Consultants, Parsons Brinckerhoff, ARCADIS, Biohabitats

LIVING BREAKWATERS
Location: Staten Island, New York
Date: 2013–ongoing
Client: Rebuild by Design (competition phase): Henk Ovink, Scott Davis, former HUD secretary Shaun Donovan, Eric Klinenberg; for more information on the competition see: http://www.rebuildbydesign.org)
New York State Governor's Office of Storm Recovery (ongoing implementation phase): Lisa Bova-Hiatt, Jamie Rubin, Betsy Mallow, Kate Dineen, Kris Van Orsdel, Daniel Greene, Alex Zablocki, Chris McNamara
Design Team (ongoing implementation phase): Parsons Brinckerhoff, ARCADIS, Ocean and Coastal Consultants, SeArc Ecological Marine Consulting, The New York Harbor Foundation, LOT-EK Architects, MFS Engineers, Prudent Engineering
For updates on the project, please visit: http://www.stormrecovery.ny.gov/living-breakwaters-tottenville

MILSTEIN HALL
Location: Ithaca, New York
Date: 2007–2011
Client: Cornell University School of Architecture
Project Team: Office for Metropolitan Architecture, Kendall/Heaton Associates, TG Miller

NEW YORK RISING COMMUNITY PLANNING
Location: Brooklyn and Queens, New York
Date: 2014
Client: New York State Governor's Office of Storm Recovery
Project Team: Parsons Brinckerhoff, HR&A

PAVE ACADEMY
Location: Brooklyn, New York
Date: 2012–2013
Client: PAVE Academy
Project Team: Mitchell/Giurgola Architects, Civic Builders

OSPREY NEST STRUCTURES
Location: Brooklyn, New York
Date: 2011–2013
Project Team: Bart Chezar, Phoenix Marine, AECOM Construction

OYSTER-TECTURE
Location: New York, New York
Date: 2009–2010
Client: Museum of Modern Art, *Rising Currents* exhibition (Barry Bergdoll, curator)
Project Team: MTWTF, Paul Mankiewicz, New York Harbor School, Phil Simmons, Hydroqual, NY/NJ Baykeeper, Bart Chezar

SAFARI 7
Location: New York, New York
Date: 2008–2009
Project Team: Urban Landscape Lab at Columbia University GSAPP (Janette Kim and Kate Orff), MTWTF (Glen Cummings)
Research and Design Associates: Dr. Steven Handel, YoungJi Bae, Jordan Carver, Susan Choe, Aliza Dzik, Lisa Ekle, Robin Fitzgerald-Green, Steven Garcia, Margaux Groux, Kathryn Hotler, Helen Kongsgaard, Sayli Korgaonkar, Monique Marion, Jenny Noguchi, Jonathan Payne, Jonathan Pettibone, Evan Sharp, Lily Saporta-Tagiuri, Sydney Talcott, Gena Wirth, Peter Li-Yang Wu, Soohyun Park.
Select podcasts were created in Janette Kim's seminar at the Barnard and Columbia Colleges Architecture Program. Students: Andrew Balmer, Julia Burgi, Alex Cook, Rick Fudge, Charlotte Furet, Emily Glass, Aaron Hsieh, Ryan Johns, Alyssa Kahn, Meg Kelly, Sayli Korgaonkar, Lesley Merz, Stephanie Odenheimer, Marc Rios, Grace Robinson-Leo, Evelyn Ting, Alexandre Vial, and Alison Von Glinow.
See http://www.safari7.org for a full list of contributors.

SIMS HABITAT PILOT PIER
Location: Brooklyn, New York
Date: 2011–ongoing
Client: Sims Metal Management
Collaborators: Bart Chezar, Dr. Michael Judge, SeArc Marine Ecological Consulting, Tom Outerbridge

SIRR COASTAL PROTECTION PLAN
Location: New York, New York
Date: 2013
Client: NYC Economic Development Corporation, the Mayor's Office of Long Term Planning & Sustainability, Dan Zarrilli, Michael Marrella
Project Team: Parsons Brinckerhoff, ARCADIS, Stevens Institute of Technology
This team developed the information and studies for the Coastal Protection chapter of "A Stronger, More Resilient New York." Download the full report here: http://www.nyc.gov/html/sirr/html/report/report.shtml

THE SHALLOWS: REGIONAL STRATEGY AND BAY NOURISHMENT
Location: New York and New Jersey
Date: 2013–2014
Client: Rebuild by Design
Project Team (RBD Competition Phase): Parsons Brinckerhoff, Dr. Philip Orton/Stevens Institute of Technology, Ocean and Coastal Consultants, SeArc Ecological Marine Consulting, The New York Harbor School, LOT-EK Architects, MTWTF, Paul Greenberg

TOWN BRANCH COMMONS
Location: Lexington, Kentucky
Date: 2012–ongoing
Client: Lexington Downtown Development Authority
Project Team: Sherwood Design Engineers (competition phase), MTWTF Graphic Design, James Lima Planning + Development, EHI Consultants, Strand Associates

TOWN BRANCH WATER WALK
Location: Lexington, Kentucky
Date: 2015
Client: LFUCG Stormwater Incentive Grant Program
Project Team: MTWTF Graphic Design, Lexington Downtown Development Authority, Bluegrass Greensource, Peach Technology, University of Kentucky Landscape Architecture Program
Additional Support: Fayette Alliance, Town Branch Trail, Lord Aeck Sargent

WATER WORKS
Location: Minneapolis, Minnesota
Date: 2013–ongoing
Client: Minneapolis Parks Foundation, Minneapolis Park & Recreation Board, Bruce Chamberlain, Tom Evers, MPF, Tyler Pederson
Project Team: Rogers Partners, James Lima Planning + Design, SRF Consulting Group

Image Credits

All reasonable efforts have been made to ascertain and obtain licenses to use third party images and materials. All images of Safari 7 (pp. 150–65) are provided by Urban Landscape Lab/MTWTF. All images of Living Breakwaters (pp. 237–59) are provided by the SCAPE Team. All other images, unless noted below, are provided by SCAPE / LANDSCAPE ARCHITECTURE PLLC.

American Littoral Society, Northeast Chapter: 13
Brenna Angel: 66–67
Arcadis US: 219 (bottom right)
Cameron Blaylock: 184–5
Bart Chezar: 109, 115, 121, 128–9
Ty Cole Studio Inc.: 54–55, 126–7, 174–5 (center, top right), 176–7
Eymund Diegel: 112, 205, 259 (bottom right)
Terry Doss: 219 (top)
Sarah Dunham: 48
Gisele Grenier (ShareAlike 2.0 Generic CC license): 42 (sidebar)
Google Earth: 23, 120 (bottom left)
Hudson-Raritan Estuary Comprehensive Restoration Plan: 250 (top sidebar)
Rick Huffman: 124
Tom Jost: 249 (lower right)
Rachel Kaplan: 68–69
Kentucky Geological Survey: 28–29 (lower)
Alex Matthew (Online Collections Database record made possible by the Staten Island Historical Society, 2012): 248 (top)
Minnesota Historical Society: 74–75
MTWTF Graphic Design: 252 (top), 253 (top right, middle right)
New York Harbor Foundation: 195–6, 252 (bottom)
New York Historical Society: 90 (sidebar)
Jon Reis Photography: 56 (top)
SeArc Marine Ecological Consulting: 250 (bottom sidebar)
Ido Sella: 226
Special Initiative for Rebuilding and Resiliency (SIRR): 216
Mierle Laderman Ukeles: 188–9
U.S. Fish and Wildlife Service: 134
Virginia State Parks Staff (Albert Herring Creative Commons Attribution 2.0 Generic License): 120